Cavell's *Must We Mean What We Say?* at 50

In 1969 Stanley Cavell's *Must We Mean What We Say?* revolutionized philosophy of ordinary language, aesthetics, ethics, tragedy, literature, music, art criticism, and modernism. This volume of new essays offers a multifaceted exploration of Cavell's first and most important book, fifty years after its publication. The key subjects which animate Cavell's book are explored in detail: ordinary language, aesthetics, modernism, skepticism, forms of life, philosophy and literature, tragedy and the self, the questions of voice and audience, jazz and sound, Wittgenstein, Austin, Beckett, Kierkegaard, Shakespeare. The essays make Cavell's complex style and sometimes difficult thought accessible to a new generation of students and scholars. They offer a way into Cavell's unique philosophical voice, conveying its seminal importance as an intellectual intervention in American thought and culture, and showing how its philosophical radicality remains of lasting significance for contemporary philosophy, American philosophy, literary studies, and cultural studies.

Greg Chase is a visiting assistant professor of English at the College of the Holy Cross. He is the author of *Wittgenstein and Modernist Fiction: The Language of Acknowledgment* (2022), and has published articles in *Modernism/Modernity*, *African American Review*, and other journals.

Juliet Floyd is Professor of Philosophy at Boston University. She is the author of *Wittgenstein's Philosophy of Mathematics* (2021), and co-editor of *Philosophical Explorations of the Legacy of Alan Turing* (with A. Bokulich, 2017) and *Philosophy of Emerging Media* (with J. Katz, 2016).

Sandra Laugier is Professor of Philosophy at the University of Paris 1 Panthéon-Sorbonne. The translator of Cavell's work into French, she is also the author of *Why We Need Ordinary Language Philosophy* (2013) and co-editor of Cavell's posthumous volume *Here and There* (2022).

T0384656

Cambridge Philosophical Anniversaries

The volumes in this series reflect on classic philosophy books from the second half of the twentieth century, assessing their achievements, their influence on the field, and their lasting significance.

Titles Published in This Series

Cavell's *Must We Mean What We Say?* at 50
Edited by Greg Chase, Juliet Floyd, and Sandra Laugier

This list can also be seen at www.cambridge.org/cpa

Cavell's *Must We Mean What We Say?* at 50

Edited by

Greg Chase
College of the Holy Cross

Juliet Floyd
Boston University

Sandra Laugier
University of Paris 1 Panthéon-Sorbonne

CAMBRIDGE
UNIVERSITY PRESS

Shaftesbury Road, Cambridge CB2 8EA, United Kingdom

One Liberty Plaza, 20th Floor, New York, NY 10006, USA

477 Williamstown Road, Port Melbourne, VIC 3207, Australia

314–321, 3rd Floor, Plot 3, Splendor Forum, Jasola District Centre, New Delhi – 110025, India

103 Penang Road, #05–06/07, Visioncrest Commercial, Singapore 238467

Cambridge University Press is part of Cambridge University Press & Assessment, a department of the University of Cambridge.

We share the University's mission to contribute to society through the pursuit of education, learning and research at the highest international levels of excellence.

www.cambridge.org
Information on this title: www.cambridge.org/9781009096546

DOI: 10.1017/9781009099714

First published 2022
First paperback edition 2024

A catalogue record for this publication is available from the British Library

Library of Congress Cataloging-in-Publication data
Names: Chase, Greg, editor. | Floyd, Juliet, 1960- editor. | Laugier, Sandra, editor.
Title: Cavell's Must we mean what we say? at 50 / edited by Greg Chase, College of the Holy Cross, Massachusetts, Juliet Floyd, Boston University, Sandra Laugier, University of Paris, Panthéon-Sorbonne.
Description: Cambridge, United Kingdom ; New York, NY, USA : Cambridge University Press, 2022. | Series: Cambridge philosophical anniversaries | Includes bibliographical references and index.
Identifiers: LCCN 2021039258 (print) | LCCN 2021039259 (ebook) | ISBN 9781316515259 (hardback) | ISBN 9781009096546 (paperback) | ISBN 9781009099714 (epub)
Subjects: LCSH: Cavell, Stanley, 1926-2018. Must we mean what we say? | Philosophy, Modern. | Cavell, Stanley, 1926-2018. | BISAC: PHILOSOPHY / Mind & Body
Classification: LCC B945.C273 M873 2022 (print) | LCC B945.C273 (ebook) | DDC 191–dc23/eng/20211014
LC record available at https://lccn.loc.gov/2021039258
LC ebook record available at https://lccn.loc.gov/2021039259

ISBN   978-1-316-51525-9   Hardback
ISBN   978-1-009-09654-6   Paperback

Contents

Contributors

SARAH BECKWITH, Duke University

GREG CHASE, College of the Holy Cross

VINCENT COLAPIETRO, Pennsylvania State University and University of Rhode Island

ROBERT ENGELMAN, Vanderbilt University

JULIET FLOYD, Boston University

ELI FRIEDLANDER, Tel Aviv University

ARATA HAMAWAKI, Auburn University

KELLY JOLLEY, Auburn University

VICTOR J. KREBS, Pontifical Catholic University of Peru, School of Education

SANDRA LAUGIER, University of Paris 1 Panthéon-Sorbonne

JEAN-PHILIPPE NARBOUX, Bordeaux Montaigne University

NAOKO SAITO, University of Kyoto

PAUL STANDISH, University College London Institute of Education

Acknowledgments

The editors thank the Boston University Humanities Center and the Boston University Andrew W. Mellon Sawyer Seminar for supporting the fiftieth anniversary conference "Continuing Cavell: *Must We Mean What We Say?* at Fifty," held at Boston University, February 9–10, 2019, which laid the groundwork for this volume. We are grateful to Cathleen Cavell, Paul Standish, Naoko Saito, Susan Mizruchi, and all the participants and staff members who contributed so much to this conference. Finally, we are grateful to Jordan D. Kokot for his masterly and quick work on the index.

Abbreviations for Cavell's Works

CHU   *Conditions Handsome and Unhandsome: The Constitution of Emersonian Perfectionism* (University of Chicago Press, 1990).

CR   *The Claim of Reason: Wittgenstein, Skepticism, Morality, and Tragedy*, new edn (Oxford University Press, 1999; 1st edn 1979).

CW   *Cities of Words: Pedagogical Letters on a Register of the Moral Life* (Cambridge, MA: Harvard University Press, 2004).

DK   *Disowning Knowledge in Seven Plays of Shakespeare*, updated edn (Cambridge University Press, 2003; 1st edn 1987).

LDIK   *Little Did I Know: Excerpts from Memory* (Stanford University Press, 2010).

MWM   *Must We Mean What We Say?*, 2nd edn (Cambridge University Press, 2002; 1st edn 1969).

PDAT   *Philosophy the Day after Tomorrow* (Cambridge, MA: Harvard University Press, 2005).

PP   *A Pitch of Philosophy: Autobiographical Exercises* (Cambridge, MA: Harvard University Press, 1994).

PH   *Pursuits of Happiness: The Hollywood Comedy of Remarriage* (Cambridge, MA: Harvard University Press, 1981).

SW   *The Senses of Walden*, expanded edn (University of Chicago Press, 1992; 1st edn 1972).

TNYUA   *This New Yet Unapproachable America: Lectures after Emerson after Wittgenstein* (University of Chicago Press, 1989).

WV   *The World Viewed: Reflections on the Ontology of Film* (New York: Viking, 1971).

Introduction

A half-century ago appeared one of the most remarkable and innovative works in English-speaking philosophy of the twentieth century, *Must We Mean What We Say?* (1969, hereafter *MWM*). The occasion for our volume is to celebrate the fiftieth anniversary of its publication by providing a handbook to it, and thus a guide to entering the early thought of its author, Stanley Cavell (1926–2018). *MWM* is a firecracker of a book, exploding in multiple directions, colorful and ambitious. But it is neither esoteric nor obscure nor eclectic. We have gathered this collection of essays to help readers of *MWM* come to appreciate its lasting significance for many different fields – philosophy of language, anthropology, literary studies, history, epistemology, literature, and literary theory. Together, the chapters that follow demonstrate the relevance of Cavell's ways of thinking to issues with which we all struggle: the power of words, art and human personality, claims to objectivity that go awry in crisis, expressions of intent and excuse in a world of passions and values, skepticism about truth and meaning. *MWM* is a classic: it does what philosophical works at their best, throughout human history, are able to do. It is a revolutionary book (literally), transforming its audience by presenting the emancipatory powers of thought and art and language:

> Wherever there really is a love of wisdom – or call it the passion for truth – it is inherently, if usually ineffectively, revolutionary; because it is the same as a hatred of the falseness in one's character and of the needless and unnatural compromises in one's institutions. (*MWM* xxxix)

Our aim here – to draw on a concept Cavell introduces in *MWM* – is to transform *MWM* from an object of interpretation into a means of interpretation, a self-reflexive, revolutionary work (Preface, xxiii, xxviii). Some of the analyses that follow stress overarching themes in Cavell's work as a whole, demonstrating the many ways in which *MWM* anticipates themes he developed in subsequent writings. Others cast *MWM* within the trio of books Cavell produced in this incredibly creative period we might call Early Cavell: soon after *MWM* came *The World Viewed:*

1

Reflections on the Ontology of Film (1971) and *The Senses of Walden* (1972), and during this time he also finished his dissertation, the platform upon which, several years later, he would construct *The Claim of Reason* (1979). Yet the main focus of the essays that follow is *MWM* itself and the deep transformation in philosophy and in culture it claims.[1] Cavell starts from Austin and Wittgenstein, remarkably giving them equal importance in the book as preparatory for the democratic method of *MWM*, which puts on an equal philosophical footing Austin, Kant, Freud, art criticism, "new music," Kierkegaard, Beckett, and Shakespeare.

MWM is an empowerment of ordinary language philosophy (OLP), both as a philosophical instrument of analysis, and as a cultural matter. Hence the importance of Cavell's claim of *MWM* as a book, not a collection of published essays. With *Must We Mean What We Say?* Cavell opens the possibility, beyond the all-too-comfortable division between "analytic" and "continental" philosophy, of a critical divide within the analytic side: between the scientist heirs of logical positivism, and the reception of Wittgenstein's and Austin's work. He reveals the deep and multiple connections of OLP to contemporary culture – from arts to politics – something that has appeared more clearly in our century.

Must We Mean What We Say? is the best entrance into Cavell's philosophy for those who are willing to struggle with the remarkable range of his ideas, each of them connected with the others. Cavell's writing is both centered and foundational, demanding rigorous attention to moral texture, perception, and detail, as well as expression and voice; radically pressing the analytic tradition forward into life, away from self-undermining logical abstractions while at the same time recovering the art of the skeptical essay in the tradition of Montaigne and Emerson (thinkers Cavell would only later begin to write about in earnest).

Must We Mean What We Say? is the first work of what is called "contemporary thought" to carry the project of ordinary language philosophy through to its end. This philosophy of language is rooted in J.L. Austin's method and goes back to Wittgenstein's first question in the Blue Book, and to Austin's question in his first essays: "What is the meaning of a word?" What is it to speak, to say anything? How and why do we talk? What are the implications of this activity for our account of what it is to be human? How do we make our words and deeds fully our own?

---

[1] See S. Mulhall, Preface to Must We Mean What We Say?, 2015 Edition, Cambridge University Press.

MWM is also built on elements of life. It appeared in 1969, just as the United States was undergoing an explosion of student protests in the face of the Vietnam War and the assassinations of Martin Luther King, Jr., Robert Kennedy, and others. By the time of the publication of the book, Cavell, already a professor of Aesthetics and Theory of Value at Harvard, was mobilized with his students. Three hundred of them had confronted the university President in protest against his support for the Vietnam War. They had been evacuated with unprecedented brutality (tear gas and beatings) by the police. As a result, the entire campus went on strike. Cavell also accompanied students' struggles for civil rights in the 1960s, traveling with them in 1964, in the tragic Freedom Summer, to Tougaloo College, in Jackson, Mississippi for a Student Nonviolent Coordinating Committee summer school. Cavell and John Rawls carried in April 1969 a motion that allowed the creation of a department of African American studies at Harvard – relaying a student campaign launched following the assassination of Martin Luther King, Jr.

But *MWM* does not confront "history," "politics," "autobiography," or "progress" in what would ordinarily be conceived of as political or biographical terms. Instead it transforms the very idea of such confrontation by focusing on aspects of reality that must be in place for confrontation to be pertinent: everyday moments of improvisation, evasion, and moral response – in short, ordinary forms of life, to use a phrase Cavell makes central to our understanding of Wittgenstein. Cavell urges by means of philosophy, literature, and conversation the kinds of self-confrontation and self-care that are preconditions for individuals and communities to lead flourishing democratic lives. *MWM* is a philosophy of culture, not by defending or characterizing any particular culture, but by bringing us a meditation on the contingencies and possibilities required for any culture: what Cavell famously calls the "whirl of organism" of our forms of life (*MWM* 52).

First and foremost, the book grapples with the fact that we mean, however incompletely and partially, sometimes perfectly clearly, sometimes obfuscating ourselves and reality. We express passions and claims to authenticity and what is true, we intend, we fail at meaning and at acting, we evade what we know and then claim to know what we most desire. This is the given of human life in language, but it is not a static given, like the sense data of the traditional twentieth-century epistemologist: the given is ordinary language.[2]

[2] See Sandra Laugier, *Why We Need Ordinary Language Philosophy*, trans. Daniela Ginsburg (University of Chicago Press, 2013).

The examination of ordinary language Cavell undertakes has its roots in an ethics and an aesthetics.[3] The attention to the ordinary detail of words and world becomes a new, revolutionary method. In this Cavell is methodologically faithful to Austin, who calls philosophy of language "a promising site for field work" and surveys, taking an anthropological view of human speaking practices. The main concepts in Austin's work, performative utterances and excuses, are as early as *MWM* seen not only in terms of propositions and meanings, but of encounters with and of others.

MWM puts together essays that, simply by being brought together, as a book, reveal a radical, original problematic that Cavell thematically developed in his later work. It offers its readers a method.

To claim *MWM* as a book meant also, for Cavell, claiming the necessity of writing and publishing books in philosophy at a moment when analytic philosophy was establishing itself as a conversation driven by polemics between articles and arguments. Cavell meant to prove that the project of analytical philosophy, to come closer to the world by examining language, could only be accomplished if we could find the conditions of truth or validity of ethical or aesthetic statements, statements of value, and real conversations; about all that we say about what actually matters to us. Cavell calls this in *MWM* the ordinary world:

I mean, of course, the ordinary world. That may not be all there is, but it is important enough: morality is that world, and so are force and love; so is art and a part of knowledge (the part which is about the world); and so is religion (wherever God is). (*MWM* 40)

The ordinary world is not everything there is in the world, "but it is important enough."

The question is again that of OLP: the philosophical force of using "what we say" appears when we ask ourselves, not only what is said, but what is this WE. How can I, do I mean what we say? Cavell has thus raised in *MWM* in the 1960s the question of our capacity for thought as constantly related to our judgment of what counts, as never being able to be outsourced to others; as being our responsibility.

Everywhere Cavell argues that the project of becoming a someone, an individual with a freely expressed personality, is not a given, is based on contingencies and casualties: art and chance, opportunities seized or forsaken, always in the details of everyday life, which is where the large ideas of philosophy (transcendence and overcoming, self-knowledge and will) find their home. This is why Cavell's tone is guarded yet

---

[3] See here Arata Hamawaki, Chapter 6.

unflinching, hopeful about honesty in reckoning with a world that is very far from perfect. He is unwilling to press to the side, but insists on working through, the skeptical sense that all claims to know oneself and others, to claim to know what is right, are to be discarded as illusions or cynical ploys. Philosophy should, does, and must articulate a person's way of finding her voice through life in an increasingly violent, uncertain, and confusing world. This seems to be fully confirmed in our lives today, pursued in a whirl of organism, disasters, pandemic, the flood of words and images in social media, and virtual selfhood and expression.[4]

Cavell's thought is a form of self-reflective realism, one dedicated to fighting the "craving for unreality" that is so characteristic of human dreams, actions, ideals, stories, and aspirations (Preface, xx). That his call for this has been heeded is confirmed in his Preface to the updated edition of *MWM*, when he notices that on two coasts of the United States the first edition of the book had been stolen so many times from two large libraries that it was deemed ineligible to be replaced (Preface, xxx). Cavell imagines droves of impoverished students grabbing for a book they desire but cannot afford. As likely is that this particular book is a very personal treasure, sparking in its readers the desire to achieve community through achieving individuality in tone, expression, and gesture. That is a heady, ambitious promise: that we may hope for a life in community with others precisely by following our deepest, most private desires to the end.

We have divided the essays into three groups.

Part I, "Ordinary Language and Its Philosophy," focuses on method and the philosophical essentials earmarking Cavell's thought as a defense of ordinary language philosophy. We initiate the collection with an explanation of why and in what ways generally *MWM* constitutes a turn in philosophy that still matters today. Sandra Laugier places the radicality of Cavell's intervention in philosophy of language into relief, explaining why this mattered in 1969, and why it matters today. An independent fashioner of ethics, philosophy of language, and politics in her own right, Laugier explains why *MWM* is a book, not merely of historical, but of actual, living, importance. As she emphasizes, we still lack answers to the questions, "What is the meaning of a word?", "What is it to speak, and how do we talk?" and "What are the implications of this activity for our

---

[4] See Juliet Floyd and James E. Katz (eds.), *Philosophy of Emerging Media: Understanding, Appreciation, Application* (Oxford University Press, 2015); see also Veena Das, *Life and Words: Violence and the Descent into the Ordinary* (Berkeley: University of California Press, 2007) and *Textures of the Ordinary: Doing Anthropology After Wittgenstein* (New York: Fordham University Press, 2020).

account of what it is to be human?" Cavell brought together so many different themes in attacking these questions, showing how each forms a crucial part of the answer that must be addressed, not from a grand theoretical perspective, but through a working through of our ordinary lives with care and attention. Laugier hence defends the very idea of "ordinary language philosophy," not as it is caricatured in philosophy since the 1960s, but as an actual alternative to what mainstream philosophy of language has become.

Juliet Floyd shows how Cavell uses his masterful rereadings of Wittgenstein throughout *MWM* to create this alternative, founding what thirty years later would come to be called the "New Wittgenstein," a philosopher who was not ending philosophy, but calling for more of it, better done, by everyone – and precisely by insisting on a wider focus on concepts and moral problems we care about in life, the power of our "forms of life." In *MWM* Cavell overcame the end-of-philosophy reading of Wittgenstein. He also anticipated by over a decade Kripke's focus on the idea of following a rule in Wittgenstein as closely affiliated with Wittgenstein's remarks on skepticism. In Cavell, the idea that meaning is constituted by a set of rules for utilizing words is overturned, not through an appeal to the force of consensus or convention, but its opposite: the overcoming of convention's tyrannies. Wittgenstein's response to a formalized, conventionalized, or contractual idea of meaning is to turn it on its head: it is not the forms themselves, given to us independently of our actions and responses, but the lives we live with them that make for their rigor. That we face the endless responsibility of keeping our words intelligible, of reinventing meaning as we go, is an idea at the heart of Cavell's novel form of ordinary language philosophizing, developed in his subsequent work.

The endless responsibilities we face in everyday life with words is also the subject of Jean-Philippe Narboux's essay on what he calls "elaboratives" in Cavell. Picking up on Cavell's appropriation of Austin's thought in "Excuses," Narboux shows how Cavell unfolds the thought that in the context of everyday life, actions must find proper descriptions that are not constitutive of the actions, or tied to their essences, but instead open themselves up to intelligible elaboration in conversation with others. No action is what it is apart from its situating in the ongoing stream of discussion, the whirl of the ordinary, where what we care about and find objectionable find themselves intimately tied to what we are prepared to count as a description of an action. This is evident in law courts, as Austin noted, where the establishing of the nature, proper description of, and significance of an action will depend upon a whole range of considerations that are familiar from a careful study of cases. Narboux draws connections between the thought of Cavell and that of Elizabeth Anscombe and more recent work in philosophy of action where elaboratives are explored.

In "Faces of the Ordinary" Eli Friedlander takes up the parallel Cavell explores in "Aesthetic Problems of Modern Philosophy" between an aesthetic judgment construed as an expression with a claim to universality (Kant) and the claims of ordinary language philosophizing insofar as it takes a stand on "what we would say". In both cases there is the claim to universality and necessity but without the anticipation of agreement in conclusions or the determinate application of concepts. In Cavell, as in Wittgenstein, the hope or dimension of possible agreement is moved, Friedlander argues, into the ground of our lives in language, in our inhabiting a life, a world, of meaning. The remarkable twofold resonance of Cavell's worked-out parallel has been one of the most influential parts of *MWM*'s legacy in academic philosophy. Conversely, the liberation of ordinary language philosophy from the very idea of a straitjacket of rules precisely through an exploration of art proved fertile, not only for Cavell but for the ordinary language tradition itself, which has inherited its multifaceted forms of response and ability to shift our sensibilities from precisely the point at which "Aesthetic Problems of Modern Philosophy" entered the tradition.

Part II, "Aesthetics and the Modern," brings us face to face with an inescapable aspect of the philosophical habitat that Cavell asks us to explore and acknowledge as real: the need for a first-person perspective on one's own stance, one's own sense of things, one's own meaning, and the power of art and culture to fill the demands of this need. This major theme in Cavell's thought is figured in the autobiographical moments of his writing, expressed in literary forms.

In "'Language-Games' and 'Forms of Life': Cavell's Reading of Wittgenstein and Its Relevance to Literary Studies," Greg Chase, a scholar of modern and contemporary American literature, returns to Cavell's pioneering interpretation of Wittgenstein's *Investigations* (also a focus of Floyd's essay) and highlights what the field of literary studies stands to gain from engaging with this aspect of Cavell's thought. Chase begins by describing how Jean-François Lyotard's influential book *The Postmodern Condition* (1979) puts forward an oversimplified account of Wittgensteinian "language-games." Next, Chase discusses how "The Availability of Wittgenstein's Later Philosophy," the second essay in *MWM*, exposes the problems with this postmodern conception of Wittgenstein. Chase closes with a reading of Sherwood Anderson's modernist short story cycle *Winesburg, Ohio* (1919), demonstrating how – when read in the spirit of Cavell's Wittgenstein – this work illuminates the "form of life" that Anderson's isolated characters all share.

Epistemologist and Kant scholar Arata Hamawaki shows how we must not think that this first-person aspect somehow pollutes objectivity in our claims. Instead objectivity, the meaning and saying of genuine things, requires a voice speaking, a perspective, and a response. Picking up on the parallel in "Aesthetic Problems of Modern Philosophy" explored by Friedlander, Hamawaki shows how Cavell extends Kant's idea that "it must be possible for the 'I think' to accompany all my representations." Judgments of what one would say when, like aesthetic judgments, evince a certain freedom of response that Kant calls "heautonomy": not merely the giving of rules to oneself (as in the "autonomy" of ethics), but the subjective self-picturing of our own responses with concepts and rules. Hamawaki thus shows how Cavell transforms the structure of Kant's "universal voice" into a thoroughgoing dimension of speech, and so the focus of the ordinary language philosopher's claims. The point is not agreement on what is true, but the need for harmony among us in our sensibilities with words, in what we each mean, one by one: what Kant and Wittgenstein call *Übereinstimmung*. Hence the constant threat, as Hamawaki emphasizes, of "alienation" in our speech with others.

Robert Engelman's contribution, "Reading Into It or Hearing It Out? Cavell on Modernism and the Art Critic's Hermeneutical Risk," also addresses the inextricability of the first-person perspective from the making of aesthetic claims. In "Aesthetic Problems of Modern Philosophy" Cavell writes that the critic must not "discount" her own subjectivity but must instead "master it in exemplary ways" (*MWM* 94). Exploring the implications of this comment, Engelman draws a distinction between imposing upon and finding meaning in an artwork: what he describes as the line between "reading into" and "hearing out." To illustrate this distinction, he looks at Cavell's analysis of Beckett's *Endgame* in "Ending the Waiting Game," wondering whether Cavell has extracted an interpretive framework from the play or imposed his own views upon it. Building on Cavell's own observations about modernism, Engelman also suggests that the situation of modernism makes the distinction between "reading into" and "hearing out" more tenuous than ever before.

In his "Must We Sing What We Mean?" philosopher Vincent Colapietro argues for the centrality of "Music Discomposed" and "A Matter of Meaning It" to *MWM*, drawing out most parallels between musical composition and philosophical authorship: voice, timing, extemporaneity, contingency, deep listening, rule-following, and an uncompromising affirmation of the radical nature of human responsibility. He highlights Cavell's resistance to the idea of "science chic" in music theory, the idea that all may be written down in a kind of mathematical mechanism. Already in *MWM* Cavell anticipated a way past the so-called culture wars that have become so pointless since the 1980s. Colapietro shows how scat instantiates Cavell's dynamic view of culture, the everyday, and revolution, its rhythms available to be read back into remarks from Thoreau's *Walden*. Cavell's sense of tradition should be contrasted with, e.g., Allan Bloom's attacks on Louis Armstrong and others for their apparently ignorant appropriations of German music (e.g., "Mack the Knife").[5] Already in 1969, Cavell had an answer to Bloom: Armstrong's power is the power to respond to his own culture through another, it is mastery, spontaneity, and the creation of culture from within.

Part III of the volume turns to the themes of "Tragedy and the Self." Naoko Saito's essay "Philosophy as Autobiography: From *Must We Mean What We Say?* to *Little Did I Know*" revisits the theme of the autobiographical in Cavell's way of practicing philosophy, focusing on the concept of "voice" in ordinary language philosophy. The autobiographical dimensions of Cavell's writing involve not only self-education, she explains, but also a radical re-placement of the subject of and in philosophy. The idea of finding one's voice tends to be associated with a foundationalist view of the self. Such a misreading misses the radicality of Cavell's reconstruction of philosophy and assimilates his writing into the dominant idea of education through narrative, with its inward turn. In contrast, Saito brings forward an idea of "tonality" in philosophy, showing how it comes to the fore in "Aesthetic Problems of Modern Philosophy." Saito also explains how Cavell's early and later works reinforce one another, realizing an understanding of the nature of voice that transforms philosophy.

In "The Finer Weapon: Cavell, Philosophy, and Praise" Victor Krebs shows how Cavell shifts the possibilities for philosophy by replacing traditional themes of epistemology with a very different idea of focusing on, and discussing aloud, what is important to us. Instead of taking the impossibility of certain knowledge in experience as an intellectual problem, Cavell understands it as an existential condition. Philosophers have traditionally disavowed and thereby avoided the problems and conditions of life by turning skepticism into an intellectual problem. The pathology

---

[5] Allan Bloom, *The Closing of the American Mind: How Higher Education Has Failed Democracy and Impoverished the Souls of Today's Students* (New York: Simon & Schuster, 1987). See S. Cavell, "Who Disappoints Whom", *Critical Inquiry*, Vol. 15, No. 3 (Spring, 1989), pp. 606–610.

behind that disavowal becomes the center of what Krebs calls Cavell's "clinical turn": a radical change in attitude, where thinking is – as Cavell puts it – a mode of praise. Krebs sees thinking as praise as a philosophical way to transform the very idea of receptiveness to experience in philosophy, away from a traditional epistemological problem and toward reconnection with feeling and passion. This allows Cavell to bring the feeling, expressing human body back into philosophy.

In "On Cavell's 'Kierkegaard's *On Authority and Revelation*' – with Constant Reference to Austen" poet and philosopher Kelly Jolley explores the themes brought to salience by Cavell in his earliest explicit response to religious writing. What is it to forget a concept, confuse one, or lose one? These are familiar terms of criticism from Kierkegaard, but they can seem strangely otiose or themselves confused. Cavell emphasizes in *MWM* both the familiarity and the unfamiliarity of their contours in our lives, exploring the very ideas of "revelation" and "religious authority." Jolley gauges Cavell's elucidations of these terms, their critical purport in Kierkegaard's practice, and his assessment of their worth, which turns on whether they may find a philosophical or merely a psychological use. Jolley explores Cavell's assessment of the connection between the religious and the psychological and (later) the connection between the aesthetic and the political, endorsing (with qualifications) the first, while worrying (with qualifications) about the latter. The essay ends with a brief discussion of authorial indirection.

In "Tragic Implication," Sarah Beckwith looks at the links between the first and last essay in *MWM*. Cavell's concept of acknowledgment as it emerges in the book's last two essays has received a fair amount of scholarly attention. Beckwith's essay, by contrast, looks at the links between his work on and in ordinary language philosophy as it emerges in his first extension and radicalization of Austin's work in the book's titular essay, "Must We Mean What We Say?" She highlights the latency of tragedy in this early work, even as Cavell finds Austin's thought unable to accommodate tragedy. Ultimately, she argues that Cavell's account of moral encounter and response in *King Lear* teaches him his differences with Austin – differences that emerge in his later engagement with Austin: in, for example, *A Pitch of Philosophy* (1994).

Our volume closes with Paul Standish's "Gored States and Theatrical Guises," an extended examination of "The Avoidance of Love," *MWM*'s final, far-reaching essay (also discussed by Beckwith), which moves from *King Lear* to a more general discussion of the relation between theater and theatricality before, in its final pages, reading the American experiment as tragedy. Standish considers a pair of comments from *MWM*'s preface, wherein Cavell connects problems of theatricalization to the "all but unappeasable craving for unreality" (*MWM* xx) and notes the human tendency to drift into a state of "exile from our words" (xxi). As Standish shows, these matters return in newly explicit ways in "The Avoidance of Love." The pivotal court scene, where Lear is distributing his kingdom, provides a theatricalization of the expression of love, and Standish links this moment to the Gloucester-Edgar-Edmund subplot, showing how Cavell brings out the play's recurrent concerns with issues of nakedness (literal and metaphorical) and "shame" (*MWM* 286). The subplot amplifies questions of legitimacy and succession, but it also democratizes these through its focus on bastardy and baseness, such that the problems of inheritance raised in Cavell's discussion reverberate through political settlements in the modern world. Standish closes by linking Cavell's comments on American theatricality to the work of Ralph Ellison, who saw the founders' acceptance of slavery as initiating America's ongoing "drama of conscience."

This "drama of conscience" is the reality we face today. Democracy and civil disobedience, the dialectic between authoritarian and liberatory conceptions, the frightening loss of self to a fast-moving, technologically and commercially driven world, the tendency to flee from the responsibilities associated with "meaning what we say," of acknowledging others and our differences from others – these are central problems of our time. There is no path forward, no power to philosophy, without a focus on the to and fro of what we say and mean and do not say in ordinary life. Our creativity with meaning, exemplified in the arts and philosophy – and popular culture and digital practice – show that action, passion, and value find their essential home here, in the burden on each one of us to become who we are. It was the central contribution of *Must We Mean What We Say?* to call for a positive, human-centered focus on voice, on real conversation about real things that matter. We and all contributors here are convinced that *Must We Mean What We Say?* is exactly what philosophy needs now.

Part I

Ordinary Language and Its Philosophy

1   *Must We Mean What We Say?* and Ordinary Language Philosophy

Sandra Laugier

Must We Mean What We Say?, Stanley Cavell's first and most important book, contains all the themes that Cavell continued to develop masterfully throughout his philosophy, but it stands out now as a crucial moment, and as a turning point, in philosophy of language. The particular importance of *Must We Mean What We Say?* lies in bringing together essays that, simply by being brought together, reveal a radical, original problematic. It is a classic and a book that is not only of historical importance, but of actual importance. *Must We Mean What We Say?* is the first work of what is called "contemporary thought" to carry the project of ordinary language philosophy (OLP) through to its end. This philosophy of language is rooted in J.L. Austin's method and goes back to Wittgenstein's first question in the *Blue Book*, and to Austin's question in his first essays: "What is the meaning of a word?" What is it to say anything?

When Cavell published what he deliberately called a "book of essays" in 1969, he knew he was upsetting a well-established American philosophical tradition, namely, analytic philosophy as it had emerged out of the arrival of Vienna Circle philosophers, epistemologists, and logicians fleeing Nazism onto the American philosophical scene. In *Must We Mean What We Say?*, analytic philosophy was called into question from within and for the first time in America, where it had become dominant.

Cavell writes at a specific moment indeed. The late 1960s were precisely the moment when "OLP bashing" began.[1] For the rest of the twentieth century, to call a thinker an "ordinary language philosopher" has been to insult them. Actually, the term itself began as a term of derision coined by detractors, and an accusation, not a claim nor an objective term of classification. Cavell's ambition was to reclaim the term and turn it around – a well-known political move today. His aim was to present and defend OLP at a moment when philosophy of language was

---

[1] See Alice Crary and Joel de Lara, "Who's Afraid of Ordinary Language Philosophy?" *Graduate Faculty Philosophy Journal* 39/2 (2019), 317–99.

at a crossroads. Attacks such as Gellner's *Words and Things: An Examination of, and an Attack on, Linguistic Philosophy* were so poorly argued that no real discussion followed. The book is nicely dismissed in *MWM* – in what may have been the first genuine response to it. But there never was an actual debate on what philosophy of language could and should become. Searle's and Grice's analytic interpretations of Austin became mainstream by simply replacing the original, and ignoring other readings.

So we need to keep in mind the historical context of *MWM*, and its deep engagements with American culture in the 1960s. The philosophical culture was becoming deeply divided, with a new complexity added to the ever-caricatural division between "analytic" and "continental" philosophy, and an emergent internal divide within the analytic side: between the scientist reception of logical positivism, and the reception of Wittgenstein's later work, to which *MWM* explicitly adds, and at an equal level of importance, Austin's work. This first theoretical "coup de force" is the mission of the four first essays, all crucial to the further development of OLP and its emancipatory power. But *MWM* attempts a second "coup," just as crucial, but whose importance would appear only in the next century: to reveal the deep and multiple connections of OLP to the preoccupations of contemporary culture (way beyond philosophical culture) – as they are expressed in modernism (the challenges of "new music," New Criticism, abstract expressionism), in modern theater and Shakespearean tragedy, and, in a less explicit way, in political and moral ruptures and wars.

MWM is thus a long-term empowerment of OLP, both as a philosophical instrument of analysis, and as a cultural matter. Hence the importance of Cavell's claim of *MWM* as a book, not a collection of published essays: he mentions his

> ... conviction in the importance of Austin's practice of philosophizing out of a perpetual imagination of what is said when, why it is said, hence how, in what context. I note that my first extended readings of literary works that I felt warranted publication are devoted to two dramas, *Endgame* and *King Lear*, both included in, and in a sense provide a structure for my *Must We Mean What We Say?* and in that sense served to convince me that [it] *added up to a book*. (*LDIK*217, my emphasis)

All the essays *add up to* a book, because there is no hierarchy of subject. Cavell had fancied putting the book in a newspaper format, so that each essay could begin on the front page. Such an interweaving of thought, art, actuality, words, sounds ... makes the book itself a modernist and democratic work.

Austin's Powers

For all these reasons, the essays on Austin and on Wittgenstein, which constitute the opening of *Must We Mean What We Say?*, are crucial to the book. They expressed a defense and illustration of the philosophy of ordinary language, to which Cavell had been converted during a series of lectures given by Austin at Harvard, in 1955. Cavell was teaching the new material and method he had discovered. I'd like to say he was an activist of OLP. As he recalls in *Little Did I Know*:

I had been invited the early spring of my first year of teaching at Berkeley – ordered was more like it – to participate in a panel some eight months later for that year's Christmas meetings of the Pacific Division of the American Philosophical Association, to be held at Stanford University. My insistence on the treasures I was finding Austin to have brought to philosophy was getting on the nerves of some accomplished teachers in and around my senior colleagues in the Berkeley department and it was their idea, whose point it was not hard for me to appreciate, even agree with, that it was time for me to justify my confidence before a public of professional colleagues. (*LDIK*360)

The occasion was a reply to a paper to be prepared by his Berkeley colleague Benson Mates criticizing the procedures of the "philosophers of ordinary language" and "the appeal to ordinary language as such." Actually the presentation went very well, leading to a publication of the exchange in the then newly founded journal *Inquiry* and later to the publication of the essay "Must We Mean What We Say?" as the first chapter of *MWM*.

In the days after the papers were delivered, during the break between semesters, ideas for expanding the thoughts I had arrived at in the paper began coming at a greater pace than I had ever before experienced with any philosophical material. For some days it seemed that I could hardly sit still for ten minutes without beginning to scribble down further suggestions. Many came to nothing; some found their way into work years later; some went immediately into new or expanded paragraphs of the talk. (*LDIK* 360–61)

In Cavell's brief first summary of his life at the beginning of *Little Did I Know*, the meeting with Austin is mentioned as a founding event – which will take him away from his initial destiny, from his first talent, music. Cavell mentions "The crisis precipitated by Austin's appearance on the scene"; his work in philosophy "had yet again to begin again" (he had started, and discarded, a half dissertation). OLP appeared as a solution to the loss (or ending) of a career in music – as if it could fulfill the aspiration to finding the right tone, or pitch, or to having a real "ear" – "to what is said when, why it is said, hence how, in what context."

The examination of ordinary language is close to an aesthetics and this makes it a kind of criticism (cf. the title "Austin at criticism").

The aim, for Cavell and Austin, is to get free from an aesthetics of "an obsession with the beautiful and the sublime" and to attend to "the dainty and the dumpy." The attention to the ordinary detail of words and world becomes a new, revolutionary method. In this Cavell is methodologically faithful to Austin, who calls philosophy of language "a promising site for field work" and surveys, taking an anthropological view of the human speaking practice. The main concepts in Austin's work, performative utterances and excuses, are as early as *MWM* seen not only in terms of propositions and meanings, but "ways we encounter each other".[2]

So Cavell in his teaching at Berkeley was trying to communicate his own experience of Austin's method, in the way it had communicated itself to him. *MWM* is a development and expression of this encounter with OLP. It starts a reflection on ordinary language as voice, a theme that appears throughout his later works as well (such as *In Quest of the Ordinary* and *A Pitch of Philosophy*[3]); and the original aesthetic approach that defines Cavell's work, through his objects – which range from William Shakespeare to Samuel Beckett and later, Hollywood comedies and melodrama, as well as opera. But everything starts from this passionate expression of the *importance* and *power* of Austin. *MWM* puts together essays that, simply by being brought together, as *a book, a singular expression*, reveal a radical, original stance that has been thematically developed in the later work. It is a method.

To claim *MWM* as a book meant also, for Cavell, claiming the necessity to write and to publish books in philosophy at a moment when analytic philosophy was establishing itself as a conversation and polemics between articles and arguments. Cavell meant to prove that inheriting analytic philosophy (the works of Frege and Wittgenstein, and the power of logic, which were his first discovery in philosophy and played an important role in his formation) could be something else.

Or rather: to demonstrate that the project of analytical philosophy, to come closer to the world by examining language, could only be accomplished if we could find the conditions of truth or validity of ethical or aesthetic statements, statements of value, conversations; about *all that we*

---

[2] J.L. Austin, *Philosophical Papers*, ed. J.O. Urmson and G.J. Warnock (Oxford University Press, 1979; 1st edn 1961). See also Austin, "How to Talk: Some Simple Ways," *Proceedings of the Aristotelian Society* 53 (1953), 227–46.

[3] See Naoko Saito (Chapter 9) and Paul Standish (Chapter 13).

say about what actually matters to us (or matters to us because we say it). This reality is what Cavell calls in *MWM the ordinary world*:

I mean, of course, the ordinary world. That may not be all there is, but it is important enough: morality is that world, and so are force and love; so is art and a part of knowledge (the part which is about the world); and so is religion (wherever God is). (*MWM* 40)

The ordinary world is not *everything* there is in the world, "but it is important enough": it is the world of what matters. So the necessity of exploring importance becomes the key to OLP.

Early Cavell

MWM can be integrated into a first part of Cavell's work, which we may see now as the "Early Cavell." It is a specific emotion to study it, because even if many later works are remarkable (of course *The Claim of Reason*, but also *Pursuits of Happiness*, *This New Yet Unapproachable America*, *A Pitch of Philosophy*), this early period is certainly the most exciting, because it expresses the moment when Cavell begins to make his philosophical voice heard within violent doubts (almost worries of fraudulence) about his ability to continue and the validity of his approach, completely new in fact. The following works may be seen as founded on this first work – and on the comfort of an early tenured position at Harvard acquired through these early papers and the dissertation that grew from them. But this first work, as well as the other parallel early works (*The Senses of Walden*, 1972, and *The World Viewed*, 1971), were exploring new territory. The two articles that constitute the point of discussion, Austinian and Wittgensteinian, of *MWM* were written in uncertainty and controversy, and in an intellectual outburst motivated first by the defense of Austin and his method in philosophy, then by the irritation caused by conformist readings of Wittgenstein.

In the months before I showed up to teach in Emerson Hall, the philosophers J. Fodor and J. Katz attacked the two articles I had submitted (in addition to my dissertation) as evidence in the case for my tenure appointment to Harvard, asserting (I believe I recall the exact words) that the articles were "deleterious to the future of philosophy." When two years after *MWM The World Viewed* appeared, one of the two reviews that came my way declared that the book was sickening, the other granted that my friends might like talking with me about movies but that this should not be grounds for publishing what was said privately. (*LDIK*, 442)

This is where OLP really comes into being. Still, "ordinary language philosophy" is a term that has never been claimed centrally by

Wittgenstein or even Austin; Cavell himself uses the term with caution, well aware that his work is not part of Oxford's school of "conceptual analysis" either. It is significant that his exchanges with Austin took place entirely in the USA and that he was seldom in contact with the British – who very quickly buried Austin, a philosopher who is nowadays very little discussed or studied or used in England, while Wittgenstein's studies are flourishing there.

At the outset, extending the scope of ordinary language philosophy is Cavell's philosophical project. Cavell embraces Austin's procedures, but extends them to the limit of their applicability by bringing them to an explicit self-consciousness. As William Rothman says illuminatingly in comparing *MWM* to *The World Viewed*: "The essays that comprise *Must We Mean What We Say?* not only embrace the procedures of ordinary language philosophy, they also investigate, philosophically, the very procedures they embrace."[4] The title essay, "Must We Mean What We Say?", which develops a theory of meaning in opposition to propositional sense and to psychological intention, as well as "The Availability of Wittgenstein's Later Philosophy," are articles of historical importance that revived OLP and determined many current readings of Wittgenstein. These two essays, symmetrically, contain the seed of all of *The Claim of Reason*, and exhibit the radicality and simplicity that characterize Cavell's approach. This approach reflects an important displacement in philosophy of language: one must not only attend to meaning as an entity, analyzing the empirical content and logical structure of statements; one must also look at *what we say* – explaining who "we" are and what "saying" is. That is, we must ask ourselves what we do with our language, and how what we do in a situation is part of what we say. And this is not merely "contextualism." *MWM* was the first work to ask questions about the *relevance* of our statements *to ourselves*, by drawing from various domains and by turning to unexpected sources, such as Beckett, Shakespeare, Kierkegaard, or the discourse of music or art criticism.[5] Since then, this notion of relevance has been more or less absorbed into a mentalist philosophy of communication, but we must not let that prevent us from seeing the importance of the model that Cavell, with great fidelity to the Austinian method, proposes here. The central

---

[4] William Rothman, in "Cavell's Philosophical Procedures and *Must We Mean*," 262, the Appendix to Rothman and Marian Keane, *Reading Cavell's The World Viewed* (Detroit, MI: Wayne State University Press, 2000), 261–77, confronts *MWM*'s and *WV*'s methods and provides a masterful analysis of this point.

[5] I have discussed this in my introduction to the French translation of *MWM*, *Dire et vouloir dire* (Paris: Le Cerf, 2009). See Sandra Laugier, "Introduction to the French edition of *Must We Mean What We Say?*," *Critical Inquiry* 37/4 (2011), 627–51.

question of *MWM* is not the question of a proposition's objective, semantic, or empirical content, but rather of the fortunes and misfortunes of ordinary expression. The issue is no longer what propositions *mean* or even what they *do*. Cavell changes the subject. To understand what it is to mean, you have to give up meaning (what is said) as an entity[6] and to proceed from "the fact *that* a thing is said; that it is (or can be) said (in certain circumstances) is as significant as what it says; its being said then and there is as determinative of what it says as the meanings of its individual words are" (*MWM* 167). The point is not "to provide some new sense to be attached to a word," but "to clarify what the word does mean, as we use it in our lives." It is Wittgenstein's lesson in the *Blue Book*, and Cavell also follows him whan he describes bringing words back from their metaphysical to their ordinary use: to *bring them home*. But… "there's no place like home" (as Dorothy knows all too well).

Cavell maintains in *MWM* that we know neither what we think nor what we mean, and that the task of philosophy is to bring us back to ourselves, that is, to bring words back to their everyday use and to bring knowledge of the world back to our ordinary knowledge of or proximity to ourselves. This is a response to the threat of skepticism, that loss of or distancing from the world that film also explores, as shown by *The World Viewed*. The goal, in both contexts, is clarity, and it is achieved, Cavell puts it, by "mapping the fields of consciousness lit by the occasions of a word, not through analyzing it or replacing a given word by others" (*MWM* 103).

New Realism

The appeal to the ordinary and to "our" uses of words is not obvious; it is shot through with this skepticism, with what Cavell defines as the "uncanniness of the ordinary." Thus, the ordinary is neither the common sense that empiricist philosophy sometimes claims for itself, nor does it have anything to do with a rationalized and descriptive version of ordinary language philosophy, or a semantics of ordinary language. For Cavell, as early as *MWM*, the ordinary is lost or distant.

Cavell's originality in *MWM* thus lies in defining the ordinary on the basis of a redefinition of ordinary language. It is his reading of Austin that makes such an approach possible – Cavell was the first to bring out Austin's realism. To talk about language is to talk about what language talks about.

---

[6] Here there is a weird convergence with Quine; see Laugier, *Why We Need Ordinary Language Philosophy*, trans. Daniela Ginsburg (University of Chicago Press, 2013), e.g., Chapter 6.

As Cavell says: "The philosophy of ordinary language is not about language, anyway not in any sense in which it is not also about the world. Ordinary language philosophy is about whatever ordinary language is about" (*MWM* 95). Examining ordinary language offers us a "sharpened perception of phenomena" (Austin, *Philosophical Papers*, 29). It is this sharpening of visual and auditory perception that Cavell seeks in *MWM*. What is at stake in OLP is "the internality of words and world to one another" (*PH* 204). This is an intimacy that cannot be demonstrated, or posited by a metaphysical thesis, but can only be brought out by attending to the differences traced by language.

In exploring the uses of words, Austin is searching for a natural, or as he calls it, "boring," relation between words and the world. He rejects arguments that would validate this relation in terms of a structure common to language and the world: "If it is admitted (*if*) that the rather *boring* yet satisfactory relation between words and world which has here been discussed does genuinely occur, why should the phrase 'is true' not be our way of describing it?" (*Philosophical Papers*, 133). Hence Austin's mention of "linguistic phenomenology" (182) as "some less misleading name than those given above" for "this way of doing philosophy." As he puts it:

> When we examine what we should say when, what words we should use in what situations, we are looking again not *merely* at words (or 'meanings' whatever they may be) but also *at the realities we use the words to talk about*: we are using a sharpened awareness of words to sharpen our perception of, though not as the final arbiter of, the phenomena. (182)

The relationship between language and the world is characterized by Austin in terms of a *given*. The problem is not agreeing on an opinion, but on a point of departure, a *given*, data. This given is *language* – conceived of not as a body of statements or words, but as *agreement* on "what we should say when" to make us conscious of differences of which we had not been conscious, to render them *perspicuous* (*MWM* 103). As Austin explains:

> For me, it is essential at the beginning to come to an agreement on the question of "what we should say when." To my mind, experience proves amply that we do come to agreement on "what we should say when" such or such a thing, though I grant you it is often long and difficult. No matter how long it may take, one can nevertheless succeed, and on the basis of this agreement, this given, this established knowledge, we can begin to clear our little part of the garden. I should add that too often this is what is missing in philosophy: a preliminary *datum* on which one might agree at the outset.[7]

---

[7] J.L. Austin, *Sense and Sensibilia* (Oxford University Press, 1962), 5.

The aesthetic perspective of *MWM* starts from the method of OLP. The philosopher's purpose in comparing and contrasting our uses of words "resembles the art critic's purpose in comparing and distinguishing works of art." It is a matter of attention. "Namely, that in this cross-light the capacities and salience of an individual object in question are brought to attention and focus." In making critical claims about art works, we mean: "Don't you see, don't you hear, don't you dig? The best critic will know the best points. Because if you do not see something, without explanation, then there is nothing further to discuss" (*MWM* 93).

Here, the agreement Austin is talking about concerning what we should say and what we mean is normative. This *normativity of the ordinary* is also a main theme by which *MWM* reformulates OLP[8]. It is normative because ordinary language "embodies all the distinctions men have found worth drawing and the connections they have found worth marking in the lifetimes of many generations" (Austin, *Philosophical Papers*, 182). This capacity to mark differences is Cavell's obsession; in order for us to have something to say and mean, there must be differences that hook onto us and are important to us, differences that matter. As he puts it: "Further, the world must exhibit (we must observe) similarities and dissimilarities ... if everything were either absolutely indistinguishable from anything else or completely unlike anything else, there would be *nothing to say*" (Austin, *Philosophical Papers*, 121). Austin's realism consists in this conception of differences and resemblances. In the chapter "Austin at Criticism" Cavell insists on the reality of the distinctions in Austin, in contrast with the distinctions usually established by philosophers.

One of Austin's most furious perceptions is of the slovenliness, grotesque crudity, and fatuousness of the usual distinctions philosophers have traditionally thrown up. Consequently, one form his investigations take is that of repudiating the distinctions lying around philosophy – dispossessing them, as it were, by revealing better ones. These are better not merely because they are finer, but because they are more solid, having, so to speak, a greater natural weight. They appear normal, even inevitable, while the others are luridly arbitrary; they are useful where the others seem twisted; they are real where the others are academic; they are fruitful where the others stop cold. (*MWM* 102–3)

In "Austin at Criticism" Cavell spells out *differences* between philosophical appeals to ordinary language and empirical investigations of

[8] Cf. Sandra Laugier, "The Vulnerability of Reality – Austin, Normativity, and Excuses," in *Interpreting Austin*, ed. Savas L. Tsohatzidis (Cambridge University Press, 2017), 119–42.

language. For Austin, "true" designates one of the possible ways of expressing the harmony between language and the world. "Fitting" designates a concept not of correspondence or even of correctness, but rather of the appropriateness of a statement within the circumstances – the fact that it is proper. "The statements fit the facts always more or less loosely, in different ways on different occasions" (*Philosophical Papers*, 130). Wittgenstein also has a say in formulating what proved to be Cavell's obsession throughout his work: the search for the right, fitting tone – conceptually, morally, and perceptually – that Cavell mentions in his autobiographical writings with regard to his mother's musical talent and his father's jokes. This search gives ordinary language realism its musical dimension. For Austin, "true" designates one of the possible ways of expressing the harmony between language and the world.

It is a matter of finding a fine (musical) sensitivity to things and the fit of words at the heart of ordinary uses. In this agreement between (what is) "achieved through mapping the fields of consciousness lit by the occasions of a word" (*MWM* 100), Austin registers the possibility of finding an ordinary adequacy to the world. This possibility is founded on the reality of language as the social activity of maintaining the world. Ordinary language is a (refined) tool; it represents experience and inherited perspicacity – a tool to mark differentiations. Consider, for example, the classification of actions in "Excuses" or the distinction at work in "Three Ways of Spilling Ink" between spilling intentionally, deliberately, or purposely – the minute detail of human action in its capacity for disaster, for *casualty* (a term coined later by Cavell, bringing together disaster, the casual, the ordinary).

What Cavell introduces in *MWM*, and expands on later as the object of his reflection on voice, is the connection of rightness of tone, of the adequacy of expression to knowledge of self (already a form of self-reliance). This is what he will call perfect *pitch*. He navigates adroitly between the Austinian critique of psychologism on one hand, and, on the other hand, caricature forms of emotivism that separate the content of our words from the emotion associated with them: "It is what human beings say that is true or false."[9]

Cavell answers the need expressed by Wittgenstein and Austin to take into account *what is said* and *the fact* that it is said when determining meaning. What pertains to expression and what pertains to description cannot be separated within a statement, as if one could break statements

[9] Ludwig Wittgenstein, *Philosophical Investigations*, rev. 4th edn, trans. G.E.M. Anscombe, P.M.S. Hacker, and Joachim Schulte, ed. Hacker (New York: Wiley-Blackwell, 2009; 1st edn 1953), §241; hereafter abbreviated parenthetically as *PI*.

down into stabilized propositions and some "additional" force – some psychological stand-in, as pitiful to Cavell as striking a table or one's chest to legitimate or reinforce a contestable or insincere affirmation. Turning to literature and to the stage, where ordinary language is brought to life, goes directly against this approach. The problem is semantic, ethical, and also political; in one of the very rare mentions of politics in *MWM*, Cavell denounces a "moral philosophy which distinguishes between the assessment of individual actions and of social practices" (*MWM* 47). This is a transparent critique of John Rawls' 1955 article "Two Concepts of Rules," very influential at the moment Cavell composed these essays included in *MWM*. Rawls aimed at distinguishing between agreeing to, or following, a rule or principle internal to a practice and general agreement to a practice. Committing to a practice leads to learning the rules that define it and to recognizing that "its rules define it." For Rawls, "it doesn't make sense for a person to raise the question of whether or not a rule of a practice applies correctly"; as long as "the action he contemplates is a form of action defined by a practice ... the only legitimate question concerns the nature of the practice itself."[10] Cavell's point is not only, first, that not all practices are governed by rules (*MWM* 52) but also, furthermore, that agreement to a practice, such as language, is never given but always under discussion. We have not agreed to everything, in language use and in political practice. This makes *MWM* a work, and OLP a method, of political philosophy – an early heterodox criticism of analytical political thought.

Relevance and Voice

Cavell has made it his goal to "reinsert ... the human voice in philosophical thinking." The goal of ordinary language philosophy is indeed to make it understood that language is spoken, pronounced by a human voice within a "form of life," a concept made central in *MWM* (84). It then becomes a matter of shifting away from the question of the common use of language – central to the *Philosophical Investigations* – to the new question of the relation between an individual speaker and the language community. For Cavell, this leads to a reintroduction of the voice into philosophy, and to a redefinition of subjectivity in language precisely on the basis of the relationship of the individual voice to the linguistic community: the relation of voice to voices. The philosopher's task, to bring our words back to earth, is neither easy nor obvious, and the quest

---

[10] John Rawls, "Two Concepts of Rules," *Philosophical Review* 64/1 (1955), 3–32 (at 26).

for the ordinary is the most difficult of all, even if (and precisely because) it is available to anyone.

No man is in any better position for knowing it than any other man – unless wanting to know is a special position. And this discovery about himself is the same as the discovery of philosophy, when it is the effort to find answers, and permit questions, which nobody knows the way to nor the answer to any better than you yourself. (*MWM* xlii)

Ordinary language philosophy responds to skepticism not with new knowledge or beliefs, but by acknowledging our condition, which, to quote one of Cavell's puns, is also our diction together. Skepticism, far from dissolving in this community of language, takes on its most radical sense here: What allows me to speak in the name of others? How do I know what we mean by a word or world, to take another of Cavell's puns? *MWM* explores our form of life in language in all its diversity; "language is everywhere we find ourselves, which means everywhere in philosophy (like sexuality in psychoanalysis)" (*TNYUA* 118).

The philosophical interest of turning to *what we say* appears when we ask ourselves not only what it is to say but what this *we* is. For Cavell, this is the question at the opening of the *Philosophical Investigations*. But it is also Thoreau (and later Emerson), through his attention to the ordinary and the common, who underwrites the practices of Wittgenstein and Austin. *The Senses of Walden* (1972) is contemporary to *MWM*; without Thoreau, there would not be this passage from the Austinian ordinary to the Wittgensteinian criteria; there would not be this need for a change in how we hear language, a change in our sensitivity to what is said.

This was the task Thoreau set for himself in *Walden*: "Our reading, our conversation and thinking, are all on a very low level, worthy only of pygmies and manikins."[11]

The falsity, the hopeless inadequacy of our tone and our language, are left unexplained both by the analytic notion of truth and by the correspondence to reality that semantic approaches, continued by contemporary representationalism, emphasize. Against these approaches Cavell proposes his version of realism, which is *realistic* (in Cora Diamond's sense), and grounded in attention to the adequacy or inadequacy of our expressions to ourselves. "Yet no intervention in philosophy more clearly than Austin's prompted an awareness of our apparent failures to mean what we say" (*LDIK* 360). Cavell takes up the discovery of one's own relevance and one's relation to the real, again with regard to the ontology

[11] Henry David Thoreau, *Walden*, ed. Jeffrey Cramer (New Haven, CT: Yale University Press, 2004), 104.

of cinema, in "What Becomes of Things on Film" (1978). There, he says that the *given* is made up of "the appearance and significance of just those objects and people that are in fact to be found in the succession of films, or passages of films, that matter to us" (*Themes Out of School*, 183).

For Cavell, there can be no definition of relevance without an examination of what is important. Here, the risk of subjectivism arises: what is relevant for one is not, or is not always, relevant for others. But this is the whole combined argument of *MWM*, *The Senses of Walden*, and *The World Viewed*: the point in Early Cavell is to show how importance for me and importance for others are logically connected; how what is important for me is important for others and vice versa. We also find here, once again (in this volume see Arata Hamawaki and Eli Friedlander from a more Kantian perspective), a parallel between ordinary language (sensitivity to what we should say when) and aesthetic judgment. No relevance without importance, without an investment in what counts. *MWM* suggests the path to replacing or refining truth with relevance, with our perception of what is relevant to us, of what counts. As Cavell puts it in his original Foreword:

> But relevance and worth may not be the point. The effort is irrelevant and worthless until it becomes necessary to you to know such things. There is the audience of philosophy; but there also, while it lasts, is its performance. (*MWM* xlii)

This is why modern criticism is an enterprise in self-knowledge. According to Cavell, this is a defining characteristic of "writing the modern": "The exercise of criticism is not to determine whether the thing is good that way but why you want it that way" (*CR* 95). He proposes a conception of criticism and objectivity according to which "these questions are always together." By radically associating "the scrupulous exactitude" of artistic desire with "a moral and intellectual imperative," Cavell redefines meaning through the conjunction of desire, importance, and value.

> When in earlier writing of mine [*MWM*] I broach the topic of the modern, I am broaching the topic of art as one in which the connection between expression and desire is purified. In the modern neither the producer nor the consumer has anything to go on (history, convention, genre, form, medium, physiognomy, composition …) that secures the value or the significance of an object apart from one's wanting the thing to be as it is. (*CR*94–95)

The Universal Voice

So what then are the criteria for what is important or significant? Our words and concepts are *dead* without their criteria for use. Wittgenstein and Austin look for these criteria on the basis of their perception of uses. Cavell asks: how can one claim to accomplish this? It is this question – of the essential lack of foundation to this claim – that defines the sense of criteria and the task of criticism.

Cavell asks in "The Availability of Wittgenstein's Later Philosophy": "The question is: Why are some claims about myself expressed in the form 'We …'? About what can I speak for others on the basis of what I have learned about myself? Then suppose it is asked: 'But how do I know others speak as I do?'" (*MWM* 67). OLP thus consists in searching for means to recognize and find one's voice, to find agreement in language and the right, fitting expression – but also to find means of expressing inadequacy and disagreement. On what is the appeal to ordinary language based? All that we have is *what we say* and our agreements in language. Cavell recollects this discovery in his autobiography.

At the same time it showed me that this "we" is essentially open to shifts and moreover that the matter of "speaking for" is never an epistemological certainty but something like a moral claim, an arrogation of right, which others may grant or refuse. That Austin's and Wittgenstein's ways of appealing to what we say demonstrate the practicality and power of such appeals has been essential to my exhilaration in discovering their modes of philosophizing. The beginnings of this exhilaration are evident even in my first published philosophical paper of continuing significance for me, "Must We Mean What We Say?" (*LDIK* 432)

Ordinary language philosophy thus consists in searching for means to recognize and find one's voice, to find agreement in language and the right, fitting expression – but also to find means of expressing inadequacy and disagreement. On what is the appeal to ordinary language based? All that we have is *what we say* and our agreements in language. The agreement Austin and Wittgenstein speak of is in no way an intersubjective agreement. It is as objective as an agreement can be. But where does this agreement come from? In "The Availability of Wittgenstein's Later Philosophy" Cavell makes the following remark about Wittgenstein, which would go on to have great resonance for other philosophers, including Hilary Putnam, John McDowell, Cora Diamond, and Veena Das:

We learn and we teach certain words in certain contexts, and then we are expected, and expect others, to be able to project them into further contexts. Nothing insures that this projection will take place (in particular, not the grasping of universals nor the grasping of books of rules), just as nothing insures that we will make, and understand, the same projections. That on the whole we do is a matter of our sharing routes of interest and feeling, modes of response … of when an utterance is an assertion, when an appeal, when an explanation – all the whirl of organism Wittgenstein calls 'forms of life.' Human speech and activity, sanity and community, rest upon nothing more, but nothing less, than this. It is a vision as simple as it is difficult, and as difficult as it is (and because it is) terrifying. (*MWM* 52)

Cavell shows at once the fragility and the depth of our agreements, and focuses on the nature of the necessities that emerge from our forms of life. That our ordinary language is founded on nothing but itself is not only a source of disquiet about the validity of what we do and say, but also the revelation of a truth about ourselves. The fact is that I am the only source of such validity. This is not an "existential" interpretation of Wittgenstein, but an understanding of the fact that language is a form of life. The acceptance of this fact – which Cavell defines as "the absence of foundation or guarantee for creatures endowed with language and subject to its powers and weaknesses, subject to their mortal condition" – is an acknowledgment of finitude and of the everyday.

The realism of *MWM*[12] lies in the connection it establishes between the nature of language and *human nature*. In this sense, the question of agreement in language reformulates ad infinitum the question of the human condition, and acceptance of the latter goes hand-in-hand with acknowledgment of the former.

The philosophical problem raised by the philosophy of ordinary language is hence double. First, by what right do we base ourselves on what we say ordinarily? Next, on what or on whom do we base our determination of what we ordinarily say? But – and here lies the genius of Cavell's questioning in *MWM* – these two questions are but one. The central enigma of rationality and the community is whether it is possible for me to speak *in the name of others*. This furthers the shift in Wittgenstein from the paradigm of description to that of confession, and the particular autobiographical tone of the *Philosophical Investigations*. In *MWM* and in its method, the idea that all philosophy is autobiographical was born, and it is here that Cavell's later project to realize this idea by writing an autobiography began. In *The Senses of Walden* he reclaims this tone of confidence:

The writer has secrets to tell which can only be told to strangers. The secrets are not his, and they are not the confidences of others. They are secrets because few are anxious to know them. Only those who recognize themselves as strangers can be told them, because those who think themselves familiars will think they have already heard what the writer is saying. They will not understand his speaking in confidence. (92)

---

[12] This section of the chapter partly relies on Laugier, *Why We Need Ordinary Language Philosophy*, chap. 7.

This remark brings us back to the notion of voice and the question of the foundations of agreement – the I as the ability to speak in my own name (cf. Hamawaki and Saito in this volume). It is important for the early Cavell that Wittgenstein says we agree *in* language and not *on* language. This means that we are not agents of the agreement; language precedes this agreement just as much as it is produced by it, and this very circularity constitutes an element of skepticism. The answer will not be found in convention, for convention is not an explanation of language's functioning, but rather a difficulty within it. The idea of convention cannot account for the practice of language. Our agreement – with others, with myself – is an agreement of voices; for Wittgenstein our *Übereinstimmung* is a "harmonic" agreement. Cavell defines an agreement that is neither logical, nor semantic, nor psychological, nor intersubjective. Instead, it is founded on nothing more than the validity of a voice. My individual voice claims to be a "universal voice"; this is what a voice does when it bases itself on itself alone, instead of on any condition of reason, in order to establish universal agreement. "Aesthetic Problems of Modern Philosophy" puts the question of the foundation of language in these Kantian terms, showing the proximity of Wittgenstein's and Austin's methods to a paradox inherent in aesthetic judgment: basing oneself on I in order to say what we say. In aesthetic judgment, Kant leads us to discover "a property of our faculty of cognition that without this analysis would have remained unknown": the "claim to universality" proper to judgments of taste.[13] Kant distinguishes the agreeable from the beautiful, which claims universal agreement, in terms of private versus public judgment. How can a judgment that has all the characteristics of being private claim to be public, to be valid for all? Kant noted the strange, "disconcerting" nature of this fact, whose *Unheimlichkeit* Wittgenstein took to the limit. It is what Kant calls the universal voice that supports such a claim; it is the *Stimme* heard in *übereinstimmen* – the very verb Wittgenstein uses when speaking of agreeing. The question of the universal voice is in *MWM* the question of the voice itself and of its arrogation. And this question becomes also the point of criticism.[14]

There is an unhappy dimension, a dimension of failure, in OLP, an obsession with cases where language fails us, where it is inadequate, inexpressive, inarticulate. Austin's classification of "infelicities" in his account of performatives in *How to Do Things with Words* is the

[13] Immanuel Kant, *Critique of the Power of Judgment*, trans. and ed. Paul Guyer and Eric Matthews (Cambridge University Press, 2000), 99.
[14] On this point, see the developments in Laugier, "Introduction to the French Edition."

background for Cavell's analyses. The ever-possible failure of performatives defines language as a human activity. One of the goals of OLP will be, then, to determine the ordinary ways in which an utterance can be infelicitous. The ever-present and sometimes tragic possibility of the failure of language and action is at the center of Austin's concerns.[15] Cavell takes it further in *MWM*. Skepticism runs throughout our ordinary use of language. I am constantly tempted and threatened by inexpressiveness. In *MWM* Cavell brings together Freud and Wittgenstein in their shared awareness of the impossibility of controlling what we say (reinforced by our will to master).

> Because the breaking of such control is a constant purpose of the later Wittgenstein, his writing is deeply practical and negative, the way Freud's is. And like Freud's therapy, it wishes to prevent understanding which is unaccompanied by inner change. In both, such misfortune is betrayed in the incongruence between what is said and what is meant or expressed; for both, the self is concealed in assertion and action and revealed in temptation and wish. (*MWM* 72)

Whether it is through ordinary language philosophy or psychoanalysis, the examination of our statements does not give us any greater mastery over our lives or words. This is the radical shift Cavell makes in *MWM*. In asking how *to mean* what I say, Cavell, far from reestablishing subjectivity by defining it as voice, turns the question of private language around. The problem lies not in being able to express what I have inside me – thinking or feeling something without being able to say it – but rather the opposite; it is to *mean what I say*. To say, as *How to Do Things with Words* demonstrated, that language is also action, does not mean I control language (for, as is clear from the central role excuses play in our lives, I do not control my actions any better). This summarizes an intuition expressed in *MWM*: the impossibility of speaking the world masks a refusal to know oneself and to *mean or be meaningful*. "What they had not realized was what they were saying, or, what they were really saying, and so had not known *what they meant*. To this extent, they had not known themselves, and not known the world" (*MWM* 40). Cavell adds here interestingly the definition, quoted before, of the ordinary world. The ordinary world is not everything there is in the world, "but it is important enough": it is the world of what matters – Cavell's world, the world we inherit from him, the world of *MWM*.

---

[15] On this, see Sandra Laugier, "The Vulnerability of the Ordinary: Goffman, Reader of Austin," *Graduate Faculty Philosophy Journal* 39/2 (2019), 367–401.

Revolutions

However, a new reading of Wittgenstein – the presentation of which is the purpose of "The Availability of Wittgenstein's Later Philosophy" – is necessary to bring out the way in which the voice is part of our human form of life. To do this, Cavell proposes that we redefine what we understand by grammar. There is a certain reading of Wittgenstein that leads to focusing on the rules that would constitute grammar, a grammar of the norms of language's functioning and its "normal" uses, that is acquired like any other form of knowledge. In contrast, Cavell proposes a reading of Wittgenstein in which learning is initiation into the "relevant forms of life." "In learning language, you do not merely learn the pronunciation of sounds, and their grammatical orders, but the 'forms of life' which make those sounds the words they are, do what they do" (*CR* 177–78).

With his first systematic study of Wittgenstein, first published in a collection dedicated to the *Philosophical Investigations*, Cavell found the tone for his reading of Wittgenstein, which would go on revolutionize the field of Wittgenstein studies (see Floyd's contribution to this volume). In "The Availability" he tells us how Wittgenstein's later philosophy teaches us things we know but do not want to know. Cavell subverts the recourse to the notion of a rule, replacing it with the notion of forms of life – the fabric/texture/whirl of human existence. We agree in forms of life, but this agreement neither explains nor justifies anything. All that we have is *what we say*, nothing else. In "The Availability" we see clearly Cavell's transition from the question of common language to that of shared forms of life, in which not only social structures are shared, but also everything that makes up the fabric of human lives and activities. Cavell shows both the fragility and the depth of our agreements, and focuses on the very nature of the necessities that emerge out of our forms of life. To agree in language means that language – our form of life – produces our understanding just as much as it is the product of an agreement. In this sense, it is natural to us, and the idea of convention is there to at once mimic and mask this necessity. Cavell's insistence on reading the concept of forms of life as *life*-forms, not simply *forms* of life, turns the given of Austin's datum into the given of life-forms – a second vertical dimension of form of life, coordinated to the first, horizontal, social agreement. Discussions of conventionalism have occluded the force of the "natural" sense of life-forms in Wittgenstein, the casual/fatal character of the ordinary that Wittgenstein evokes in his mention of "the natural history of humanity" – realities and structures of life, to which the beautiful epigraph from Jean Giraudoux also refers (*MWM* 44).

This allows us to understand – beyond banalities about a Wittgensteinian "therapeutic" – how reading Wittgenstein can transform us (how it is revolutionary). "When [Wittgenstein or the ordinary language philosopher] asks 'What would we say (what would we call) ... ?' ... he is asking something which can be answered by remembering *what is said and meant*" (*MWM* 64).

This sheds light on the relationship between grammar and "transcendental" knowledge. Grammar is not a philosophical method – unless it consists in asking, "what would we say if ... ?" or, "but would someone call ... ?" These are questions that ask one to say something about herself.

So the different methods are methods for acquiring self-knowledge ... perhaps more shocking, and certainly more important, than any of Freud or Wittgenstein's particular conclusions is their discovery that knowing oneself is something for which there are methods – something, therefore, that can be taught (though not in obvious ways) and practiced. (*MWM* 66–67)

Cavell's first reading of Wittgenstein's *Investigations* shows that "the nature of self-knowledge – and therewith the nature of the self – is one of the great subjects of the *Investigations* as a whole" (*MWM* 68). *The Claim of Reason* develops this line of thinking masterfully. But it is nevertheless the case that "The Availability" on its own established the principles of an unorthodox reading of Wittgenstein that continues to inspire us. By exploring our relevance to ourselves, *MWM* reveals the connection between the words we pronounce and hear, the truth we search for, and the life we want to lead – which was revolutionary in the philosophy, and in the culture, and in the politics of the late 1960s, and remains so today.

In fact, "revolutionary" is the word Cavell uses in his Foreword to describe "Wittgenstein's and Austin's sense of their ... tasks [as] ... a recognizable version of the wish 'to establish the truth of this world'":

Wherever there really is a love of wisdom – or call it the passion for truth – it is inherently, if usually ineffectively, revolutionary; because it is the same as a hatred of the falseness in one's character and of the needless and unnatural compromises in one's institutions. (*MWM* xxxix)

This revolutionary character, which Cavell attributes to Wittgenstein and Austin, to their capacity to transform us, is that of *MWM*. Thus, already in *MWM*, finding the real conditions of truth in politics and in ethics is the most urgent question. And that is what makes this book of essays the starting point of any inheritance of philosophy of language. This is, in a sense, all there is to understand in order to understand why and how it still matters.

2   Revolutionary Uses of Wittgenstein in *Must We Mean What We Say?*

Juliet Floyd

Introduction

Every remark Cavell makes in *Must We Mean What We Say?* (*MWM*) about Wittgenstein is significant, for he is at work throughout the book transforming philosophy through Wittgenstein. The idea is to exemplify, model, and extend Wittgenstein's "practice" with and in philosophy, morphologizing him (and so Cavell) into a revolutionary, fruitful philosopher of central relevance to our lives, politics, and culture. Cavell concertedly pries Wittgenstein out from the boxes of logical behaviorism, conventionalism/formalism, positivism, nihilism, cultural/social/linguistic conservatism, and rule-constrained "language-game" theories of meaning into which he was (and often still is) crammed.

Cavell accomplishes this not only by attending to the texts with care and brilliance, but also by opening up his American audience to European roots of Wittgenstein's philosophy. At the same time, he invites his European and American audiences to take up the most recent discoveries of Anglo-American philosophy through Wittgenstein. Finally, Cavell makes Wittgenstein's work with the whole tradition of analytic philosophy – with its European and American-imported admixtures of logical positivism and pragmatism – responsive to, and relevant for, American philosophy conceived as a larger, indigenous tradition – a matter he would pursue in *The Senses of Walden*, *The Claim of Reason*, *The World Viewed*, and his subsequent writings on Romanticism and Emerson. The lenses of Thoreau and Emerson would take Cavell beyond *MWM*, allowing him to pursue the "transcendental," "perfectionist"

I am grateful for the support of the Andrew W. Mellon Foundation for their Boston University Sawyer Seminar funding, 2016–19, and to Rebeccah Leiby, who helped organize the conference "Continuing Cavell: *Must We Mean* at Fifty," February 9, 2019. The Boston University Humanities Foundation generously helped fund that occasion and also gave me a Jeffrey Henderson Senior Research Fellowship that funded my fall 2020 writing of this essay. Members of the Boston University Center for the Humanities faculty seminar in fall 2020 gave me enormously helpful comments that led to improvements in the essay, as did my co-editors Greg Chase and Sandra Laugier.

quality of everyday life as a normative field for philosophical thought and criticism, and this would, incidentally, allow Cavell to work with their responses ("however inexpert") to Eastern philosophy: Cavell reads the *Bhagavad Gita*'s structure as an inspiration for *Walden*'s; Gandhi's thinking with "Civil Disobedience" interweaves with his own reading of *Walden*.

This progression of readings reveals numerous potentialities latent in all these thinkers and traditions and texts. But Wittgenstein is the fulcrum on which the most memorable and complex echoes and transformations turn. Cavell contrasts Wittgenstein's "writing" with Austin's "practice," and Wittgenstein's "practice" with Austin's "teachings" (*MWM*, xii, xxv), giving himself a path of regression toward what is most important and fundamental through his reception of them both – and this is the path that the first four essays in *MWM*, as a package, follow (the second half of the book injects Wittgenstein into the heart of literature). From Austin, Cavell draws out the pertinence of ordinary language philosophy (hereafter OLP) as a method, utilizing it in every branch of philosophy. Next, he complicates Austin by taking Wittgenstein to have deepened the roots of OLP by pressing it to explore problems of life and sources of skepticism. In "Austin at Criticism," the fourth essay in the first half of *MWM*, Cavell revisits Austin through this argumentative line.

MWM makes out this step from Austin to Wittgenstein. From them, Cavell says, he learned how to take his own recurrent doubts about the relevance of philosophy to life into philosophy, making it thereby relevant to life after all. This is done by showing us how deeply entrenched are our human tendencies to avoid life as it is, to make our talk empty, highblown, irrelevant, evasive, especially in philosophy. The grand and comprehensive systems of modern European philosophy, even Nietzsche's "Superman" (*Übermensch*), brought us the idea of "super-orders" (*Überordnungen*) for "super concepts" (*Überbegriffe*), concepts like "will," "freedom," and "action." Kant's critique of the "transcendent" use of concepts in metaphysics was an essential brake on uncritical metaphysics, and yet Kant did not carry the critique through, landing us, as Hegel observed, in Idealism and Skepticism. Hegel reached for Reality, but landed us, according to Kierkegaard, in falsely rationalistic structures of "history" and "freedom."

Can an appeal to "everyday language" alone free us from these misrationalized structures? Cavell's answer here is that we cannot appeal flatly to "language-games" with which we are familiar when we aim to shepherd our living concepts back home: this idea of OLP fails. He applies this insight in the second group of essays in *MWM*: e.g., the question of whether Kierkegaard liberates us from Hegel by means of the "heightened" angle he takes on concepts of "revelation" and "authority" in "On Authority and Revelation" is the subject of Cavell's essay "Kierkegaard's *On Authority and Revelation*." Here Cavell tests OLP, subjecting Kierkegaard's "qualitative" dialectical uses of these concepts to a Wittgensteinian investigation of their "grammar" (see Chapter 11). The point is to highlight our ability to go on and over and out with our familiar concepts, to emphasize the work involved in making sense of what a person means, making it salient, putting it to use in our own lives. And this is something that does not come for free, automatically, with "mastery" of a language or membership in a faith. Cavell shows us that what "mastery of a language" involves is just this ability to project forward, creatively, with concepts, to submit ourselves to the working through of others' words, including their "high" words – even if the use of high words may make us feel at times uncomfortable, emptied out.[1]

It is not enough, Cavell suggests – with a small swipe at Kierkegaard and a bow to Marx – to condemn in one's innermost heart the public and society as corrupt (*MWM* 174). One must take on the age as it comes, and work one's way through its specific forms of oppression, taking oneself to be at work within, and on behalf of, a community of speakers. And here we can and must make sense of what does not fall easily into our presently imagined language-games, especially in poetic regions of uses of language, especially in discussing our ultimate fates, or ultimate values, e.g., in religious and spiritual life. In such regions of our language concepts may receive what Wittgenstein elsewhere calls an "intransitive," as opposed to a "transitive" use[2]: no particular qualification or object or "what" is available to spell out the meaning. In his essay on Lear, Cavell cites Wittgenstein's citation of Luther, "Faith resides under the left nipple" (*MWM* 271) – these are invitations to enter into this sense-making within ordinary life.

History shows, Cavell reminds us, that modern European philosophy has fostered illusions and skeptical turns as often as it has revealed realities; its depths may be regarded as "superficial" – a point made by Wittgenstein, playing on the dialectic of the "deep" and the "shallow"[3]; "superficial" is a recurrent term of criticism throughout *MWM*.

[1] Robert Chodat, *The Matter of High Words: Naturalism, Normativity, and the Postwar Sage* (Oxford University Press, 2017).
[2] Ludwig Wittgenstein, *Preliminary Studies for the 'Philosophical Investigations': Generally Known as the Blue and Brown Books* (Oxford: Basil Blackwell, 1969), §15.
[3] Ludwig Wittgenstein, *Philosophical Investigations*, rev. 4th edn, trans. G.E.M. Anscombe, P.M.S. Hacker, and Joachim Schulte, ed. Hacker (Malden, MA: Wiley-Blackwell, 2009; 1st edn 1953), §97; hereafter cited parenthetically as *PI* (*PPF* = *Philosophy of Psychology – A Fragment*, within *PI*).

Wittgenstein's reminder that philosophy sometimes results in emptiness, in what Heidegger called "chatter," and what Wittgenstein labels mere "structures of air" (*PI* §118), Cavell admits and explores; and yet he takes the motto of *PI* from Nestroy – "progress always looks greater than it is" – to overturn, rather than endorse, Spenglerian pessimism about declines of civilizations. For Wittgenstein's motto implies that there is progress in philosophy, even if philosophy must gauge its grammar of "progress" differently, with more attention to the complex potential uses of "reality" and "illusion," than do science and history. Cavell cites with approval Hegel's idea that history is "cunning," and observes that it may even be "just" when he discusses the idea of modernism, with its radical machinations with, and exploitations of, the very idea of "progress" (*MWM* 207).

Austin and Wittgenstein showed Cavell how to "investigate philosophically the very topic of irrelevance" (*MWM* xxiii), the specific ways in which our ideas of a "super order" (including the straight denial that there is such a thing) lead us to miss what is before our eyes, the ground of words evolving, with us, in life. This frames the most central questions pursued in *MWM*: Why is it that our practices of speaking with a point, for a purpose, with reason, meaning what we say – or our failing to speak with these, speaking emptily or evasively or disguisedly or thoughtlessly or vaguely or irrelevantly – matter? *Why* is it that one person's appeal to what we ought to say or do, or what is logically necessary, may be comforting and releasing for her, but intolerably confining for another? And finally, *Why* are these issues so difficult to keep in view in philosophy?

Cavell makes Wittgenstein easier to recognize philosophically by painting him as a natural and needed step onward from Austin. This is not a correction of Austin, but an elaboration of his work's significance. Austin was sometimes "impatient" with philosophy, did not allow it to be called forth from his practice into its full power (*MWM* 107). His greatness in carrying out "fieldwork" in our everyday uses of language, in singling out contrasts of significance and calling out failures of words to mean, goes beyond this, providing a pathway forward that is a gift to philosophy that it is difficult, Cavell says, to imagine being "matched" (*MWM* 113). Indeed, says Cavell, "it would be something of an irony if it turned out that Wittgenstein's manner were easier to imitate than Austin's" (*MWM* 114).

Wittgenstein's writing does seem to call forth, more readily than Austin's, weak imitation ("jargon," as Wittgenstein once warned).[4] Too often he is accused of being a "master" who, like Svengali, draws

---

[4] Ludwig Wittgenstein, *Wittgenstein's Lectures on the Foundations of Mathematics: Cambridge, 1939*, ed. Cora Diamond (University of Chicago Press, 1989; 1st edn 1976), Lecture XXXI, 293.

people into uncritical requotation of his most beautiful metaphors, a "guru" who is needlessly obscure. But in Cavell's hands, things stand in the opposite way. Wittgenstein's mature interlocutor style, with its dynamism of multilogues and voice, shows us a way to "go on" in philosophy, a way to *find our own voice*, to test our own sense of relevance and irrelevance in philosophical argumentation, analogization, and criticism, and to allow ourselves to become vulnerable to our own responses to others' responses to us.[5]

Cavell takes Wittgenstein to build on the kind of attentiveness to our uses of words in life characteristic of Austin's teaching. But Cavell's Wittgenstein furthers the value of this teaching by exploring the many-colored character and dimensions of the nearly unlimited variety of human impulses toward emptiness, our fallenness in language. Readers can see right away that in *PI* Wittgenstein never explores ordinary uses of words in the field in the careful, micro-focused ways Austin does: the *Investigations* contains little of OLP in this sense. Instead, Wittgenstein invites his readers to investigate the extent and roots of, and possibilities for, OLP's methods insofar as philosophy aspires to address itself to what he calls our *"forms of life"* (*PI* §§19, 23–25, 240–42, *PPF* i). And his words live in the wild, or beyond it, beyond any particular place or time or context. This transforms Austin's fieldwork. Cavell stresses in every essay of *MWM* that Wittgenstein wants to make sense of, fill in, get the right angle on, important emptinesses in life and speech, rather than declaring them "meaningless" according to this or that criterial theory of meaning, in the manner of the positivists. Lack of meaningfulness comes instead through, e.g., sonorous claims as to "What we ought to do" in contexts that make these words merely hortatory and private to the speaker (*MWM* 11). The only truth to the "emotive" theory of ethics is that such emptiness is possible: but for Cavell, it must be overcome through philosophical investigation.

Forms of Life

The most significant and lasting move Cavell makes with Wittgenstein is to highlight the concept of "form of life," *Lebensform*, as central to his philosophy. Though the term only occurs five times in *PI*, the idea is

---

5 See Sandra Laugier, "Voice as Form of Life and Life Form," *Nordic Wittgenstein Review* 4 (2015), 63–81; Sandra Laugier, "Wittgenstein: Ordinary Language as Lifeform," in *Language, Form(s) of Life, and Logic: Investigations after Wittgenstein*, ed. Christian Martin (Berlin: De Gruyter, 2018), 277–304; Juliet Floyd, "*Lebensformen*: Living Logic," in *Language, Form(s) of Life, and Logic*, ed. Martin, 59–92.

central and centrally structured the maturation of Wittgenstein's later philosophy.[6] "One of [Wittgenstein's] best mottoes," Cavell tells us, is that "To imagine a language is to imagine a form of life" (*MWM* 172; *PI* §19); he quotes the remark twice (*MWM* 84). Forms of life, and not pre-given rules of language-games, concepts, cultures, or theses, are, Cavell insists, "always the ultimate appeal for Wittgenstein" (*MWM* 50). Cavell takes Wittgenstein's appeal to work with possibilities and necessities ("form"), rather than actualities or empirical facts. It is thus to our possibilities, positive and negative – our prospects and fears – that philosophy must devote itself. And "forms of life" are not merely immediate givens, but call forth our reflection on the very idea of givenness itself: this concept is thus really a norm of elucidation for the speaking human body.

That body is the "best" picture, as Wittgenstein says, of the human soul: one is not "of the opinion" that a body is ensouled; rather one lives and responds to and expresses "forms" (possibilities) of ensoulings with one's body, with one's expressions and words (*PI PPF* iv §25, see *MWM* 84, 240). Expression, tone, gesture, gait, and responses to responses shape one another, the "ordinary" of everyday life forming a dynamic arena of constant repairs, adjustments, and realignments. For Cavell the fragility of meaning is exemplified in the "given" drive for human love and acknowledgment – including the acknowledgment of human separateness and unlovedness, investigated and characterized in his essays on *Lear* and *Othello*.

An "investigation" in Wittgenstein is never sparked by a well-demarcated question, problem context, or empirical query (as it is, e.g., in the "normal science" Kuhn characterized in his *The Structure of Scientific Revolutions*). Instead, an investigation (*Untersuchung*, a "search beneath/amongst") responds to a situation in which we find ourselves lost ("a philosophical problem has the form, I don't know my way about/I don't recognize myself," *PI* §123, cf. §203), the "grammar" of the question unclear. Our thread out of the "labyrinth" of our lives with language requires the sorting through of several different paths, directing our attention toward the *Fragestellungen*, our possible question-positionings themselves, to allude to what was already an explicit aim of Wittgenstein's in his early philosophy.[7]

---

[6] Juliet Floyd, "Chains of Life: Turing, *Lebensform*, and the Emergence of Wittgenstein's Later Style," *Nordic Wittgenstein Review* 5/2 (2016), 7–89.

[7] Ludwig Wittgenstein, *Tractatus Logico-Philosophicus*, trans. C.K. Ogden (London: Routledge & Kegan Paul, 1922), Preface; hereafter cited parenthetically as *TLP*.

It is the "possibilities of phenomena," rather than actualities, that are to be explored: the logic, the "grammar" of the questions themselves (*PI* §90). This does not take us away from the world, but to it. Cavell's ways of investigating these things, of getting to reality by attending to a variety of possibilities before us, is one of the most important motifs in his book, the notion of possibility invoked throughout the text (*MWM* 65, 73–74, 116, 174, 194, 200, 221, 330, 342). This serves to undercut the empiricist, verificationist, and conventionalist understandings of Wittgenstein's thought that still cling to it today.[8]

"Form of life" and "technique" enter as terms into Wittgenstein's writing rather late, in 1937; they express major keynotes of his mature philosophy.[9] These notions only appeared, in fact, after Wittgenstein won through to the interlocutory, dynamic literary style of *PI*. The image of logic or "grammar" here is not "gap free" (*lückenlos*, a term from Frege; cf. *PI* Foreword). Instead, logic itself is rendered and reflected through glimpses, sketches, partial routines, questions, and claims that are broken off, recontextualized, moved, contested, and rearranged: through *life*. Cavell shows us how Wittgenstein's voice is all the voices of his interlocutors, and none of them fully, as if there is a Last Word that is unelaboratable – one is reminded here of the ending of Toni Morrison's *Beloved* (1987). *PI* expresses through its literary form a spirit of questioning, a response to philosophy as a "need of questioning" (*CR* 34). One of Cavell's typically inventive moves distinguishes what he calls "the voice of temptation" (the temptation toward questions leading us toward the super-concepts of dogmatism and skepticism) from the voice of "correctness," the voice that tries to bring these demands down to earth (*MWM* 71). These, he states, are "antagonists" in the drama of *Philosophical Investigations*, neither one winning the field once and for all, each living through the other (*MWM* 71). And they are hardly the only voices.

I have urged elsewhere, following Cavell's lead, that the interlocutory style of the *PI* was a necessary response to the mechanization of human rule-following placed at the foundations of mathematics by Alan Turing in 1936.[10] Turing's machine-casting of logic created novel possibilities for human forms of life with words (and/as computations), as we know:

---

[8] Timothy Williamson, *The Philosophy of Philosophy* (Malden, MA: Blackwell, 2007); compare Avner Baz, *When Words Are Called For: A Defense of Ordinary Language Philosophy* (Cambridge, MA: Harvard University Press, 2012).

[9] Floyd, "Chains of Life"; Juliet Floyd, "Wittgenstein on Ethics: Working through *Lebensformen*," *Philosophy and Social Criticism* 46/2 (2020), 115–30.

[10] Juliet Floyd, "Turing on 'Common Sense': Cambridge Resonances," in *Philosophical Explorations of the Legacy of Alan Turing: Turing 100*, ed. Juliet Floyd and Alisa Bokulich,

overwhelming floods of data and "information" becoming noise, social media's new complexities of self-presentation and expression, the weaponization of speech, the fraying of democracy, etc. As Wittgenstein surely knew, massive computational power was required to create atomic weapons, whose dropping in 1945 on civilians – this "dark time", as Wittgenstein calls it (*PI* Foreword) – enacted the full specter of what Cavell calls in *MWM* "skepticism": human beings' recurrent impulses to destroy meaning and life as they are given, often in the name of hope and salvation ("these dark times" include the concentration camps in Wittgenstein's native culture), a strange determination to be obsessed by catastrophe. Cavell's essay on Beckett's *Endgame* invokes the need for a "phenomenology of the Bomb" (*MWM* 136). The interplay between the phenomena of hope and catastrophic despair is one of the most important themes in *MWM*, as it is in *PI*.

Wherein lies the possibility of progress? The issue for Cavell (as for Wittgenstein) is the progress, not primarily of science – which will be as it may – but of ourselves. In the image Wittgenstein lays out in *Philosophical Investigations* (alluding to Turing) we have made *ourselves* into machines, symbolizing our *own* modes of operating in a particular way (*PI* §§190ff.).[11] As Cavell puts it, we subject ourselves to "spiritlessness" (*MWM* xxvii). The mad dream of solving the problems of meaning through our offloading ourselves and our difficulties to mechanization and general theory is recurrent not only in *PI* but in *MWM*. The idea is linked by Cavell to modernism in the arts, which he construes as a crisis in which the very idea of fraudulence, the destruction of art through new art, the destruction of theatre through real theatre, is intensified, and "science chic" (rules, theories, mechanisms) results (*MWM* 208–09). Cavell's pairing of modernism and mechanism (or flat literalism) is most explicitly articulated in "Music Discomposed" and in "Ending the Waiting Game," where demands for literalism fail altogether to overcome the wash of emptiness to which words may be subjected. The lesson of these essays, and Wittgenstein most of all, is that the corruptions of a tradition – its misuses – require us to work through it, use it (maybe by flipping it), and not pretend that we stand outside or above it by way of a theory.

Boston Studies in the Philosophy of Science (Dordrecht: Springer, 2017), 103–52; Juliet Floyd, "Turing, Wittgenstein and Types: Philosophical Aspects of Turing's 'The Reform of Mathematical Notation' (1944–45)," in *Alan Turing: His Work and Impact*, ed. S. Barry Cooper and Jan van Leeuwen (Amsterdam and Burlington, MA: Elsevier, 2013), 250–53.

[11] Juliet Floyd, "Teaching and Learning with Wittgenstein and Turing: Sailing the Seas of Social Media," *Journal of Philosophy of Education* 53/4 (2019), 715–33.

The second, equally pioneering half of *MWM* brings these Wittgensteinian points to bear on literature. They predict, and show, that OLP in general – Austin and Wittgenstein in particular – have a perennial philosophical relevance to the study of literature, and, more widely, to general education in a democratic culture.[12] Resisting as they do emptinesses in theories of significance (metaphor, myth, symbolism, and so on), Austin and Wittgenstein give us an indispensable skill and performative art: the ability to wriggle words free from the blindnesses always latent in our uses of them.[13] The detailed, sensitive "alignment" with reality of which Cavell writes is what is required for criticism and the uses of literature in life and self-education. Any author of criticism must subject his or her criticism to honest accounting with his or her life. And this can only be done by reflecting on what she is doing, not only with the texts, but with the theories and concepts, hence with the life and words, that she brings to them.

The Importance of Wittgenstein's Style of Writing

One of the most central contributions of Cavell's title essay "Must We Mean What We Say?" is his insistence that Wittgenstein's "literary achievement" is necessary to his purpose and thoroughly philosophical, not merely a matter of "style" alone – much less straight mysticism and obfuscation, which we still recurrently hear at times (*MWM* 70ff.). Wittgenstein's response to our self-mechanizations is to transform philosophical problematics into explorations of the logic, or "grammar," of concepts: what it is to speak, use them, apply them, with spirit and life. In exploring how we use them, we are exploring "reality," taking seriously that reality contains the words, whose uses evolve. Cavell: "ordinary language is not about language, anyway not in any sense in which it is not also about the world. Ordinary language philosophy is about whatever ordinary language is about" (*MWM* 95).

Cavell spells out a variety of ways of going beyond our tendency – especially the analytic tradition's tendency (though every philosophical tradition exhibits it) – to self-mechanize in philosophy, to fall back into

---

[12] See Paul Standish and Naoko Saito (eds.), *Stanley Cavell and the Education of Grownups* (New York: Fordham University Press, 2011).
[13] Compare Sarah Beckwith, *Shakespeare and the Grammar of Forgiveness* (Ithaca, NY: Cornell University Press, 2011); and Toril Moi, *Revolution of the Ordinary: Literary Studies after Wittgenstein, Austin, and Cavell* (University of Chicago Press, 2017). For a recent book bringing life in an especially à propos way into the uses of grammar and its pitfalls in our time, see Ibram X. Kendi, *How to Be an Antiracist* (New York: One World, 2019).

what Kant calls a school-concept of philosophy (*Schulbegriff*) as opposed to a world-concept (*Weltbegriff*).[14] We – we educators, we citizens, we teachers, we speakers – suppose that some other structure than our reflection on, or discussion of, our lives as *these* lives, *in* real life, with real possibilities and needs, can resolve our philosophical problems.

The peculiar pathology bequeathed to us by Frege and Russell (and by means of their work, modern computer science) is one of transforming structures of reasoning into a formalized deductive arrangement of argumentative inferences – mechanizing argumentation in that way. Wittgenstein's response requires us to explore what logic really *is, in life.* To accomplish this he must constantly ask us to make out the contrast between genuine claims and formalized patterns, empty insistence and dogmatism, joke and serious claim, to explore how we feel about, use, and respond to logic in our own mouths and the mouths of others. We must see how our lives are figured in and by others, make ourselves vulnerable in that way *to* logic, for there to be logic. There is much precise argumentation in *PI*, just as there is much precise argumentation in Austin and Cavell: we must not let the beauty of their writing and the fact that it is not always arranged in familiar, formalizable ways distract us from this. The purpose of their argumentation is, however, not to achieve certainty or dogmatic correctness. Nor is it aimed at depriving us of what certainties and evident truths we can make out. Rather, the *Investigations* is concerned to explore the many varieties of ways in which we miscast and misuse the "must" in what we mean, especially when we take ourselves to be "arguing" or "overcoming" mysticism and superstition. We often subject ourselves to our own trances with the "must" and the "must not".

The price of our dreams of mechanizing (or scientizing, or literalizing, or "objectively" arguing, or legislating) our way out of our situation is a loss of receptiveness to what Cavell – calling and responding to African American 1960s vernacular through Wittgenstein – calls *soul.*[15] In *PI*, Wittgenstein's interlocutory exchanges among voices – like jazz's improvisations, like the emerging blues to R&B to funk of James Brown in 1969 – is a way to get us to get back soul where it has been denied and cast out, to achieve honesty, express anger, deal with history, and find ways to joy, ecstasy, and praise (the concepts of joy, enjoyment, and

---

[14] Immanuel Kant, *Critique of Pure Reason,* trans. Allen W. Wood and Paul Guyer (Cambridge University Press, 1998), A838/B866f.

[15] American vernacular appears glancingly in *MWM,* e.g., 93: "It is essential to making an aesthetic judgment that at some point we be prepared to say in its support: don't you see, don't you hear, don't you dig?"

praise are crucial in *MWM*, though not yet ecstasy – that notion is left to be connected later on to Emerson, Thoreau, and the Romantics). Wittgenstein radicalizes the dialogue form, which goes at least back to Plato, allowing it a newfangled dynamism and multidimensionality: his method is to get into motion. It is a radicalization designed to defeat the usual mechanizations (evasions and hidings) of academic philosophical argumentation and interpretation, just as Plato's was, but engineered, so to speak, for a new era.

In *PI* there are no particular settings or characters or recognizable situations: the everyday contexts of dinners, familiar acquaintances, walks, and encounters in the agora are obliterated, occluded from view. Life is sped up, clipped, and slowed down to a nearly intolerable and broken-up pace: time is nearly forgotten, and must be brought back to each interlocutory exchange by the reader. Wittgenstein's words and questions in the *PI* find themselves crying out for our help, demanding that their use be embedded in a meaningful context: in short, to be *used* or "brought home." The souls in our words, the very idea of culture itself, have been obliterated or eclipsed beyond recognition (the term *Kultur*, warped by the Nazis, does not occur in *PI*, having been quite intentionally eliminated by Wittgenstein from his manuscript in 1937; it is replaced by *Lebensform*).[16] Wittgenstein is a "philosopher of culture" only in a very special sense: he sees what was called "culture" in his era to be obliterated, to require the growth of new forms of life.[17]

Like funk, *PI*'s literary form invites our bringing of a bodily lived context to it: we are asked to "Get Up Offa that Thing" (James Brown) and sing and dance. We must bring soul *to* words (cf. *PI PPF* iv). Cavell stresses the importance of the spirit of questioning, exploring the ways human response may be *made* relevant or irrelevant, drawing in at the center the notion of voice, the weaving and embedding and binding of words, things, and communities in life. This fruitful and dynamic idea of form of life as voice has been drawn out recently by Sandra Laugier, who has remixed Cavell's thoughts and deployed them in fields such as anthropology, popular culture, feminism, ethics, and social critique, imbibing the dynamic sense of the "social" that Cavell forwards.[18]

---

[16] Floyd, "*Lebensformen*," 75.
[17] See also Cavell, "Declining Decline," in *TNYUA* 29–76.
[18] Sandra Laugier, "Popular Cultures, Ordinary Criticism: A Philosophy of Minor Genres," trans. Daniela Ginsburg, *MLN* 127/5 (2012), 997–1012; *Why We Need Ordinary Language Philosophy*, trans. Daniela Ginsburg (University of Chicago Press, 2013); "The Ethics of Care as a Politics of the Ordinary," *New Literary History* 46/2 (2015), 217–40; "This Is Us: Wittgenstein and the Social," *Philosophical Investigations* 4/2 (2018), 204–22.

"I am not of the *opinion*" that my friend has a soul, as Wittgenstein writes – the very idea of soul is deeper than opinions, as every genuine ethics has always taught (*PI PPF* iv §22; *MWM* 240). At the same time, "one human being can be a complete enigma to another" (*PI PPF* iv §19). And it can make sense to say of some man or child that he is "an automaton" (*PI* §420, *PPF* xi §325). Skepticism, the fragility of what Cavell famously calls our "attunements" in judgment, can destroy worlds: the stuff of tragedy and, later on in Cavell's work on film and gender, melodrama. (*Contesting Tears* explores Cavell's experience that women are not so good as men at being world-breakers; they are more often "unknown.")

Fanaticism and Passion for Truth; Realism

The *realism* of Cavell's thought lies in his facing head-on, as a starting point, the dynamic "whirl of organism" of our forms of life with words (*MWM* 52). Our skills and sensitivities with worlds are part of the evolving reality in which we live, part of what is important. This world is both conceptual and biological: we live animal lives that are human, and Cavell was ultimately led to write on companionship and animal life.[19] As he puts it in a later essay on Wittgenstein as a philosopher of culture, the notion of "form of life" has at least two dimensions, the horizontal, ethological one, and the vertical, top-to-bottom biological one (*TNYUA* 41). We must add to this the possibilities for realism in the theatre of the self in a virtual world.

Cavell invites us to see that it is in the everyday – "diurnally," so to speak, day by day – that we work through the philosophy of our own and others' natures, to achieve the "peace" that philosophy, Wittgenstein remarks, should bring us (*PI* §133; cf. *TNYUA* "Declining Decline"). While Cavell embraces the idea that this "peace" may be figured as our deaths – so that he can accept that philosophy is for him, as it was for Pierre Hadot, an ancient form of life[20] – there is also the "realism" involved in getting through the day as our best self. In Wittgenstein's drafts of his remark about "peace" in the *Investigations* the more hopeful reading comes through: "peace" is what one achieves when one organizes the drawers in one's desk, so that one can sit down and write peacefully, pulling out thoughts and creating new ones and breaking off whenever

[19] Stanley Cavell, "Companionable Thinking," *Wittgenstein and the Moral Life: Essays in Honor of Cora Diamond*, ed. Alice Crary (Cambridge, MA: MIT Press, 2007), 281–98.
[20] Pierre Hadot, *Philosophy as a Way of Life: Spiritual Exercises from Socrates to Foucault*, ed. Arnold Davidson, trans. M. Chase (Oxford and Cambridge, MA: Blackwell, 1995).

one wishes to, never rifling through a disordered pile of words in a frenzy of anxiety.

The anxiety will not be quelled by formal theories of language. Anglo-American philosophers of language and mind have increasingly turned away from a single-minded focus on compositional, formalized theories of syntax and semantics to look at what is sometimes called "applied" philosophy of language: neuro and cognitive science as philosophy; the evolution of in-group and out-group morality; the analysis of slurs, hate speech, falsities, and disinformation.[21] More positively, there is an increasing interest of late in the ethics and language of care, of vulnerability, and of loss: words that we find to repair forms of life that have faced catastrophic loss.

Following Cavell, we should take such widenings to verify the power of OLP, rather than reinforcing the idea that a "semantics"/"pragmatics" distinction tells us about the "core" of philosophy of language (*MWM* 11, 18). Cavell's Austin–Wittgenstein OLP is not "applied philosophy of language," as if a kind of marginal subbranch of something larger. From the point of view he erects in *MWM*, the formal development of seman-tics is instead a mathematical "application" of ordinary language, and it is the latter that is prior and preeminent as a field of critical focus.

This is another main thrust of the title essay in *MWM*. Political and ethical concerns lie at the center of this, as Cavell periodically reminds us. They lie at the origins of OLP as well. Austin, a brilliant tactical mind, was in 1944 vested by the British army with the large responsibility of deter-mining the German order of battle on D-Day (like Ryle, another Oxford philosopher, he was trusted to administer and direct). Cavell praises Austin's teaching, his "didactic directions for profitable study," his "lists of exercises," his "liking for sound preparation," and his "disapproval of sloppy work and lazy efforts" (*MWM* 113–14). These were devoted to inculcating in Austin's Oxford students – future civil servants and academ-ics – a suspicion of high-flown, ideologized "cackle," a willingness to question authority, in short, a respect for the genuine work of truth.

Genuine responsibility to truth requires, Austin shows us, the import-ance of establishing and urging, from occasion to given occasion, that we do mean what we say. And this in turn requires the skill and courage to explore the rub and responsibility of slow, careful scrutiny of sometimes stubborn facts, about our own lives with words and those of others.

Cavell stresses in his Foreword to *MWM* the importance of OLP's power to draw out our "passion for truth" by bringing us "to a

[21] Luvell Anderson and Ernie LePore, "Slurring Words," *Noûs* 47/1 (2013), 25–48; Samia Hesni, "Illocutionary Frustration," *Mind* 127/508 (2018), 947–76.

consciousness of the words we must have, and hence of the lives we have" which, he writes, "represents for me a recognizable version of the wish to establish the truth of this world" (*MWM* xxv). This part of the work of truth is never done, because the tendencies we all have to evade the unending responsibility for apt and appropriately meaningful speech in life, in our institutions, and in our conduct are endless tasks.

Just here Cavell fingers a confusion in philosophy: the idea that science alone can exhaustively and preeminently realize our passion for truth. This is the idea, for example, that empirical psychology and/or sociology are *the* ways to come to know ourselves, and to know what we mean, and how, and how far obligated by this we are. Far from it. Cavell argues that it is instead the very successes of science, its evident excellence, that generates the problem: it shifts our focus away from our given forms of life, from the passion for truth itself. "Science chic," as Cavell nicely calls it, "leave[s] us dryly ignorant of ourselves":

> Our problem is not that we lack adequate methods for acquiring knowledge of nature, but that we are unable to prevent our best ideas – including our ideas about our knowledge of nature – from becoming ideologized. Our incapacity here results not from the supposed fact that ordinary language is vague; to say so is an excuse for not recognizing that (and when) we speak vaguely, imprecisely, thoughtlessly, unjustly, in the absence of feeling, and so forth. (*MWM* 69)

Cavell's uses of OLP to resist "ideologization" lie at the center of OLP as Cavell construes it, and with such prescience. What words could better diagnose the ways thoughtlessness and untruth in speech have become a mode of life on the Internet today, where psychological profiles are constructed for each one of us with each click of a button, software generating further content targeted at our individualized desires? As Gramsci warned, the production of consumption has come to replace the consumption of production, and the risk run by our inability to prevent our best ideas from being hijacked, commercialized, weaponized, and/or ideologized is everywhere acknowledged, often as a problem for science itself. We must learn, practically, how we may surmount the challenges and mean what we say.

In going beyond the confines of the Vienna Circle, Wittgenstein addressed himself to the "kink" in history presented to philosophy by the successes of modern science, the transition from "great philosophers" to "skillful" ones, but he denied that ethics could be a matter of skill alone.[22] Reworking Thomas Kuhn's famed appropriation of

---

[22] Ludwig Wittgenstein, *Wittgenstein: Lectures, Cambridge 1930–1933: From the Notes of G.E. Moore*, ed. David G. Stern, Brian Rogers, and Gabriel Citron (Cambridge University Press, 2016), 5:2.

Wittgenstein's notion of a "paradigm" to capture what is at stake in the ideas of "tradition" and of "revolution" – an appropriation Kuhn partly worked out in conversation with Cavell, when they were together on the faculty at Berkeley – Cavell widens this sense of a "kink" into a program for philosophy: the path is not straight, but requires a starting point in "forms of life," and the "skill" of "aligning" words with reality (*MWM* 20).

The importance of OLP as Cavell understands it lies in its connection with what Ryle called "know how": our skills in working relevantly (sensitively, authentically, openly, receptively, artfully, carefully ...) with words in particular contexts, projecting them into life and the world (to use a notion Cavell develops at length in *CR*). "Contexts" are not givens like boxes into which we insert words according to pre-given rules or programs: they are built up in our lives with words (the World Wide Web is not a context, but an opportunity (and obligation) to try to create new ones).

This emphasis on our ability to "fit" our concepts to reality has been developed in the substantial body of work by Cora Diamond, with her idea of a "realistic spirit" which transverses ethics and moral philosophy through philosophy of logic.[23] It was also emphasized by Hilary Putnam, in his post-1990 forms of "realism." Both of these influential philosophers are deeply and explicitly indebted to Cavell's readings of Wittgenstein.[24] Their work reinforces the importance of securing and furthering a novel understanding of Wittgenstein that goes beyond the positivism and nihilisms of earlier interpretations. John McDowell's attack on the "non-cognitivism" associated with conventionalist understandings of rule-following in ethics illustrates another way of working with Cavell's ideas among his contemporaries.[25] Scholarly extensions by those who followed Cavell, Putnam, and Diamond congealed in the early 2000s what has come to be known as "the New Wittgenstein."[26] The heart of this approach's novelty, as I understand it, is a rejection of conventionalism and pessimism as hallmark Wittgensteinian ideas, a

[23] Cora Diamond, *The Realistic Spirit: Wittgenstein, Philosophy and the Mind* (Cambridge, MA: MIT Press, 1991).

[24] Hilary Putnam, *The Threefold Cord: Mind, Body and World* (New York: Columbia University Press, 1999) and *Philosophy in an Age of Science: Physics, Mathematics, and Skepticism* (Cambridge, MA: Harvard University Press, 2012); for realism in philosophy of mathematics, see Juliet Floyd, "Aspects of the Real Numbers: Putnam, Wittgenstein, and Nonextensionalism," *Monist* 103 (2020), 427–41.

[25] See John McDowell, "Non-Cognitivism and Rule-Following," in *The New Wittgenstein*, ed. Alice Crary and Rupert Read (New York: Routledge, 2000), 38–52 (at 43).

[26] See Crary and Read (eds.), *New Wittgenstein*.

refusal to regard his work as "all about language (or concepts)" rather than a call for sensitivity in "aligning" words with realities. Even where recent Wittgenstein scholars may criticize Cavell for being too naively optimistic, or differ amongst themselves about how to read Wittgenstein's notion of "grammar," they are everywhere indebted to his release of Wittgenstein (and OLP more generally) from the fixed box of "rules of language."[27] This release allows us to do the work of actually working through *hard* discussions, difficulties we face in life, through reflection on the importance of what we mean, say, and do with words. So in this way, following Cavell (but not always doing what Cavell did), they open up Wittgenstein's philosophy, projecting it to new realms.

Cavell insists on reading philosophers as thinkers on journeys who move along not only by means of theses and corrections of theses. One of the most important of his contributions to Wittgenstein scholarship was to suggest that we learn how to read the *Tractatus* through the later philosophy, as the beginning of an unfolding of thought, and not simply regard the *Tractatus* as a work of logical empiricism and the later philosophy as having evolved beyond, or wholly negated it (*TNYUA* 31–32). This idea had a great impact on the so-called New Wittgenstein generation: they went back in the early 1980s, under the influence of Cavell, Hidé Ishiguro, Brian McGuinness, and Cora Diamond, to interpret the *Tractatus* anew: no longer as primarily a work of logical empiricism, or an application of Kantian or Russellian ideas, but also as a first step in the unfolding of a certain recasting of certain ideas of what philosophy can – and cannot – be.[28]

Rule-Following

We are always doing philosophy *in* life. In doing philosophy the ways Cavell does it, we are constantly exploring what Cora Diamond called, in one of her most important essays, "faces" of necessities of words and actions – in brief, their *character*.[29] *PI* analogizes words with faces in many places: the words "look out" at us, crying for interpretation; they show us aspects, features, drawing in our responses, rearranging grammar through rejuxtapositions of words. Cavell often asks us to let

---

[27] Steven G. Affeldt, "The Ground of Mutuality: Criteria, Judgment and Intelligibility in Stephen Mulhall and Stanley Cavell," *European Journal of Philosophy* 6/1 (1998), 1–31; Stephen Mulhall, "The Givenness of Grammar: A Reply to Steven Affeldt," *European Journal of Philosophy* 6/1 (1998), 32–44.

[28] The literature is vast; on Cavell, see Victor Krebs, "Around the Axis of Our Real Need," *European Journal of Philosophy* 9/3 (2001), 344–74.

[29] "The Face of Necessity," in Diamond, *Realistic Spirit*, 243–66.

the texts (or films, or artworks) read us, to "make ourselves vulnerable" to them, to see what peers out at us from the words used, e.g., by Shakespeare or Emerson (cf. *CR* 495), to see our own potentialities in what we make of them. As Karl Kraus said, "if a monkey looks in (to a book), then a monkey looks out." In philosophy we are working on ourselves, with our characterizations of words and actions and ourselves, seeing what aspects these are capable of showing us, to show ourselves who we are and might become.[30]

Calling attention to the fact that the "ultimate appeal" in Wittgenstein is not to rules or arbitrary decisions, but to the importance of our *forms of life* with language – our embodiments of meaning through speech and gesture and characterization – is the main focus of the second essay in *MWM*, "The Availability of Wittgenstein's Later Philosophy," a searing criticism of David Pole's interpretation of Wittgenstein. Pole made the fateful mistake of taking the notions of "rule" and "language-game" to be basic for Wittgenstein, reading into him precisely the idea Cavell is concerned to deny: that "ordinary language philosophy" depends upon the thesis that there is a pre-given set of rules for the language-games we play, and that the job of philosophy is to unearth them, and that therefore the idea of "following a rule" is clear and uncontested in the later Wittgenstein. According to this reading, "language-games" *are* our language, and Wittgenstein's philosophy is devoted solely to their description. Pole infers, as so many other (mis)readers of Wittgenstein do, that this is ultimately a form of conventionalism in which necessities lie in arbitrary "linguistic" "decisions" and "conventions" of coordinated response. This would be a kind of postmodernist formalism, but (as Greg Chase explains in Chapter 5) Wittgenstein is actually engaged in *PI* in *defeating* convention and formalism, in overcoming the legacy not only of the Vienna Circle's positivism but of the postmodern formalism that would eventually emerge in thinkers such as Lyotard.

Not long after *MWM* appeared, Saul Kripke began to develop an influential criticism of the idea that Wittgenstein unproblematically subscribes to a clear idea of "following a rule."[31] Like Cavell, Kripke took skepticism about necessity and concepts to be a central feature of Wittgenstein's later thought. "Rule-following" or "Meaning Skepticism" has generated an increasingly intricate literature deriving from Kripke's Humean reading of Wittgenstein, according to which

---

[30] Juliet Floyd, "Aspects of Aspects," in *The Cambridge Companion to Wittgenstein*, ed. Hans Sluga and David Stern (Cambridge University Press, 2017), 361–88.

[31] Saul A. Kripke, *Wittgenstein on Rules and Private Language: An Elementary Exposition* (Cambridge, MA.: Harvard University Press, 1982).

there is "no fact of the matter" about what I "ought" to do if I really mean to follow a rule of a series such as "+2" (2, 4, 6 ...). Kripke argues that if we meet a skeptic (or deviant child, as in *PI* §§185ff.) who insists that she meant by "+2" (2, 4, 6 ... and then 1004, 1008 ...) there is nothing to which we may appeal in calling the child "wrong". Our meaning, much less the child's intentions, do not determine or fix all the steps, and cannot. Kripke concludes that Wittgenstein's "skeptical solution," in the manner of Hume and Berkeley, is to insist that the only uniformity in meaning we may demand is a consensus forged through our insistence on "going on in the same way." As Wittgenstein puts it in *The Brown Book* – but, interestingly, not in *PI* – we exclude the deviant child and treat him as a "lunatic."[32]

Cavell's response to this remark in *The Claim of Reason* was to feel "rather anxious" about it: "these people are in a great hurry to separate out lunatics" (*CR* 112). On the other hand, in our society children who will not add as we do, who will not go along, are "set apart," "ostraci[zed]" (*CR* 112). In a later essay (in *CHU*) Cavell explicitly developed this response to Kripke, once again emphasizing the lived reality of our constant efforts to treat our "goings on" with words as a matter for repair, invention, shared routes of feeling and response, and so on: the work, in part, of art and certainly more generally of the activity of giving words to one another in life.[33] The main difference between Kripke's and Cavell's explorations of skepticism and rule-following in Wittgenstein remains what is at the heart of *MWM*: Cavell places front and center the idea that it is the dynamism of our forms of life, the continual reembedding and weaving of words in life and creating reattunements in meaning – rather than fixed rules of language-games – that characterizes the starting and ending point of human lives with logic.

For Cavell investigations of "grammar" are dynamic, an arena of theatricalization, pleading, contesting, repairing, excusing, and so on: all the many ways we have of binding ourselves to our words, and to each other, and to reality, in life. Kripke's more narrow focus leaves Wittgenstein in a skeptical form of denial, a denial that "there is a fact of the matter" about how one should "go on" with a rule. But this form of skepticism leaves our ordinary practices ultimately unexamined. Cavell, more self-reflexively, takes Wittgenstein to be working through the sources of skepticism itself, showing how the power of skepticism lies precisely in its refusal of obviousness, and the difficulties of our attempts

---

[32] Wittgenstein, *Preliminary Studies*, §30, 92; CHU 92–93.
[33] Stanley Cavell, "The Argument of the Ordinary: Scenes of Instruction in Wittgenstein and in Kripke," in *CHU* 64–100.

to catch and characterize what *is* "obvious," which is what is most difficult to clearly *see*.

This shows that Kripke *deprives* working philosophy of the concept of the obvious itself. His refusal to explore or work with this concept prevents an investigation of it, one of Wittgenstein's major tasks. As Cavell writes: "Wittgenstein's later philosophy can be thought of as investigations of obviousness" (*MWM* 312), where what is "obvious" may not remain so very long. In Cavell's understanding skepticism also eclipses our understanding of what the "real" is, for it denies the relevance of forms of life, of realities (dispositions, claims, biological tendencies, histories) *to* meaning. By contrast, for Cavell the most powerful antidotes to the powers of skepticism lie not the claims of abstract rules or truth-as-such, but the promise of the quotidian itself. This requires us to constantly re-explore and test our attunements in language.

That this exploration of the grammar of attunement has a precursor in Kant, in particular in his *Critique of Judgement* – a work devoted to a critique of aesthetic and teleological judgment – is the focus of the third essay in *MWM*, "Aesthetic Problems of Modern Philosophy." Because other essays in this volume explore its importance, I shall not say much more about this essay, except to stress that what Kant calls the *heautonomy*, or self-reflexive, self-picturing nature of aesthetic and teleological judgment, when we claim to speak "with a universal voice" ("this is beautiful!" as opposed to "this is beautiful to me") lies close to the heart of what Cavell wishes to draw from Wittgenstein's philosophical procedures.[34] This implies that philosophy involves using words for myself, reflecting *on* myself *through* my responses to and with words, in other words, that the writing of philosophy has – just as Plato and Wittgenstein suggest – an autobiographical purpose. In both philosophers, the interlocutory exchanges record, presumably, conversations each philosopher really had, and/or tell us what they themselves made of what they remembered: they are confessions as much as directives. To accommodate all our voicings "with a universal voice" we must attend to forms of life, rather than shooting for unanimity directly.

At this point we see how central to Cavell's reception of Wittgenstein is his turning toward literature, music, and theatre in the second half of *MWM*. For here we may educate our responses to ourselves, to our own responses, and share these with others, testing and exploring

---

[34] Juliet Floyd, "Heautonomy and the Critique of Sound Judgment: Kant on Reflective Judgment and Systematicity," in *Kants Ästhetik/Kant's Aesthetics/L'esthétique de Kant*, ed. Herman Parret (Berlin and Boston, MA: De Gruyter, 1998), 192–218.

attunements. The concepts of love, joy, and what Cavell calls "acknowledgment" are central to all these essays, and I will say a brief word or two about this in closing.

Joy and Social Change

The frequency with which Cavell speaks of "enjoyment" in *MWM* develops Wittgenstein's remark in the *Tractatus'* Preface that the purpose of his writing was to give the reader who understands him "pleasure" (*TLP* Preface). Cavell works into his discussion of Wittgenstein a reading of the *Tractatus* remark that "The world of the happy man is a different one from that of the unhappy man" (*TLP* 6.43). The specific pleasure at stake is the pleasure of philosophizing, of reflecting, learning how to enjoy going on with oneself, to *become* someone. It is fascinating to see that the Black Lives Matter movement, particularly in the heated street exchanges during the contestation of the 2020 presidential election, chose joy as the signal concept to express the excitement of nonviolent protest for change. Joy is an alternative to rage and a force for alteration and transformation.[35]

Cavell's turn toward literature and poetry in the second bouquet of essays in *MWM* is to bring us pleasure. But this pleasure, including especially the pleasure of tragedy as Cavell construes it in his most memorable essays on *Lear* and *Othello* (for more on the latter, see *CR* 481–96), is not generally a matter of working with pleasant things: it is not a pleasure of subject matter, but of allowing oneself to be hit by something, to incorporate the sense of being touched and moved into a movement in oneself. To incorporate tragedy, as in these plays, is to see that it is as real a thing in our lives as the bread boxes and tables and chairs we ordinarily find ourselves discussing in epistemology class, and to see also that the most fundamental problems of knowledge in life are faced as problems of what others know, see, say, and feel. This is not, as Wittgenstein emphasizes in the *Investigations*, a matter of observation in the sense of an induction from experience. It is a matter of making something of one's own experience, and doing so in an exemplary way, so that a community home, some kind of form of life, is available to one's making.

As Cavell puts it, we do not *have* to "go on enjoying the proceedings" in *Othello*, "and yet the empirical and the transcendental are not as clearly

---

[35] Note that in the Philadelphia resistance to the overturning of the American election in November 2020, joy was developed as an explicit concept for resistance by the Black Lives Matter movement. See www.blmphilly.com/galleries/black-joy-matters.

separate as, so to speak, we thought they were" (*MWM* 329). To reassure ourselves, once we are involved in the performance and see the horror of Desdemona's murder, that "they are only pretending" is childlike. The purpose of the play is to help us grow into a form of life, to align the idea of love as it is in our world with our lives and our words with others, to align us with the concept's reality. The important point is not that play-acting happens in a play, or that we find love in our own lives (if we do, it is a favor of fate), but that the performance activates a whole field of related concepts, feelings, and sensibilities that form the true "grammar" of the forms of life in which human grief and joy can have a place. The question of whether a dog can feel grief is suggested in Wittgenstein, but not posed, when he writes in the *Investigations* that

"Grief" describes a pattern which recurs, with different variations, in the tapestry of Life [*Lebensteppich*]. If a man's bodily expression of sorrow and of joy alternated, say with the ticking of a clock, here we would not have the characteristic course of the pattern of sorrow or of the pattern of joy (*PI PPF* I §2).

It is Cavell's contention, I have argued, that a freeing of ourselves from mechanization is part of the purpose of philosophizing in the manner of Austin and Wittgenstein. This is crucial, as he argues, for what he calls "the good of society" (*MWM* 347). His sense that the good of society is bound up with the plasticity and drive for good in the self is inherited from pragmatism, but Cavell turns and pressures this by means of Wittgenstein. The need to become a particular individual in a society that tells itself that there are no castes (when surely, empirically, there are) and no history (when we know that there is) requires the work of each self embedding itself over and over again in the community.

In *MWM* Cavell tethered his sense of the function of the arts to the time of the Vietnam era in the United States, but his move toward the figure of the child is as current now as it could be:

we had hardly expected, what now is apparently coming to be the case, that the ordinary citizen's ordinary faithfulness to his children may become a radical political act. We have known, anyway since eighteenth-century France and nineteenth-century America and Russia that high art can be motivated by a thirst for social change. But in an age in which the organs of news, in the very totality and talent of their coverage, become distractions from what is happening, presenting everything happening as overwhelmingly present, like events in old theater – in such an age the intention to serious art can itself become a political act: not because it can label the poison in public words, purify the dialect of the tribe – perhaps it can't, for all words now are public and there is no known tribe; but because it is the intention to make an object which bears one's conviction and which might bring another to himself. (*MWM* 347)

This idea of bringing "another to oneself" is refracted here through the Wittgensteinian idea of "bringing words home." In learning to watch how words and wishes may be embedded in particular lives, we shepherd ourselves back to others, become worthy of being brought to: we become worthy of speech itself, worthy of what words can mean. Nothing guarantees that absorption in art or religion will bring this about. But the artist (playwright, philosopher, filmmaker, painter, everyday person) who makes an object (or a field of significance) that is designed to "bear conviction" produces something which is an "attestation," Cavell says: faith and knowledge through the hope of self-knowledge (*MWM* 348). This deep understanding of what I would call the practical import of Wittgenstein's later philosophy is unique to Cavell, and one of the greatest gifts he leaves us in *MWM*.

3   Actions and Their Elaboration

Jean-Philippe Narboux

That the description of human actions is inherently problematic, even litigious, is perhaps Cavell's single most important contention concerning the concept of action. He writes:

Actions, unlike envelopes and goldfinches, do not come named for assessment, nor, like apples, ripe for grading. (*CR*265)

This makes "naming actions" a most "sensitive occupation" (*MWM* 35). This thesis runs through many of the essays collected in *MWM*. It comes to the fore in the eponymous essay of the collection (Chapter 1) and in "A Matter of Meaning It" (Chapter 8). It also supplies the leading thread of Part Three of *CR*. Cavell builds on Anscombe's observation that human actions do not qualify as intentional or voluntary except insofar as they are brought under a description and on Austin's related study of excuses as factors reducing or abrogating human agency (which they do only relative to a description), but pushes the inquiry further back by asking *how we arrive at descriptions of actions in the first place*.

According to Cavell, it belongs to the nature of human actions that they should both admit of and call for *further descriptions* – "elaboratives," i.e., explanations, justifications, excuses – whenever they prove questionable (*CR* 296; *MWM* 8). These are never entered as a matter of course, or as a foregone conclusion (cf. *CR* 122). What makes it possible and necessary to dwell on what one is doing or has done by way of such redescriptions is precisely that the descriptions under which it is to be brought are not determined. Cavell contends that we need to come to terms with this grammatical feature of the concept of human action if we are to comprehend the nature of practical reasoning and practical knowledge, hence that of moral reasoning and moral knowledge (*CR* 293, 310–12, 315; *MWM* 231–33).

Cavell never lost sight of "the opening issue" of his first plan for a dissertation, "The Concept of a Human Action in Kant and Spinoza" (*LDIK* 55ff., 318f., 338; *CR* xv, xix), viz., "how one determined, in Kant's view, what the maxim of an action is out of the infinite number of things I can be said to be doing at any moment" (*LDIK* 318–19). In both *MWM* and *CR*, echoing Anscombe's qualms in "Modern Moral Philosophy,"[1] he reproaches Kant for having failed to take proper measure of the special difficulty that the description of action poses: "This categorial formulation does not tell us how to determine what was done; neither does Kant's categorical formulation, although, by speaking of "the" maxim of an action, it pretends to, or anyway makes it seem less problematical than it is" (*MWM* 25; see *CR* 265). In this essay, I expound Cavell's early account of action and moral reasoning by bringing together strands of *MWM* (especially Chapters 1, 2, 7, and 8) and *CR* (especially Part Three) whose intrinsic importance and mutual relevance remain to this day underappreciated. I defend his account against various objections to the conception of practical knowledge around which it revolves: that "to know what you are doing is to be able to elaborate the action" (*CR* 311).

This requires reconstruction since none of the above-mentioned writing is primarily concerned with developing a positive and unified account of human action. If an interest in the topic of human agency systematically recurs in these writings, this is because Cavell traces a number of seemingly unrelated philosophical misconceptions to a single false alternative concerning action: the alternative between construing intentional action as an external physical movement whose efficient cause lies in a prior mental event (this Cavell regards as a "disastrous" picture of action) and regarding it as a game-like move whose rationalization lies in a certain set of defining rules (a prima facie more promising, but equally inadequate, picture of action). The variegated topics of these misconceptions include statements about ordinary language and their invocation for the purpose of philosophical criticism, the relation of rules to imperatives, the place of intention in works of art and our relation to them, the rise and decline of theater in general and tragedy in particular, the rationality of morality, and the relation of facts to values. What this false alternative obscures is the nature of the relation between saying and doing, the distinct albeit closely related senses in which both are (must be) meant, intended and so are (must be) ascribable to us (*MWM* 32). Pulling together the main threads of Cavell's account of action helps bring out the internal unity of *MWM*.

---

[1] "[Kant's] rule about universalizable maxims is useless without stipulations as to what shall count as a relevant description of an action with a view to constructing a maxim about it." Elizabeth Anscombe, *Collected Philosophical Papers*, 3 vols. (Oxford: Blackwell, 1981), vol. III: *Ethics and Politics*, 27; hereafter cited as *CPP* III.

Elaboratives and the Rationality of Moral Disputes

Elaboratives Defined

The concept of an elaborative is meant to circumscribe a class of utterances by which an agent *further articulates* or *redescribes* what he is doing or has done in response to a query. Cavell equates elaboratives with "the defenses we learn in learning to defend any of our conduct which comes to grief: those excuses, explanations, justifications ... which make up the bulk of moral defense" (*CR* 295f., xvi, 163).

Elaboratives are thus first-person utterances proffered in response to the question "Why?" in the special sense in which this question asks for a *reason for acting* and is applicable to an action if and only if this action counts as intentional *under the description* that it mentions.[2] Thus an agent can often justify, or at least explain, what he is in the course of doing intentionally by supplying a *wider description* of what he is doing that mentions some further intention with which he is acting ("Why are you breaking these eggs?" – "I am making an omelet").[3] Elaboratives possess third-person counterparts, to which they are internally related: these third-person counterparts are typically entered *on behalf of* the agent whose action they concern.

To produce a moral defense is "to undertake to show that an action which on the surface, or viewed one way, appears callous or wanton, is nevertheless justified or anyway excusable" (*MWM* 163). The division of moral defenses into excuses and justifications can be traced to Austin. In justifications, "we accept responsibility but deny that it was bad" whereas in excuses "we admit that it was bad but don't accept full, or even any, responsibility."[4] Excuses can be defined as "the different ways, and different words, in which on occasion we may try to get out of things, to show that we didn't act 'freely' or were not 'responsible'" (Austin, *Papers*, 273). Thus, "the tenor of so many excuses is that I did it but only *in a way*, not just flatly like that" (187). In excuses, instead of vindicating what was done by way of a fuller description of it, we implicitly "admit that it wasn't a good thing to have done" but submit a fuller description of it in order to "argue that it is not quite fair or correct to say *baldly* 'X did A'" (176). In Hart's words, an excuse marks "our refusal to say

---

[2] See Elizabeth Anscombe, *Intention* (Cambridge, MA: Harvard University Press, 1957), §§15, 18.

[3] *Ibid.*, §§22, 26; Michael Thompson, *Life and Action: Elementary Structures of Practice and Practical Thought* (Cambridge, MA: Harvard University Press, 2008).

[4] J.L. Austin, "A Plea for Excuses," in *Philosophical Papers*, ed. J.O. Urmson and G.J. Warnock (Oxford University Press, 1979; 1st edn 1961), 175–205 (at 176).

'He did it' without qualification."[5] The question "Why?" is rejected, if not as inappropriate, nevertheless as inapplicable *as it stands*, without further qualification. In this respect, the manner in which an excuse challenges an unqualified ascription of action is analogous to the manner in which a legal plea challenges a legal accusation.

The issue of *the fairness of speech* thus proves indiscernible from the issue of fairness *simpliciter*, i.e., *justice*. Indeed, terms of excuses bear an internal relation to terms of aggravations, such as "deliberately" or "on purpose": aggravations can be regarded as the "opposite numbers" of excuses insofar as an excuse "often takes the form of a rebuttal of one of these" and aggravations "often bring in the very things that excuses, if we had any, would be designed to rule out" (*Papers*, 177, 273). Conversely, statements of the form "I did it" or "He did it" are often in the business of admitting or ascribing or making accusations of responsibility. In moral life "our interest in intention, given the need to confront someone's conduct, is to localize his responsibility within the shift of events" (*MWM* 236). As a form of description, the concept of intention designates a whole dimension of assessment to which human actions are subject.

Insofar as the study of excuses brings into focus the many ways in which an action can fail to do moral wrong even though, or rather precisely because, it goes wrong, i.e., is performed incorrectly (*MWM* 22) – "at least as many as the myriad excuses we are entitled to proffer when what we have done has resulted in some unhappiness" (26) – it can be regarded as a salutary corrective to the exclusive focus on obligation and justification. To the extent that this exclusive focus is written into the accusatory or "categorical" character of speech, the study of excuses remedies "the injustice of our speech" (*CW* 333, *CR* 262f.; Austin, *Papers*, 176).

The Place of Elaboratives in Moral Disputes

That "actions do not come named for assessment" is best brought out initially by displaying the logical contrast in which the assessment of claims to moral knowledge stands to the assessment of claims to theoretical knowledge (*CR* chap. 9). In turn, this contrast can be brought out by pointing to the difficulty of selecting a best case of moral knowledge, analogous to the best case of theoretical knowledge that typically comes under challenge in philosophical inquiries about our knowledge of the

---

[5] Herbert Hart, "The Ascription of Responsibilities and Rights," *Proceedings of the Aristotelian Society*, n.s. 49 (1949), 171–94 (at 192).

existence of material objects. The difficulty of producing a claim to moral knowledge satisfying the description "if I know anything at all, surely I know this" (264) suggests that it is not in fact possible to produce a skeptical inquiry about moral knowledge along the same lines as the skeptical inquiry about theoretical knowledge. If this is true, then the fact that "moral arguments can always break down" does not point to a skeptical conclusion.

When it comes to moral knowledge, a best case would have to consist in either a particular rule or principle of action ("Promises are to be kept") or a particular action to be done ("You ought to have kept your promise to support her"). But the description of a kind of action ("keeping promises") as something to be done (or, equivalently, as good) is not sufficiently determinate to provide for the possibility of moral agreement, while conversely the description of a particular action ("keeping your promise to support her") as to be done (i.e., as good) is too determinate not to prejudge the possibility of such agreement (264f.).

What this simple dilemma shows is that the difficulty of fastening on a best case of moral knowledge can be traced to a difficulty about *how actions are to be described*.

This suggests that the worry about how to describe actions is not a skeptical one, not something "beyond the field of everyday life." It is a worry to which everyday moral life is exposed, whose disclosure does not await philosophical reflection. It bespeaks, not the restrictedness of ordinary moral life but, on the contrary, its lack of restriction, its exposure. In turn, this suggests that appeals to ordinary language, in the moral register, are not fated to be irrelevant as direct criticisms of the tradition (265), unlike their counterpart in the theoretical register (146). This legitimates the philosophical method employed here.

Play and Morality

The Analogy between Morality and Games

In order to get clearer about the place of elaboratives within moral life, it will help to proceed negatively. We first inquire into the significance of the fact that elaboratives are systematically out of place in competitive games. This claim would carry no force if the analogy between moral conduct and competitive games were simply misguided. Cavell's contention is not that this analogy affords no insights but rather that its limitations are as crucial as its rationale (*CR* 309).

Cavell objects to Rawls' claim that the analogy warrants assimilating a moral activity like that of promising to a special social "practice," or "institution" (*CR* 293; *CHU* 113–15), where a "practice" is characterized as an activity defined and set into existence by "rules setting up offices, specifying certain forms of action appropriate to various offices, establishing penalties for the breach of rules, and so on."[6] In short, Cavell rejects the claim that "promising is an action defined by a public system of rules" (Rawls "Two Concepts," 3–4).

But to object to the analogy on the ground that there are no counterparts in moral conduct to the rules about how the Queen moves in chess is to miss its point, which is that an *action* of a certain type must be done in a certain way, meet certain criteria, if it is to *count* as an action of that type at all, just as a move of a certain type (say, moving your Queen) must be done in a certain way, accord with certain rules, if it is to *count* as a move of that type at all (*MWM* 29–30). One must learn *how* to do an action of a certain type, just as one must learn how to make a move of a certain type within a given game, because "there are *ways* of doing all of these things" and "not just anything you do will *be* competently performing them" (*CR* 294). Thus, the successful performance of any action "depends upon ... what is normative for it" (*MWM* 22). The analogy thus casts some light on the concept of action, if only by dispelling the "vague and comforting idea" that "in the last analysis, doing an action must come down to the making of physical movements with parts of the body" (Austin, *Papers, 178*; *MWM* 29 n. 27). In the (normative) sense in which there is such a thing as "how the action is done, or how it is *to be* done," there is no such thing as how a purely physical movement is done (*MWM* 22). But the analogy by no means implies that promising is uniquely, or even primarily, a matter of following rules.

The criteria that an action must meet in order to count as an action of a certain type belong in the same logical register as the rules of a game: they are *constitutive* of the concepts whose employment they govern. If we call the utterances articulating the criteria governing an action, or the rules governing a move, "normative utterances," then it is crucial to realize, first, that these utterances being "normative" does not stand in opposition but rather in complementarity to their being "descriptive" and, second, that prescriptive utterances are not examples of "normative utterances" in this sense, however deep-seated the inclination to sort rules with imperatives may be (*MWM* 15, 22, 24).[7]

Statements setting out the constitutive rules of a game, language, or ritual are typically in the indicative, not the imperative, mood; Cavell

---

[6] John Rawls, "Two Concepts of Rules," *Philosophical Review* 64/1 (1955), 3–32 (at 25).
[7] Compare Anscombe, *Collected Philosophical Papers*, vol. I: *From Parmenides to Wittgenstein*, 118; hereafter cited parenthetically as *CPP* I.

calls them "categorial declaratives" (*MWM* 13, 15). They evince a "rule-description complementarity." Consequently, there can be "no question of going from 'is' to 'must,' but only of appreciating which of them should be said when; i.e. of appreciating the position or circumstances of the person to whom you are speaking" (27; cf. Anscombe, *CPP* III, 24, 101). That rules are not conveyed by "pure imperatives" suggests that the function of the "modal imperatives" (e.g., "must," "cannot") on which their formulation is apt to turn is not to prescribe us a new action (as an arbitrary convention does) but rather to urge us not to do badly or wrongly what we do (*MWM* 25–26). In turn, this suggests that metaphysical alienation occurs within natural language and moral alienation within morality (26).[8] The distinction between "is" (description) and "must" (rule) captures the distinction between not doing a thing at all and doing it badly (as distinct from not doing it quite well).

This complementarity should not come as a surprise. For in contrast to prescriptive utterances – whether in the form of imperatives ("You shall not…," "Don't…") or advisory rules ("One ought to…") – utterances that lay out or call attention to constitutive rules ("The Queen moves…," "You must move your Queen…") do not require but rather preclude the existence of an alternative course of action (*MWM* 28; *CR* 309; Rawls, "Two Concepts," 25). Statements containing "modal auxiliaries" like "You have to," "You must," "You can," or their negative counterparts (*MWM* 27, 30) – Anscombe calls them respectively "forcing modals" and "stopping modals" (Anscombe, *CPP* III, 100) – are not mandatory or permissive (*CPP* I, 118). Cavell registers the existence of a logical contrast between "You ought to…" and "You must…" in this respect. While neither formula is assimilable to an imperative (let alone a command, i.e., pure imperative) and both require a background of action and position into which the action is set (*MWM* 30), they differ in that the former implies, whereas the latter precludes, the existence of an alternative:

> if I say truly and appropriately, "You must…" then in a perfectly good sense nothing you then do can prove me wrong. You CAN *push the little object called the Queen* in many ways, as you can *lift* it or *throw* it across the room; not all of these will be *moving the Queen*. (*MWM* 28)

The funny sense that a "stopping modal" like "You can't" tells you that you "can't do" something you plainly *can* (you plainly can push *the little*

---

[8] Accordingly, Kant's "categorial imperative" is best cast as a "categorial declarative" capturing the logic of rational agency (rather than command), in line with Kant's insistence that it must assume the form of a command only insofar as we are not perfectly rational creatures (*MWM* 24–25; *CR* 315).

object called "the Queen" as you wish, only you won't be playing chess) (Anscombe, *CPP* III, 101) and the funny sense that it tells you that you "can't do" something that you cannot so much as *try* to do anyway (you plainly cannot so much as *try* to move your *Queen* otherwise than in straight, unobstructed paths (*MWM* 28) are a function of each other. The air of paradox that the stopping modal is apt to assume when considered under either one of these two aspects simply vanishes upon realizing their complementarity.

By the same token, the analogy is not meant to cast light on what it is to *justify* an action. For if a particular move that I have taken in the course of a game is queried – subjected to the question "Why?" in the special sense in which it asks for a *reason for acting* – then "there is nothing [I] can do but refer to the rules" ("Two Concepts," 27). But then "one doesn't so much justify one's particular action as explain, or show, that it is in accordance with the practice." To cite the rules is to *fit* my particular action (my having moved my Queen in this way) *into* the practice of playing the game (chess) ("Two Concepts," 27), "to *explain* my action, make clear what I was doing, not to justify it, say that what I did was well or rightly done" (*MWM* 29, n. 27). Defenses, whether in the guise of justifications or excuses, do not exhaust the range of elaboratives. Here, to elaborate my action is to explain it, which in turn is to place it into a certain background (*MWM* 27, 30–31; "Two Concepts" 25), by citing rules that "tell you what to do when you do the thing at all" (i.e., constitutive rules), not "rules" that "tell you how to do the thing well," i.e., what you ought to do *if* you want to do the thing well (prescriptive "rules" like principles – "advisory rules" – or maxims) (*MWM* 25, 28; "Two Concepts," 26). The distinction between "is" (rule-description) and "ought" (rule-prescription) captures the distinction between not doing a thing at all and not doing it quite well (as distinct from doing it badly). Since I would not be so much as *moving the Queen* if my move did not accord with the rule that "the Queen moves in straight, unobstructed paths," it can make no sense to (try to) justify a move falling under the concept of *moving the Queen* by appealing to this rule. Nor can it make sense to question a rule of the game in the course of playing it (*CR* 295; "Two Concepts," 26). Conversely, a statement containing a "stopping modal" that does seem to mention a *reason*, like "You can't move your Queen in this way, (because) the Queen moves in straight paths" or "You can't move your King, (because) he'd be in check" (both of which are of the same logical form as "You can't sit here, (because) it's N's place") cannot be said to mention a "reason" in the sense of "something independent which someone puts forward as his reason for what he does" (Anscombe, *CPP* III 101–02, 142). In effect, the "reason" occurring in the second half of the statement and what it is a "reason" for are not separately intelligible.[9]

When Elaboratives Are Systematically Out of Place: Morality Distinguished from Play

Cavell directs two criticisms at Rawls' interpretation of the analogy between play and life. The first is that this analogy is unable to do justice to the internal relation between actions and elaboratives because elaboratives (at least defenses, i.e., excuses and justifications) are fundamentally out of place in competitive games. The obliteration of this crucial limitation of the analogy is responsible for a distorted account of the place of elaboratives in moral life.

If a tennis player who had just failed to get his second serve within the service area argued that he should not lose the point because he simply forgot that he was equipped with a new racket or because his mind was elsewhere when he served, or because it was mere inadvertence, or awkwardness, or parody on his part, he would be deemed incompetent not just at playing tennis but at playing competitive games in general (*CR* 295–96). The same would apply to a server who had just hit an ace, yet argued that in all fairness he should not get the point because placing the ball where he did was not intentional on his part.

Elaboratives can have no place within competitive games – cannot affect the description or the evaluation of what one has done – because the constitutive rules of the game *settle* in advance how what one has done is to be described (*CR* 296, 311; *MWM* 236–37). "In competitive

---

[9] There is a converse point, apart from which the structure of Chapter 1 of *MWM* is unintelligible: to speak is to act, so "what we mean (intend) to say, like what we mean (intend) to do, is something we are responsible for" (*MWM* 32). The rule-statement complementarity displayed by normative utterances like "(we say that) the Queen moves in straight, unobstructed paths" is grounded in the fact that these utterances, qua statements, describe *how we do certain actions* (22), and describe this *from within*, i.e., in the first-person plural, *not* on the basis of observation (14, 16) or in the form of a prediction (64) – whether it be simply the action of *saying something* or also some other action (22). For "the Queen moves in straight, unobstructed paths" to *state* how the action of *using the words "moving the Queen"* is done by us just *is* for it to *lay out* how this action is to be done by us, and conversely. For this utterance to state how the action of *moving the Queen* is done by us just *is* for it to *lay it out* how it is to be done by us, and conversely. The successful performance of an action "depends upon our adopting and following the ways in which the action in question is done, upon what is normative for it" in the way that the unimpeded performance of a purely physical movement does not (22). This is true not only of the actions that are described by these utterances (like *moving the Queen*) but also of the action of *describing* itself, i.e. the action performed *by* these utterances. The latter presupposes normative utterances articulating how *describing* is (to be) done (22).

games ... *what counts as a move* is *settled* by the Rules of Play" (296), e.g., "if you swung at three pitches and failed to touch the ball on the third swing, then you *struck out*" (311). To know what you have done, it suffices to know the rules of the games and to observe what happens (311). The ascription of a move A to a player X need not and cannot be *qualified* because the possible ends, means, and circumstances of any move within the game are known beforehand (324). Thus, there is simply no logical place for those qualifications that constitute the bone of contention of so many moral arguments.

Within the arena of competitive games, intention is generally immaterial and elaboratives (at any rate defenses) are out of place because a player's responsibility for what he or she does is restricted a priori by the rules of the game, which automatically and conclusively settle how what one does is to be described (*MWM* 236). Conversely, outside the arena of competitive games, in moral life, intention is relevant and elaboratives are in order because our responsibility for what we do is not restricted a priori. There, "tracing an intention limits a man's responsibility" (*MWM* 236). In moral life, responsibility is neither restricted a priori (as in games) nor unrestricted (as in art).[10] If games contract responsibility, art dilates it completely (*MWM* 236f.).

To regard promising as the paradigmatic moral commitment and a rule-governed practice on the model of competitive games is to reduce all moral commitments to the ritual of promising and to assimilate the making of promises to the signing of legal contracts (*CR* 298). In the sphere of contracts, "commitments, liabilities, responsibilities are from the outset limited, and not total, or at any rate always in the course of being determined" and "a given conflict can be adjudicated, umpired" (*CR* 299).

The assimilation of promising to a rule-governed practice stands or falls with the assumption that all moral relationships could in principle be regimented into legal ones. Every moral conflict could be settled by reference to a set of rules that are (in Rawls' terms) "publicly known and understood as definitive." Seeing moral life as thus restricted requires construing all personal relationships as contractual ones (*CR* 299), taking the idea of a "social contract" at face value (*CR* 25–28).

Apart from the existence of elaboratives, carrying a responsibility that cannot be limited in advance would be apt to become unbearable (*CR* 324). Elaboratives "make it tolerable to act not knowing in advance

---

[10] While games contract responsibility, art dilates it completely. For "the artist is responsible for everything that happens in his work – and not just in the sense that it is done, but in the sense that it is meant" (*MWM* 236–37).

what we may do, what consequences we may be faced with" (*CR* 325). Morality is valuable insofar as "it provides a door through which someone, alienated or in danger of being alienated from another through his action, can return by the offering and the acceptance of explanation, excuses and justifications" (*CR* 269). Were it not for the existence of elaboratives, "the human necessity for action, and of action for motion" would be unbearable (*PP* 86).

In Rawls' view, the defining rules of the practice of promising specify which defenses (i.e., justifications and excuses), if any, are in order within that practice (cf. "Two Concepts," 30–31). In particular, they specify under which conditions breaking one's promise is and is not permitted (cf. Thompson, *Life*, 184), with one significant exception. The unavailability of a general utilitarian defense (i.e., the logical impossibility of justifying or excusing one's failure to keep one's word by appealing to the consideration that this was "best on the whole") is not written into the rules of the specific practice of promising, so much as into the very concept of a rule-governed practice (pace Cavell, *CR* 296, 307; cf. "Two Concepts," 30f.).

However, the fact that learning what a promise is requires learning what defenses it is appropriate to enter should one break it does not show that these defenses are provided for by the rules defining promising. Rather, it suggests, if anything, that promising is not any more a special social practice than these defenses are (*CR* 296). Defenses are by no means specific to promising (*CR* 310). The fact that one must know what elaboratives are in order to know what a promise is shows neither that the former are part of the latter nor that they obey rules, just as the fact that one must know how to *follow a rule* in order to know how to *play a game* G shows neither that the former is part of the latter nor that it obeys rules. We learn how to follow a rule against the background and in the course of innumerable activities other than game G or even games in general (*MWM* 49). In the sense in which *playing game G* obeys rules, neither *obeying a rule* nor *playing games* does (*MWM* 50; *CR* 307).

Rawls' adhesion to a conception of practice tailor-made to fit competitive games drives him to say that excusing conditions for failure to keep one's word is "*part of our practice*, somehow written into it, and thus also a part that might be written out" (184). Rawls construes the "considerable variation in the way people understand the practice" [of making and keeping promises] as a variation between a range of distinct practices (variants of the game of promising, as it were), some of which are "deviant."

This has the effect of turning any disagreement about "*whether* what you said was (tantamount) to a (serious) promise, *whether* you were really prevented from keeping it (or perhaps only succumbed to temptation or intimidation)" (*CR* 297) into a disagreement about "how it [= the practice of making and keeping promises] is best set up" ("Two Concepts," 31), i.e., into an "external question" as to which variant is to be adopted (*MWM* 47). It also has the effect of turning any such disagreement into a clash between non-overlapping definitions of "promising" (Thompson, *Life*, 185ff.) and of turning any position taken on a contentious case into the adoption of a new rule that changes the "game" (*MWM* 48).

However, disagreements of this kind make up the bulk of moral arguments (*CR* 297): they cannot be reckoned "external" to *our* practice of promising. It is far from clear that we should count the radically deviant practices of "promising" counterfactually envisioned by Rawls as embodying heterodox understandings of "promising," and so as constituting a variety of distinct practices, rather than as turning on a variety of mistaken renderings of *the* practice of *promising* (Thompson, *Life*, 185–86).

Cavell's second criticism calls into question the very conception of rules that sets the terms in which Rawls construes the analogy between moral life and rule-governed practices like competitive games (*CR* 293, 303). Rawls' concept of a *constitutive rule* is marred by a fateful unclarity. It fails to mark, first, the distinction between the *specification* (i.e. constitution) and the *definition* of a move by a rule; second, the distinction between the definition and the *determination* of a move by a rule (or, which comes to the same, the distinction between the specification of a practice and the specification of the moves) (*CR* 304f.).

First, definition is not the only form that the specification (i.e., constitution) of a move by a rule can take: the conventions that specify (i.e., constitute) the moves of a game include, along "defining rules" that lay out which moves count as playing at all, some "regulating rules" that lay out certain moves, a failure to perform which makes one liable to penalties for misplay (*CR* 305; *MWM* 25). Although both sets of conventions are constitutive of the moves of a practice in the sense that they preclude the existence of an alternative, the latter are more typically expressed by means of "must" than the former, presumably because we sense that we need to be encouraged to follow them, or deterred from circumventing them (*MWM* 25–26). Knowing how to play a game requires knowing how not to play badly (not doing things badly), not just knowing how to play at all (do things at all). It requires grasping the difference between not doing a thing well and not doing the thing (*MWM* 28, 32).

Second, the specification of a practice is not exhausted by the specification of its moves by constituting rules. In effect, "a certain mastery of a game is required in order to be said to play the game at all" (*CR* 304), which mastery involves an understanding of certain principles or maxims of strategy and a knowledge of how and when to apply them.[11] Although these two sets of "rules" (in the broad sense) prescribe rather than constitute moves (they leave room for an alternative move and so are expressible by means of "ought"), a mastery of them "is as essential to being described as *playing the game* as a mastery of its moves is" (306). Knowing how to play a game requires knowing how to play well (doing things well), not just knowing how to play at all (doing things at all). It requires grasping the difference between doing a thing badly and not doing the thing (*MWM* 26, 32).

This belies Rawls' claim that a query about a move whose form is specified by the practice cannot be made from within the practice itself, out of a concern for the validity of the move in question, but only through incompetence (i.e., ignorance of the constitutive rules of the practice or that someone is engaged in the practice), from which it follows that the answer to such a query cannot take the form of a justification, but only that of an explanation adducing a constitutive rule so as to fit the move into the practice. As Cavell points out, the query "Why did you do that?" *can* be competently entered from within the game, with a view to questioning the strategic pertinence of a move that one knows to be in accord with the defining rules of the game. For the rules defining a move do not determine it: there is no alternative to the definition, since a "move" not in accord with it is simply not a *move*, but there are alternative moves in accord with the definition (*CR* 304f.). A corresponding defense will invoke a principle or maxim that says what we ought to do in order to play well rather than a rule (in the narrow sense) that says what we must do in order to play at all. For all that, the "rule" (in the broad sense that includes principles and maxims) invoked in the defense may be one that someone must master to some degree in order to count as playing the game at all. The analogues of both kinds of "rules" (constitutive and guiding) in moral conduct (or in language) are equally essential to it, just as both kinds of "rules" are equally essential to play (*CR* 308; *MWM* 49f.).

This extension of the scope of the analogy does not support Rawls' account of promising as a rule-governed practice. On the contrary, it points to a crucial disanalogy:

Part of what gives games their special quality – what, one may say, allows them to be practiced and *played* – is that within them what we must do is (ideally) completely specified and radically marked off from considerations of what we ought to (or should not) do. (*CR*308)

---

[11] Maxims of strategy, "which may be thought of as formulating strategies as though they were moves" (*MWM* 29), coincide with what Rawls calls "summary rules" (*CR* 305).

As the division between moves (rules) and strategies (principles) is fixed
(or at least not up to the players themselves), whether X has done A and
whether A is a better course of action than B are equally settled by the
game. The players are thereby set free to concentrate on the quest for the
best way to win, i.e., on *playing* (*CR* 324).[12] Moral conduct is not playful
because it is confronted at every juncture with the *necessity of a choice*
between "must" and "ought." As a moral agent, you have yourself to
draw the line because "unlike the case of games, what is and is not an
alternative open to you is not fixed" (309). No alternative is blocked in
itself. Hence "what alternatives we can and must take are not *fixed*, but
chosen, and thereby fix us" (*CR* 324).

It follows from the foregoing that "no rule or principle could function
in a moral context the way regulatory or defining rules function in
games" (*CR* 307). In both games and morality, I supply another human
being with reasons why he "ought to do X" or why he "must do X" given
his position. But in morality I do not articulate these reasons in terms of
the defining rules and strategic principles of *the* game, but in terms of *his*
cares and commitments (*CR* 325).

The ultimate and deepest implication of this criticism of Rawls' comparison between play and moral life is that it obscures the nature of *our
practical knowledge of what we have done* (*CR* 293, 310–12):

Outside the arena of defined practices, in the moral world, what we are doing has
no such defined descriptions, and our intentions often fail, one way or another, in
execution. There, knowing what you are doing and what you are going to do and
what you have not done, cannot fully be told by looking at what in fact, in the
world, you do. To know what you are doing is to be able to elaborate the action:
say why you are doing it, if that is competently asked; or excuse or justify it if that
becomes necessary. (*CR* 311)

Before we turn to this radical claim, we need to register another way in
which elaboratives can be out of place: contextually.

The Role of Elaboratives in Practical Knowledge

When Elaboratives Are Contextually Out of Place: The Concept of Normal Action

We saw that elaboratives are as indispensable to the moral register as they
are extraneous to competitive games, within the confines of which they

---

[12] Traditional art is playful insofar as it can take its medium for granted and indulge in
improvisation (*MWM* 200f.).

are systematically out of place. But this does not imply that outside the arenas of competitive games elaboratives are systematically in place – i.e., that each and every of our actions calls for and admits of elaboration by way of justification, mitigation, or explanation. The reason why this implication should be rejected is not primarily that some actions lie *beyond the reach* of elaboratives, although this is both true and important: *tragic* actions can be characterized as those that lie beyond the compass of the justifiable, the excusable, and the explainable, hence beyond morality in its civil guise (*PP* 86). Rather, elaboratives are *normally* – that is to say, *by default*, pending the provision of some reason to the contrary – simply *not* in order: only occasionally is it at all intelligible to enter one.

This is a direct corollary to Austin's point that modifying expressions whose function is to *qualify* an action-ascription are *normally* not in order (such modifying expressions include, along with those on which elaboratives turn, the various expressions of aggravation that are the "opposite numbers" of expressions of attenuation). Setting aside cases covered by "verbs of omen" such as murder, "Only if we do the action named in some special way or circumstances, different from those in which such an act is naturally done ..., is a modifying expression called for, or even in order" (Austin, *Papers*, 190).

Austin's insight – "No modification without aberration" (189, 284) – is a generalization of such remarks as that "When we ask whether an action is voluntary we imply that the action is fishy" (*MWM* 12). To say that we imply as much in raising or addressing the question whether an action is voluntary is in effect to say that "the condition for applying the term 'voluntary' is that there be something (real or imagined) fishy about any performance intelligibly so characterized" (*MWM* 7). When Ryle maintains that in their ordinary employment "voluntary" and "involuntary" are only applicable to "actions that ought not to be done," he is wrong to the extent that he construes the condition too narrowly (by assuming that there must be something morally fishy about the action) and he conflates the non-voluntary and the involuntary, thereby implying "that (responsible) actions which are not contemptible must be admirable" (*MWM* 7).

The general point is fundamental enough to Cavell to prompt him to speak of "Austin's discovery (for our time and place, anyway) of normal action" and to regard it as "holding the clue to the riddle of Freedom" (*MWM* 7, fn. 5). About such antitheses as that between the voluntary and the involuntary, Cavell writes:

[They] miss exactly those actions about which the question "Voluntary or not?" really has no sense, viz., those ordinary, unremarkable, natural things we do which make up most of our conduct and which are neither admirable nor contemptible; which, indeed, could only erroneously be said to go on, in general, in any special way. (*MWM* 7)

Normal actions are neither voluntary nor involuntary, neither intentional nor unintentional, neither careful nor careless, etc. (*MWM* 13). We can think of them as these natural, unremarkable, ordinary actions that we do not need to be encouraged to do, or discouraged from doing badly, by means of "modal imperatives" like "must" and "cannot" (*MWM* 25). They are the counterparts to the descriptive side of "categorial declaratives." This point belongs to logic: a question cannot be meaningfully asked about an action unless that action has proven questionable in some respect (*MWM* 8).

Moral philosophy is chronically *moralistic* insofar as it fails to recognize that raising a question about an action requires that this action be questionable or, equivalently, to make room for normal actions. It is thereby driven to postulate, absurdly, that every action of ours must be morally assessable, on pain of not counting as an action at all (*MWM* 8; *CR* 269; *LDIK* 281–82).

Thus, actions do not come named for assessment (*CR* 265) and naming actions is a sensitive occupation (*MWM* 35) because on those occasions when what we are doing or have done proves questionable and hence remarkable, what we are answerable for cannot be settled by appealing to the *rules* of a practice (by which we fix the extent of our cares and commitments beforehand) but rather is *for us* to circumscribe, through the offering of elaboratives. It takes nothing short of moral confrontation to achieve knowledge of what we are responsible for doing or having done, to demarcate the action-descriptions that we endorse from those that we disown, because the contours of our responsibility are neither obvious nor uncontentious (*CR* 312).

Acknowledging What One Has Done

Cavell articulates a more radical thesis: I may come to realize what I am doing or have done as a result of elaborating my action in response to some moral challenge (*MWM* 229–37; *CR* 312). Such knowledge is first-personal in nature; it is not based on observation (Austin, *Papers*, 283). Yet it is elicited by the other's query. Cavell's inquiry into practical knowledge proceeds by way of a close confrontation with Anscombe's (*MWM* 235; *LDIK* 318–19).

The difficulty as to how to describe an action is not simply or primarily a difficulty for whoever is not the agent, and it does not arise only from a lack of explicitness. It is true that the way the agent structured his action may fail to be apparent to others. Accordingly, the concept of intention has a "bracketing effect": "when the till-dipper claims that he *intended all along* to put the money back, what he is claiming is that his action – the action that he was engaged upon – is to be judged as a whole, not just a part of it carved out of the whole" (Austin, *Papers*, 285). It is also clear that "many disputes as to what excuse we should probably use arise because we will not trouble to state explicitly what is being excused" (200). Elaboratives, however, are not simply or even primarily in the business of *making explicit* what one is doing or has done.

Cavell's claim may seem puzzling (*MWM* 233). It may seem that I can only *come to realize* what I am doing or have done under those descriptions in which it does *not* count as a human action (*actus humanus*), but only as an act of a human being (*actus hominis*), i.e., under those respects in which it is not intentional or voluntary on my part. Thus I may discover that I have pushed the wrong button by mistake (i.e., due to an error *in* performance) or by accident (i.e., due to an error *of* performance) (cf. Anscombe, *Intention*, §§31–32; Austin, *Papers*, 185 n.). Moreover, among the manifold descriptions that my action admits insofar as it is "done amidst a background of circumstances" and the further ones that it collects as its effects radiate out, its results unfold, and its consequences materialize in the world, there are of course plenty that I need not be aware of and about which I might *find out* later, if ever. These are all descriptions that I recognize to be true of my action but in which I need not recognize myself.

It may seem that I cannot *come to realize* what I am doing or have done voluntarily except in the sense of bringing out further *interpretive motives* of my action by casting it in a new light. The concept of elaboration may seem paradoxical insofar as it pertains to the essence of an intention that it should have some *logical* priority over its execution. In John McDowell's apt terms, "an intention is precisely something which, in a certain sense, is entirely there in my mind before I act on its basis. I do not need to wait and see what I do before I can know what I intend to do."[13]

According to Cavell's diagnosis, we are held captive by the assumption that, as a matter of logical impossibility, "no present or future revelation can show what an earlier intention was" by "our, for some reason, not

---

[13] See John McDowell, "Towards a Reading of Hegel on Action," in *Having the World in View: Essays on Kant, Hegel, and Sellars* (Cambridge, MA: Harvard University Press, 2009).

being free to consider what 'acknowledging an intention' is, or what 'being shown relevance' is" (*MWM* 233, 184).

Suppose that a man is firing a gun outside a house (*MWM* 231). He is making a lot of noise, spending ammunition, polluting the surroundings with lead, disturbing insects, crushing grass where he is standing, wearing away his shoe-soles, etc. (236). Assuming them to be eventful enough for speech, these true descriptions are presumably among those of which our man is cognizant. Everyone, including our man, knows that firing a gun is bound to make a lot of noise, etc. Yet not only can none of these descriptions figure in an ordered series of descriptions representing the inner teleological nexus of the man's action – he is moving his index *in order to* pull the trigger and he is pulling the trigger *in order to* fire the gun, but he is not doing any of these things *in order to* make a lot of noise nor is he making a lot of noise in order to do any of these things (cf. Anscombe, *Intention*, §26) – but also none of them is so much as relevant in the first place. As things stand, none of them is remarkable enough to qualify as a *circumstance* of the man's action. That he is making a lot of noise goes without saying, but it is not eventful enough for speech. He is not involuntarily making a lot of noise. But neither is he doing so voluntarily, let alone intentionally.

Suppose that it is pointed out to him that there is a child asleep in the house, or terrified by noise, or that the unmistakable sound made by this old gun model is the rallying signal used by the local hunters or mobsters (*MWM* 231). Then it is no longer irrelevant that the man is making a lot of noise. It is shown to be relevant. If he did not know about the child, or the signal, and he persists in firing the gun, then "what he is doing will be differently described. We might say: his intention will have altered" (*MWM* 231). Further penetration into what happens requires further penetration into what he intends because it requires further penetration into what he does (*MWM* 236).

Saying that "his intention will have altered" may seem tendentious. It may appear to fly in the face of the logical priority of intention over its execution as a result of conflating a change of intention with the change of an intention (that the man exchanged an intention for another does not mean that there is any intention that changed).

This objection misses the point of Cavell's formulation. It is twofold. First, once the man's conduct is questioned, the man can never return to his former intention, resume his former position – he can disclaim the weight of the challenge but not its relevance. Second, what his intention was before is not independent from what it is after (*MWM* 231).

It helps at this point to distinguish between the intentional and the voluntary. We can say that "something is voluntary though not intentional if it is the antecedently known concomitant result of one's intentional action," yet the question "Why?" is denied application (cf. Anscombe, *Intention*, §§25, 49). Assuming a wider concept of intentional action that includes voluntary actions in the sense just defined, Cavell continues: "Suppose he has conveniently forgotten; confronted, he may vehemently deny that he had known, or that it matters; or vehemently acknowledge that he had intended to wake or terrify the child. Vehemence here measures the distance between knowing a thing and having to acknowledge it" (*MWM* 234). Does talk of the man having "conveniently forgotten" muddle the issue? It is tempting to object along these lines: either he could and should have known, or not. If it was both possible and necessary for him to know that there was a child terrified by noise, then *terrifying the child* counts as voluntary on his part even if he had no inkling of the child's presence because his ignorance counts as voluntary; otherwise it counts as involuntary (cf. Anscombe, *CPP* iii, 9).

This dilemma, however, is predicated on the very assumption that Cavell means to dislodge: that any conceivable specific way in which an action can go wrong is to be assessed against some corresponding relevant *obligation* and the agent is either to be inculpated for it or to be exculpated from it according to whether it falls within or without the scope of this obligation. If this were the case, then there would be no such thing as a *normal* action and excuses would need neither to be *proffered* nor *accepted*. Just as "it would be incorrect to suppose that we are obligated to see to it (to take precautions to insure), *whenever* we undertake to do anything, that none of these ways will come to pass" (*MWM* 26), so it would be likewise incorrect to suppose that we are obligated to see to it that none of these ways is subject to an obligation.

Reverting to Anscombe's account of the distinction between the voluntary and the intentional (*Intention*, §49), we must ask: are we really to count *every* "antecedently known concomitant result of one's intentional action" as *voluntary*, as this account implies? This would imply that crushing grass and wearing away his shoe-soles are *voluntary* actions on the man's part, on a par with terrifying the child once cognizant of its presence. Insofar as the notion of relevance is built into that of circumstance,[14] crushing the grass and wearing his shoe-soles do not seem to qualify even as *circumstances* of the man's action, let alone as voluntary

---

[14] Cf. Aquinas' definition of *circumstantia*: "In things located, that is said to surround something, which is outside it, but touches it, or is placed near it. Accordingly, whatever conditions are outside the substance of an act, and yet in some way touch the human act, are called circumstances." Aquinas, *Summa theologica*, trans. Fathers of the Dominican Province (New York: Benziger Brothers, 1947), Ia, IIae, Quest. 7, Art. 1.

actions on his part. Would the light on the wall be shown to be a *circumstance* of my action of opening the window, or a voluntary action on my part, simply by my answering the question "What are you doing making that light come on the wall?" with "Ah yes, it's the opening the window that does it," or "That always happens when one opens that window at midday if the sun is shining" (*Intention*, §28)? Isn't my reluctance to mention myself as cause, let alone as agent, a way of disowning altogether the description?

On the other hand, what inclines us to regard the description "making a series of clicking noises, which are in fact beating out a noticeable rhythm" as the description of a *circumstance* of the action of "pumping water into the cistern which supplies the drinking water of a house," when by hypothesis the reply that the question "Why?" elicits from the man is "I was not aware I was doing that" (i.e., the question "Why?" is denied application) (*Intention*, §23)? The answer is obvious: this description is *not unremarkable*. It is even tailored to figure as the positive answer to the question "Why?" in an alternative scenario ("Why are you moving your arm up and down?" – "To click out the rhythm of God save the King") (*Intention*, §26).

On closer inspection, Anscombe supplies a criterion for when an antecedently known concomitant result of one's intentional action should count as voluntary, suggesting that such a concomitant will count as voluntary if the question "Why?," although it is denied application, is not simply rejected as *inappropriate* in its demand. Then the description of an antecedently known concomitant result of one's intentional action does not count as one under which the action is voluntary unless it is in some way *remarkable* and therefore relevant.

In the typical case, acting requires doing and doing requires moving (*PP* 86). In moving, I expose myself to being moved. As Cavell puts it, "The human being is inherently clumsy, society inherently involves our bumping against each other" (*CW* 115). To act, in short, is to expose oneself to circumstances and therefore to further relevances. Cavell's account diverges from Anscombe's in that it does not construe the question "Why?" simply as a device of explication but as a means of achieving self-knowledge in the first place.

Conclusion: Practical Knowledge and Exposure

It may look as if we have to choose between two antithetical perspectives on the relation of intention to action:

In contrast to Freud's vision of the human being as a field of significance whose actions express wider meaning than we might care to be questioned about,

Austin's vision is of the human being as a field of vulnerability whose actions imply wider consequences and effects and results – if narrower meaning – than we should have to be answerable for. (*CW* S33)

For Austin the significance of a slip is to reduce an act's intentionality, for Freud to expand it. (*CW* 353)

But these perspectives are not incompatible: every human action that is eventful enough for speech is at once underdetermined and overdetermined (*LDIK* 30, 517): overdetermined because the range of relevant descriptions under which a human action may count as voluntary is not unlimited, underdetermined because that range of relevant descriptions is not limited a priori. The circumstances and turns of event that it finds itself exposed to are accidents. Yet every circumstance or turn of event that it suffers is one that it has exposed itself to. In this way, every (non-normal) human action is apt to be tragicomical.

The view that our responsibility for what we do is limited to what we do voluntarily is not wrong, so much as superficial. It has depth only insofar as it encapsulates an aspect of the problem of responsibility rather than a solution to it.[15] The Kantian vision of morality as immune to luck "is only superficially repulsive – despite appearances, it offers an inducement, solace to a sense of the world's unfairness."[16] To the extent that the difficulty about how to describe actions is ineliminable, "the idea of a duty toward others as human beings might itself be a restriction to my knowledge of their existence" (*CR* 435).

---

[15] Compare Bernard Williams, "Moral Luck," in *Moral Luck: Philosophical Papers, 1973–1980* (Cambridge University Press, 1981), 20–39 (at 29f.).
[16] *Ibid.*, 21.

4   Faces of the Ordinary

Eli Friedlander

In "Aesthetic Problems of Modern Philosophy," Stanley Cavell draws together the method of ordinary language as laid out in Wittgenstein's procedures and the grammar of aesthetic judgment, as Kant articulates it in the "Analytic of the Beautiful" of the *Critique of the Power of Judgment.* His aim in that essay is, first, as he puts it, to "outline two problems in aesthetics each of which seems to yield to the possibilities of Wittgensteinian procedures, and in turn illuminate them" (*MWM* 73). Secondly, he wishes to suggest "resemblances between one kind of judgment recognizable as aesthetic and the characteristic claim of Wittgenstein – and of ordinary language philosophers generally – to voice 'what we should ordinarily say'."

The "problems" that Cavell outlines in the first part of the essay, one about the paraphraseability of poetic language, and the other as to whether there is a possible "tonality" to so-called atonal music, take the form of an argument between opposed sides. The rigid opposition appears, most clearly in the case of paraphrase, to be the outcome of fixations on certain uses of concepts. The work of philosophy, as Cavell exemplifies it in addressing that first problem, would release us from the deadlocked positions by appealing to "what we say" in our ordinary judgments involving such concepts as "approximate," "literal," "description," "telling the meaning," "putting things another way," "knowing what an idiom means," explaining a metaphor, "showing understanding," and others still …

In the second part of the essay, Cavell reflects on the procedures of ordinary language deployed and takes the form of aesthetic judgment in Kant to provide us with an analogue or *a model* for this method of philosophy. He is well aware that some would take aesthetic judgments to be notoriously lacking in rigor or universal rationality. Yet, Cavell argues that precisely "the familiar lack of conclusiveness in aesthetic argument, rather than showing up an irrationality, shows the kind of rationality it has, and needs" (*MWM* 86). The central aspect of aesthetic judgment that Cavell singles out for attention in this context is its peculiar form of universality: "Kant's 'universal voice'," Cavell writes "is, with perhaps a slight shift of accent, what we hear recorded in the philosopher's claims about 'what we say'" (*MWM* 94).[1] Kant's universal voice is a form of subjective universality that essentially involves *representativeness* or exemplification. In judging, I take myself to speak for others, for an idea of an as-yet-unattained agreement. Just like the judge of taste, the ordinary language philosopher would speak for what we say, not by claiming empirical uniformity, but by representing our common, yet-to-be-acknowledged agreement.[2]

★

The central question I want to pursue, following this brief summary, concerns the nature of the mutual illumination of aesthetics and ordinary language philosophy, and its bearing on our understanding of the affinity of philosophy and art. But, let me start by raising some difficulties about such purported resemblances, as well as by problematizing the summary understanding I presented of the relation between the two parts of the essay.

First, even granted that there are resemblances between the aesthetic judgment and the claims to voice what we ordinarily say, is it important that the problems addressed in the first half of the essay are themselves problems of *aesthetics*? Are they not just examples, in which there is an occasion to deploy the Wittgensteinian procedures? That is, could Cavell have equally taken an illustration from the philosophy of mind, from debates about the relation of mind and body, or from arguments about our knowledge of the external world? Is there something we can learn from these *aesthetic* problems, something that specifically the sphere of art can teach us? Can *these* problems not only yield to Wittgenstein's philosophical procedures, but is it also the case that the mode of their overcoming in our experience of art would "illuminate" those very procedures?

Secondly, one might argue that an aesthetic judgment can only be vaguely analogical to the characteristic claim of ordinary language

---

[1] Cavell is very careful in articulating the affinity between the two contexts: the judgments of ordinary language philosophy are equally as close to or distant from aesthetic judgments as they are to ordinary empirical hypothesis. Further, he writes that there is an "aesthetic analogue" to the judgment of ordinary language philosophy; they both involve a claim of dependence on agreement of "the same kind." We would be tempted to conceive of the "we" in the philosopher's claim about "what we say" to require the kind of universality that we attribute to an empirical hypothesis, and yet it is closer to the "we" of the universal voice in aesthetic judgment.

[2] For an elaboration of this aspect of the aesthetic judgment in relation to Cavell's concern with exemplification, see my "On Examples, Representatives, Measures, Standards and the Ideal," in *Reading Cavell*, ed. Alice Crary and Sanford Shieh (London: Routledge, 2006), 204–17.

philosophy. For the one has to do with a work of art, or with natural beauty, and the other with the whole range of our life in common with concepts. Don't aesthetic judgments at best involve a *very restricted* subset, in the space of our linguistic practice as such? I say, at best, since some interpretations of Kant's account of beauty do not allow for *any* involvement of concepts in the judgment of taste.[3]

Thirdly, we might further insist on the difference between the two contexts, by pointing out that an aesthetic judgment is made in the *presence* of a thing of beauty, say an artwork. That work is present to us in its singularity or uniqueness, as we judge *it* to be beautiful. One might not easily find an analogue for this singular presence in the case of ordinary language procedures.

Finally, since in the practice of ordinary language philosophy, there is nothing that parallels the presence of that which is beautiful, it follows that it would merely be concerned with our confusions, with getting rid of problematic pictures. The stress would be on the "disappearance" of the false argument. This might be indeed something that we would wish to distinguish from the aesthetic judgment which rests on *true insight* into a work, or is that through which we come to see the work of art differently.

*

In order to address these difficulties and advance our understanding of "Aesthetic Problems," we need to return to Kant and seek in his view the anchor for the connection between aesthetic judgment and the ordinary. Let me first note that the account of aesthetic judgment is developed in the *Critique of the Power of Judgment*. Aesthetic judgments reveal to us the very capacity to judge in its purest manifestation, or what is at the heart of any use of that capacity. The aesthetic field should not merely be compared and contrasted to other domains in which we judge, such as theoretical cognition or moral cognition. It is not just one of several domains of judgment, but rather that one in which judging as such is manifest most succinctly. For sure, Kant argues that the aesthetic judgment is only a reflective judgment, whereas, say, the theoretical judgment is determining. But this does not preclude finding a role for reflection at the heart of the articulation of the systematic character of cognition.[4]

---

[3] For an account of the dimension of meaning in Kant's aesthetics, see my *Expressions of Judgment: An essay on Kant's Aesthetics* (Cambridge, MA: Harvard University Press, 2015).
[4] Indeed, even the difficulties that Kant brings up at the opening of the "Analytic of Principles" of the "First Critique," and his ensuing descent into the obscurities of the schematism, suggest the importance that the consideration of reflective judgment will have in addressing the issue of the application of concepts more generally. Cavell saw that very clearly when he discussed the problem of the projection of concepts, and of following a rule, as well as when he related later Wittgenstein's account of language to the Kantian

I will try to justify this claim in the discussion of common sense in what follows.

In his discussion of Kant on the grammar of the judgment of taste, Cavell primarily focuses on the second moment of the "Analytic of the Beautiful," where Kant develops the account of the universal voice. But the four different moments belong together, and in particular, I would argue, there is an internal relation between the second and the fourth moment, in which Kant shows aesthetic judgment to presuppose a *common sense*.

Without engaging in a detailed discussion of the relation between the universal voice and common sense, let me suggest that we think of it through a polarity of expression and ground. In judging with a universal voice, one takes oneself to be representative. Representativeness involves a turn to others; it demands expression, through which the communicability of one's judgment is attested. For feeling to be communicable, it must be possible for me to *articulate* my experience, to make it mean something, even if only to myself. Aesthetic judgment is not a mere evincing of feeling toward an object, occurring when some mysterious play of the mind is taking place in me, a process of which I am moreover supposed to be made aware only indirectly, inferring it from finding no interest in the object upon reflection on my state of mind.

There is indeed an expressive pole in aesthetic judgment, which as Cavell insists in the essay, is most evident in acts of criticism of art. But, it is equally important, that this expression be *of* a natural ground that underlies our common existence in language. This ground may be called natural, not in being preconceptual, but rather in being a unity of life, revealed at the heart of our existence with concepts.[5] This ground is

project of laying out the conditions of possibility of experience, "so that it speaks not alone of deducing twelve categories of the understanding but of deriving – say schematizing – every word in which we speak together" (*CHU* 39). See in this context my "Meaning Schematics in Cavell's Kantian Reading of Wittgenstein," *Revue Internationale de Philosophie* 256 (2011–12), 118–99.

[5] In Chapter 6, Arata Hamawaki suggests insightfully how the relation of universal voice and common sense, idea and ground, can be viewed in temporal terms: "We might think of aesthetic judgments as made from the perspective of a possible future community, pressing the form of life we share in new directions. And we might think of the judgments of the OLP as measuring the community of mind we already have. But the possibility of each is contained in the possibility of the other" (119). This holding together of what we already have and what is to be formed is a question raised by Kant in the fourth moment of the analytic, yet left unanswered: "whether taste is an original and natural faculty, or only the idea of one that is yet to be acquired and is artificial, so that a judgment of taste, with its expectation of universal assent, is in fact only a demand of reason to produce such a unanimity in the manner of sensing ... this we would not and cannot yet investigate here." Immanuel Kant, *Critique of the Power of Judgment*, ed. Paul Guyer, trans. Guyer and Eric Matthews (Cambridge University Press, 2000), 124 (5:240). For an elaboration of

sensed in judging, but *not* as anything specific. What is sensed as common is a unity underlying our diversity of concepts. Viewed this way, the work of art, by way of aesthetic judgment, provides an occasion to become conscious of the depth of our attunement in meaning.[6] For sure, this does not bypass considerations of the forms of art, of medium, genres, style. But as Cavell shows on many occasions so powerfully, these forms should not be taken merely formalistically. Each medium has its way to teach us what space and time are, what nature, what subjectivity, and what action are. Be it as they are refracted in the colors of painting, or revealed by the automatisms of the film.[7]

Let me try to put this important point in a slightly different way: Kant explicates in the Fourth Moment, the presupposition of a common sense, in terms of the account of the harmony of the faculties, of the imagination and the understanding. He figures a determinate cognition, the application of a concept to an object, as a specific "proportion" of imagination to understanding. This can be roughly understood as how much imagination is required for a given concept. Or put differently, how broad a field of meaning needs to be configured or schematized by the imagination in applying that concept. For the concept dog, for example, we might not need much imagination, but for the concept of love we might need more than we might have readily in mind in our unreflective existence.[8] So much so, that we would doubt that it is a determinate cognition that is at issue in our sense of what love comes to in our lives. And yet, a work of literature – *King Lear*, say – spans in the imagination the schematism of the concept of love, as it were holding it in balance with other fundamental concepts of human existence.

An aesthetic judgment rests on the ground upon which our concepts hang together.[9] It is this weave of meaning that Kant invokes in the

---

this point, see my "Common Sense, Communication and Community," in *The Palgrave Kant Handbook*, ed. Matthew Altman (London: Palgrave Macmillan, 2017), 407–24.

[6] In other words, we have here precisely the presence of a dimension that belongs to our space of meaning in common, art as a partial subset of our experience of the world requiring specialized notions. One could also say that art provides an opening to meaning that is on a par with the ambitions of philosophy. Art, Religion, and Philosophy, as Hegel would put it, all belong to absolute spirit.

[7] Cavell's most sustained discussion of the relation of form and content in an artistic medium is probably found in *The World Viewed*.

[8] This should be compared to Cavell's discussion of imaginative projection in *The Claim of Reason*.

[9] In particular consider that Kant writes in the fourth moment of the "Analytic of the Beautiful" that "since the universal communicability of a feeling presupposes a common sense, the latter must be able to be assumed with good reason, and indeed without appeal to psychological observations, but rather as the necessary condition of the universal communicability of our cognition, which is assumed in every logic and every

presupposition of common sense. And precisely in order to distinguish this ground of cognition in general from a specific cognition, he shifts from the language of proportionality to that of harmony. Harmony suggests consonance, affinities sensed, echoes over a wide range of meaning as a judgment strikes precisely the keyboard of the imagination.

Kant's term for that "consonance" is *Stimmung*. As Sandra Laugier has pointed out, it is related to *Übereinstimmung*, the term that Cavell singles out in his discussion of §241 of Wittgenstein's *Philosophical Investigations*: "It is what human beings *say* that is true and false; and they agree in the *language* they use. This is not agreement in opinion but in forms of life" (*PI* §241).[10] Cavell's gloss on this passage brings out that "The idea of agreement here is not that of coming to or arriving at an agreement on a given occasion, but of being in agreement throughout, being in harmony ... That a group of human beings *stimmen* in their language *überein* says, so to speak, that they are mutually voiced with respect to it, mutually *attuned* top to bottom" (*CR* 32).

★

In making an aesthetic judgment, whose expressive face must be articulate, nuanced, precise, and even pointed, we rest on a ground of agreement. The ground we stand on in judging is not a position, but rather a form of life in common. Moreover, our involvement with a work of art allows us, through the precision of expression in our judgment, to sense that ground of attunement. As we articulate our experience in being sensitively cued to the singularity of a work, our language is not just right, merely correct, but is pitched *just right*. Its fit to the work reveals the latter to be a place of convergence for our concepts.

In reflecting on the practice of ordinary language philosophy, we similarly must consider these two faces, the one precise and specific (as exemplified in the often repeated donkey anecdote of Austin that serves to distinguish our uses of "by mistake" and "by accident"), the other which Cavell expresses as "a matter of sharing routes of interest, and feeling, modes of response, senses of humor and of significance and of fulfillment, of what is outrageous, of what is similar to what else, what a rebuke, what a foregiveness, of when an utterance is an assertion, when an appeal, when an explanation – all the whirl of organism that Wittgenstein calls 'forms of life'" (*MWM* 52).

principle of cognition that is not skeptical." Kant, *Critique of the Power of Judgment*, 123 (5:239). For a more elaborate reading of the relation of the second and fourth moment in Kant's "Analytic of the Beautiful," see my "Common Sense."

[10] Sandra Laugier, "Voice as Form of Life and Life Form," in *Nordic Wittgenstein Review* 4 (2015), 63–81 (at 75).

The use of the term "whirl"– especially if we associate it with what induces vertigo – should not be taken to imply that we cannot pursue and thematize the dimension of a form of life in language. It is, I will argue, crucially present in the two problems of aesthetics in Cavell's essay. Indeed, it is by noticing the presence of that dimension that we recognize what is specific in these being problems of *aesthetics*, as well as notice an important difference between the two. As he patiently defuses the dispute concerning the paraphraseability of a poem, Cavell suggests that in some cases, it would in effect be just right to say "I know what it means but I can't say what it means." Speaking of lines of modernist poets such as Hart Crane and Wallace Stevens, Cavell writes:

Paraphrasing the lines, or explaining their meaning, or telling it, or putting the thought another way – all these are out of the question. One may be able to say nothing except that a feeling has been voiced by a kindred spirit and that if someone does not get it *he is not in one's world, or not of one's flesh.* (*MWM* 81, my emphasis)[11]

Nothing less than the belonging to a world, that is the sense of one's own world, is staked on that feeling.

It is no coincidence, I take it, that the lines of poetry to which Cavell refers are from modernist poets. It is in conditions of transformation or revolution, such as is characteristic of the modern in art, that we are liable to encounter the polarization of views that expresses itself in endless fruitless arguments: Is photography an art comparable to painting? Can film compete with the achievements of the theater? Is there or isn't there a form of tonality in a so-called atonal work? But while we might not want to adopt either of the positions in the argument generated by these questions, we still have to recognize that they arise from a true tension in our form of existence. This is clearly at issue as Cavell stresses how our understanding of tonality is weaved into a form of life with music:

The language of music is part of a particular form of life, one containing music we are most familiar with; associated with, or consisting of, particular ways of being trained to perform it and to listen to it; involving particular ways of being corrected, particular ways of responding to mistakes, to nuance, above all to recurrence and to variation and modification. No wonder we want to preserve the idea of tonality: to give all *that* up seems like giving up the idea of music altogether. I think it *is like* it. (*MWM* 84)

---

[11] In Chapter 6, Arata Hamawaki brings out convincingly and in detail how the account of agreement in aesthetic judgment differs significantly from the form of agreement we expect over cognitions of matters of fact. In particular he elaborates the difference between agreement on a proposition and the kind of agreement expressed by the sense of sharing the same world. As he puts it forcefully: "The 'world' that we share, or fail to share, in this sense is *shown in* what 'we say' and is not an *object* of what one says: my relation to the world in general is not one of knowing" (119).

As opposed to the problem of paraphraseability, which, phrased in general terms at least, involves certain false pictures of language, with the problem of atonal music we seem to be truly at an impasse. We are faced with a challenge, not to our liking of a certain musical style, but to our very idea of music. What I find remarkable is the way Cavell articulates the resolution of this impasse: "we may find ourselves *within* the experience of such compositions, following them; and then the question whether this is music and the problem of its tonal sense, will be – not answered or solved, but rather they will disappear, seem irrelevant" (*MWM* 84).

It has become something of a philosophical platitude to say that Wittgenstein seeks not to solve but rather to make philosophical problems disappear. But note the way in which Cavell makes this possibility depend on finding oneself *within* a new space of experience, moreover a space of experience opened, as though constructed for us, by the work of art. It is not sufficient to have a critique of metaphysically inflected claims that are shown to be problematic by an appeal to ordinary language. (As though by listing the correct ways of speaking, we would show that the metaphysical assertion is not one of them, and thus the apparent meaning vanishes into thin air.) Dissolution of the tension requires an environment in which what appeared uniquely troubling is *absorbed* in the unity of a space of experience and disappears *in that* space. Moreover, that space is to be characterized as something of a new world, even if it is our world recognized anew. A world is to be entered for the problem to disappear. That our experience can have the kind of unity of a world is most powerfully present to us in art. It is as though Cavell takes to heart Kant's claim that there can be no argument about taste and concludes from it that it is the force of the work of art to make the opposition of argument disappear in a higher positivity of experience.

The presentation of the problem of atonal music and its peculiar resolution indeed leads Cavell to align Wittgenstein's mode of criticism with Hegel's dialectic:

I had to describe the accommodation of the new music as one of naturalizing ourselves to a new form of life, a new world. That a resolution of this sort is described as the solution of a philosophical problem, and as the goal of its particular mode of criticism, represents for me the most original contribution Wittgenstein offers philosophy. I can think of no closer title for it, in an established philosophical vocabulary, than Hegel's use of the terms *Aufhebung*. We cannot translate the term: 'cancelling,' 'negating,' 'fulfilling' etc. ... are all partial, and 'sublate' transfers the problem. (*MWM* 85)

Now, with the Hegelian dialectic, it is very clear that the disappearance of an opposition internal to spirit is its transformation, its being absorbed in a

higher form, becoming a moment of a transformed space of experience.[12]
Another, maybe even more striking way to make this point than the reference to Hegel in this essay, is Cavell availing himself in this essay of the early
Wittgenstein. Indeed, it is practically the only place in which Cavell takes on
the *Tractatus*, and even though there are hardly two paragraphs referring to
that work, they are extraordinarily insightful and rich.

The region of the *Tractatus* that Cavell relates himself to is significant, even
if not surprising in retrospect. It is the only mention of skepticism in that
work, figuring toward its end in a stretch of propositions that investigates the
character of questioning. Witttgenstein has often been taken to merely
dismiss skepticism, as he writes: "Skepticism is not irrefutable, but obviously
nonsensical, when it tries to raise difficulty where no questions can be asked.
For doubt can exist only where a question exists, a question only where an
answer exists and an answer only where something can be said."[13]

"Doubt can exist only where a question exists." But spiritual suffering that
takes the form of doubt seems to be taken seriously enough by Wittgenstein
in a further proposition that clarifies the statement: "Is this not the reason
why those who have found after a long period of doubt that the sense of life
became clear to them have then been unable to say what constituted that
sense?"[14] What is the way to find peace, in the face of doubt for which no
precise question can be articulated and therefore no specific answer can be
given? For sure, in resolving that "long period of doubt," it would not be
sufficient to say something like "it was all nonsense, get over it," if only
because any resolution must be true to the struggle that led to it. For it to be
accepted as resolution, it must "answer" to the character of depth of the
problems. To be able to let go of our highest spiritual struggles, we must be
open to reorientation in, or of, our world.

Skepticism is out of the question. What is not the object of a question,
what is unquestionable, is what we call "world."[15] There is no question
for which the answer would be the existence of the world (meaning the
supposed metaphysical question: "why is there something rather than
nothing?" is no real question). But this also means that conviction can be
reached in the unquestionable, yet not by providing an answer: "You have

[12] I note that at this point we can now recognize the importance of stating the two aesthetic
problems, in the first part of the essay, as antinomial oppositions. The dialectical
resolution finds the standpoint for absorbing the oppositions in a higher unity.
[13] Ludwig Wittgenstein, *Tractatus Logico-Philosophicus*, trans. David Pears and Brian
McGuinness (London: Routledge, 2001), 6.5–6.51.
[14] *Ibid.*, 6.521.
[15] For an interpretation of the ethics of Wittgenstein's *Tractatus* developing the themes
suggested here, see my "Logic, Ethics and Existence in Wittgenstein's *Tractatus*," in
Wittgenstein's Moral Thought, ed. Reshef Agam-Sega and Edmund Dain (London:
Routledge, 2017), 97–132.

reached conviction," Cavell writes, "but not about a proposition; and consistency, but not in a theory. You are different, what you recognize as problems are different, your world is different. ('The world of the happy man is a different one from that of the unhappy man')" (*MWM* 86).

Following this last quote from the *Tractatus*, Cavell adds: "And this is the sense, the only sense in which what a work of art means cannot be *said*. Believing it is seeing it" (86).

★

The work of art teaches us, models for us, what it is to find ourselves in this unity of world, to see the world *sub specie aeterni*, as Wittgenstein also puts it. In a notebook entry from 1931, he remarks:

> The work of art compels us – as one might say – to see it in the *right* perspective ... But now it seems to me too that besides *the work* of the artist there is another through which the world may be captured *sub specie aeterni*. It is – as I believe – the way of thought which as it were flies above the world and leaves it *the way* it is, contemplating it from above *in* its flight.[16]

That way of thought is the practice of the ordinary language philosopher. So as to fly above the world and leaves it as it is, it must gather our language, so that we encompass it as the unity of a world. As the consideration of the work of art makes evident, this gathering must be anchored somewhere. What is it in the philosophical practice that corresponds to the unique concentration of meaning that the work of art affords us? Wittgenstein's enigmatic claim "The world is my world" suggests that the sense of the uniqueness of my life is inseparable from the recognition of the unity of world. Let me end then by citing the how Cavell formulates the same insight in *The Claim of Reason*:

> In philosophizing, I have to bring my own language and life into imagination. What I require is a convening of my culture's criteria, in order to confront them with my words and life as I pursue them and as I may imagine them, and at the same time confront my words and life as I pursue them with the life my culture's words may imagine for me: to confront the culture with itself along the lines in which it meets me. This seems to me a task that warrants the name of philosophy. (*CR* 125)

---

[16] Ludwig Wittgenstein, *Culture and Value*, ed. G.H. von Wright, trans. Peter Winch (Oxford: Blackwell, 1994; 1st edn 1980), 4–5, translation amended. The last lines of "Aesthetic Problems" articulate the character of the ordinary both as what is wholly in common, and ever denied and rejected: "About what we should say when, we do not expect to have to tolerate much difference, believing that if we could articulate it fully we would have spoken for all men, found the necessities common to us all. But philosophy concerns those necessities we cannot, being human, fail to know. Except that nothing is more human than to deny them" (*MWM* 96).

Part II

Aesthetics and the Modern

5   "Language-Games" and "Forms of Life"

Cavell's Reading of Wittgenstein and Its Relevance to Literary Studies

Greg Chase

Much of Stanley Cavell's most memorably original writing was prompted by his engagement with another memorably original thinker: Ludwig Wittgenstein. Cavell first outlines his pioneering interpretation of Wittgenstein's thought in the second essay of *Must We Mean What We Say?*, "The Availability of Wittgenstein's Later Philosophy" (initially published in 1963). The essay mounts a devastating critique of David Pole's book *The Later Philosophy of Wittgenstein* (1958). Early on, Cavell writes, "What I find most remarkable about this book is not the modesty of its understanding nor the pretentiousness and condescension of its criticism, but the pervasive absence of any worry that some remark of Wittgenstein's may not be utterly obvious in its meaning and implications" (*MWM* 45), and he hardly lets up in the pages that follow. The essay's title plays on two senses of the word "availability." Wittgenstein's mature philosophy is "available" (46) in the sense that *Philosophical Investigations*, the fullest encapsulation of this philosophy, was published in 1953, two years after Wittgenstein's death in 1951. However, Cavell indicates that – on the evidence of Pole's book – Wittgenstein's philosophy may still not be available, if "available" is taken to mean something like: capable of being understood, even to a modest degree. Cavell uses his disappointment with Pole's work as an occasion to offer some thoughts of his own on how to read the *Investigations*, thus maintaining hope that Wittgenstein's dense and gnomic text might still be made "available" to readers.

As a scholar of twentieth-century literature, I have looked to Wittgenstein's *Investigations*, as well as to Cavell's reading of this work, for a clarifying perspective on the expressions of alienation and linguistic skepticism frequently voiced by characters in modernist fiction.[1] However, despite the relevance of Wittgenstein's claims to literary studies, the conception of his work that Cavell presents in the "Availability"

---

[1] For example, see my "Acknowledging Addie's Pain: Language, Wittgenstein, and *As I Lay Dying*," *Twentieth- Century Literature* 63/2 (2017), 167–90.

essay has not been widely taken up by my field. Why not? The simplest answer is likely along the lines of "had we but world enough and time": I suspect that many of my colleagues in literary studies feel understandably disinclined to engage with a philosophical tradition cited only sporadically in their field, given that there are always more novels, plays, and poems (not to mention student essays) to be read. In what follows, though, I propose an even more specific explanation for this state of affairs: Cavell's reading of Wittgenstein has been obscured from view by a much more influential misreading, which has taken hold in literary-critical circles in the last forty years. The source of this misreading is Jean-François Lyotard's *The Postmodern Condition* (1979), which makes Wittgenstein's concept of "language-games"[2] central to its understanding of postmodernism's "incredulity toward metanarratives."[3]

My discussion has three sections: the first reviews how Lyotard's description of language-games has become – in a kind of self-fulfillment of his own argument – foundational to the contemporary literary-critical understanding of postmodernism, even as Lyotard's discussion relies on an unacknowledged simplification of how Wittgenstein understands the linked concepts of "language-games" and "rules" in the *Investigations*. The second section shows how Cavell's "Availability" essay exposes the problems with this postmodern reading of Wittgenstein; Cavell demonstrates that the concept of "rules" possesses only secondary importance in the *Investigations*, while bringing out the importance of a different Wittgensteinian term: "forms of life" (*PI* II, 345). Finally, the third section examines Sherwood Anderson's modernist short story cycle *Winesburg, Ohio* (1919), showing how Cavell's reading of Wittgenstein helps to elucidate the "form of life" that Winesburg's isolated speakers all share.

Lyotard's Postmodern Wittgenstein

Published in 1979, ten years after *Must We Mean What We Say?*, Lyotard's *The Postmodern Condition* soon became one of the essential texts of postmodern theory, all the more so after its translation into

---

[2] Ludwig Wittgenstein, *Philosophical Investigations*, rev. 4th edn, trans. G.E.M. Anscombe, P.M.S. Hacker, and Joachim Schulte, ed. Hacker (Malden, MA: Wiley-Blackwell, 2009; 1st edn 1953), §7; hereafter cited parenthetically as *PI*, followed by remark, rather than page, number.

[3] Jean-François Lyotard, *The Postmodern Condition: A Report on Knowledge*, trans. Geoff Bennington and Brian Massumi (Minneapolis: University of Minnesota Press, 1984), 10, xxiv; hereafter cited parenthetically as *PC*.

English in 1984.[4] Lyotard recruits Wittgenstein to support his argument that, now more than ever before, what counts as "knowledge" depends on the specific epistemological conventions of different disciplines. According to Lyotard, the spread of global capitalism reinforces the inextricable links between knowledge and power. "Nation-states ... collaborate with corporations" (*PC* 45) to fund research; as a result, "science laboratories" prioritize "the development of saleable programs," generating marketable pieces of knowledge that suit the private interests of their "financial backers" (46). Lyotard uses the *Investigations'* concept of "language-games" to explain this postmodern cultural situation. In Lyotard's account, what Wittgenstein "means" by this coinage "is that each of the various categories of utterance can be defined in terms of rules specifying their properties and the uses to which they can be put – in *exactly* the same way as the game of chess is defined by a set of rules determining the properties of each of the pieces" (*PC* 10, my emphasis). According to this account, each field of knowledge becomes its own game, with its own contingent set of rules. The rules of one discipline have no necessary bearing on those of another, and practitioners of the former may be unable to speak the language of the latter. A language-game does not merely reflect or express knowledge of the world; it produces this knowledge. Words become an arbitrary set of social conventions, with no necessary relation to any underlying reality.

Lyotard arrived at this theory against the backdrop of worrisome developments in his own professional life. In the 1970s, he taught at the Experimental University Centre at Vincennes, which had been founded in response to the protests of 1968, in which he had been "an active participant."[5] At first, the Experimental University welcomed non-traditional students and educational methods and gave students an unusual degree of control over the direction of their studies.[6] By 1979, however, the Experimental University was facing an "imminent move ... from Vincennes to St. Denis," which Lyotard saw as an attempt to restrict its autonomy and reincorporate it into the larger bureaucratic apparatus of the French state.[7] One of the targets of critique in *The Postmodern Condition* is "a kind of education under capitalism that ... socially reproduces students to fulfill the technical demands of the

---

[4] On the "continuous success" of *The Postmodern Condition*, see François Cusset, *French Theory: How Foucault, Derrida, Deleuze, & Co. Transformed the Intellectual Life of the United States*, trans. Jeff Fort (Minneapolis: University of Minnesota Press, 2008), 215.
[5] Kiff Bamford, *Jean-François Lyotard* (London: Reaktion, 2017), 66.   [6] *Ibid.*, 95–98.
[7] *Ibid.*, 95.

system,"[8] and Lyotard could personally attest to this trend toward a more market-driven model of education. So Lyotard set out to attack "the promotion of relativism, of fluctuating and nonreferential values," which he understood as symptomatic of the "virtual, global, financial capitalism" he saw emerging around him.[9]

Given that *The Postmodern Condition* offers an anti-authoritarian critique of corporate interests, it is easy to see why cultural critics would have found Lyotard's work compelling in the late twentieth century: a moment of neoliberal economic ascendency and accelerating levels of wealth inequality. In *Postmodernism* (1991), Fredric Jameson explicitly links this economic situation to developments in the realm of aesthetics, writing, "aesthetic production has been integrated into commodity production generally: the frantic economic urgency of producing fresh waves of ever more novel-seeming goods (from clothing to airplanes), at ever greater rates of turnover, now assigns an increasingly essential structural function and position to aesthetic innovation and experimentation."[10] Consistent with Lyotard's account of how each language-game operates according to its own rules, works of postmodernist fiction signal innovativeness by disregarding the conventions of earlier fictional modes, even those modernism had left in place. As an example, consider John Barth's short story "Lost in the Funhouse" (1968), which comments self-referentially on the process of its own composition. After opening with a description of a character, Ambrose M, on a family trip to Ocean City, Barth's story abruptly makes the following comment: "Description of physical appearance and mannerisms is one of several standard methods of characterization used by writers of fiction."[11] Rather than representing how its characters use words to make sense of the world around them, as earlier works of fiction had done, "Lost in the Funhouse" creates a world of words, governed by its own self-contained rules.

Given how influential Lyotard's account of the postmodern condition has been, his reading of Wittgenstein has similarly permeated the public consciousness. Before we examine the problems with Lyotard's Wittgenstein, let us consider two brief examples that testify to the enduring prominence of this reading. The first comes from the *Internet*

[8] Michael A. Peters, *Poststructuralism, Marxism, and Neoliberalism: Between Theory and Politics* (Lanham, MD: Rowman & Littlefield, 2001), 13.
[9] Cusset, *French Theory*, xvi.
[10] Fredric R. Jameson, *Postmodernism, or, The Cultural Logic of Late Capitalism* (Durham, NC: Duke University Press, 1991), 4–5.
[11] John Barth, "Lost in the Funhouse," in *Lost in the Funhouse: Fiction for Print, Tape, Live Voice* (New York: Random House, 1988), 73–74.

Encyclopedia of Philosophy, an open-access scholarly resource: the author of the entry on Lyotard writes, "For both Wittgenstein and Lyotard, language games are incommensurable, and moves in one language game cannot be translated into moves in another language game."[12] Certainly, this sentence is consistent with the way Lyotard presents the concept of "language-games" in *The Postmodern Condition*; for our purposes, however, the question would be whether it accurately represents Wittgenstein's views. The second example comes from "True Crime: A Postmodern Murder Mystery," an unsettling *New Yorker* article by the journalist David Grann; this piece tells the story of Krystian Bala, a Polish man convicted of homicide in part on the basis of "evidence" prosecutors found in his novel *Amok* (2003), which recounts a murder similar to the one Bala was suspected of having committed. As Grann recounts,

Bala ... was drawn to the radical arguments of Ludwig Wittgenstein, who maintained that language, like a game of chess, is essentially a social activity ... For Bala, such subversive ideas made particular sense after the collapse of the Soviet Empire, where language and facts had been wildly manipulated to create a false sense of history. "The end of Communism marked the death of one of the great meta-narratives," Bala later told me, paraphrasing the postmodernist Jean-François Lyotard.[13]

While the musings of a convicted murderer hardly represent a promising place to turn for a persuasive exposition of Wittgenstein's thought, what bears emphasizing about Grann's piece is that it makes no effort to contest Bala's Lyotard-inspired reading of Wittgenstein. Together, Grann's article and the entry from the *Internet Encyclopedia of Philosophy* highlight the degree to which Lyotard's work has shaped the popular understanding of Wittgenstein in the twenty-first century. On this view, Wittgenstein was a proto-postmodernist, who posited that – as Lyotard writes in another context – "there is no unity to language; there are islands of language, each of them ruled by a different regime, untranslatable into the others."[14] Particularly now that the academy's interest in

[12] Ashley Woodard, "Jean-François Lyotard (1924–1988)," *Internet Encyclopedia of Philosophy*, www.iep.utm.edu/lyotard/#SH4b.

[13] David Grann, "True Crime: A Postmodern Murder Mystery," *New Yorker*, February 4, 2008, www.newyorker.com/magazine/2008/02/11/true-crime.

[14] Jean-François Lyotard, "Wittgenstein, 'After,'" in *Political Writings*, ed. and trans. Bill Readings and Kevin Paul Geiman (Minneapolis: University of Minnesota Press, 1993), 20. For additional comparative treatments of Wittgenstein's and Lyotard's thought, see David Schalkwyk, "Knowledge, Ethics, and the Limits of Language: Wittgenstein and Lyotard," *Journal of Literary Studies* 12/1–2 (1996), 86–111; Schalkwyk, "Why the Social Bond Cannot Be a Passing Fashion: Reading Wittgenstein against Lyotard," *Theoria: A Journal of Social and Political Theory* 89 (1997), 116–31.

postmodernism has waned from its heyday in the 1980s and 1990s, this view of Wittgenstein is liable to make him seem like an out-of-touch theorist, whose abstract conception of language has little bearing on the daily lives of ordinary human subjects. Turning to Cavell, however, demonstrates that this conception of Wittgenstein's thought could hardly be farther from the truth.

From "Rules" to "Forms of Life": Cavell's Wittgenstein

The main problem with this postmodern reading of Wittgenstein is that it misrepresents how the *Investigations* actually employs the concept of "language-games." It is true that Wittgenstein compares learning the "rules" of language to learning those of chess (*PI* 197); however, as Cavell makes clear in "Availability," the differences between these two cases are just as important as the similarities. Chess has a finite set of rules; these can be (and often are) written down in the form of a list, and when a disagreement arises between players, they can refer back to this list to resolve their dispute. By contrast, as Cavell writes, "That everyday language does not, in fact or in essence, depend upon such a structure and conception of rules, and yet that the absence of such a structure in no way impairs its functioning, is what the picture of language drawn in [Wittgenstein's] later philosophy is about" (*MWM* 48). So it is not accurate to claim, as Lyotard does, that the rules of Wittgenstein's language-games are "exactly" like those of chess (*PC* 10); on the contrary, we might say that a central preoccupation of Wittgenstein's later philosophy is to understand why, in spite of its evident difference from chess, "everyday language" still works.

Early in the *Investigations*, Wittgenstein defines a language-game as "one of those games by means of which children learn their native language" (*PI* 7). He goes on to list the following examples:

> Giving orders, and acting on them –
> Describing an object by its appearance ... –
> Constructing an object from a description ... –
> Reporting an event –
> Speculating about the event –
> Forming and testing a hypothesis –
> Presenting the results of an experiment in tables and diagrams –
> Making up a story; and reading one –
> Acting in a play –
> Singing rounds –
> Guessing riddles –

Cracking a joke; telling one –
Solving a problem in applied arithmetic –
Translating from one language into another –
Requesting, thanking, cursing, greeting, praying. (*PI* 23)

As in Lyotard's account, Wittgenstein identifies a heterogeneous set of language-games, each with its own, distinct rules. Like Lyotard, Wittgenstein distinguishes between language-games associated with the sciences ("Forming and testing a hypothesis") and language-games associated with other realms of human activity ("Acting in a play"). For Wittgenstein, however, the point is that all these language-games, *taken together*, help us to understand the roles that words play in our lives. When we form and test hypotheses, we are liable to use many of the same words that we use to speculate about an event ("Maybe"; "What if?"), and we may even use them in the same ways, to mean the same things. Through the movement between these language-games, we learn conventions for how words work. Each language-game is different, but each also contributes to our broader understanding of "language and the activities into which it is woven" (*PI* 7). Furthermore, language-games as described by Wittgenstein are smaller and more concrete – more ordinary, we might say – than Lyotard's account suggests; for instance, Wittgenstein's list includes "Forming and testing a hypothesis," but it notably does not include an entry like "Scientific inquiry." (It also includes "Solving a problem in applied arithmetic," rather than "Applied arithmetic.") Put another way: in the *Investigations*, language-games tend to be played by children; in *The Postmodern Condition*, they tend to be played by corporations.

If the *Investigations* presents the relation between words and world differently than Lyotard suggests, how are we to understand Wittgenstein's repeated invocations of "games" and "rules"? As Cavell explains in "Availability," Wittgenstein does present language as a social activity, but this fact need not be taken to imply that the meanings of our words are not tied to, or grounded in, any underlying realities. The postmodern reading of Wittgenstein omits the crucial fact that, as Cavell writes in the titular essay of *Must We Mean*, "we learn language and learn the world together, that they become elaborated and distorted together, and in the same places" (*MWM* 19). In "Availability," Cavell emphasizes that "the ultimate appeal for Wittgenstein" (50) is what the *Investigations* calls "forms of life" (*PI* ii, 345). As Toril Moi has discussed, Wittgenstein's notion of "forms of life" encompasses "both our cultural practices and their connectedness to the natural conditions of our lives ... Cutting across the nature/culture divide, the concept ... is elastic enough to range from the purely biological to the completely cultural, to encompass the human body as well as the finest distinctions of the practices in a specific culture."[15] Similarly, in a later work, *This New Yet Unapproachable America* (1989), Cavell distinguishes between "the ethnological ... or horizontal sense" of forms of life and "the biological or vertical sense," writing that Wittgenstein's term includes both, and that we misunderstand the *Investigations* if we focus only on the former (*TNYUA* 41).[16] All the language-games described by Wittgenstein take place upon, and are circumscribed by, "very general facts of nature" (*PI* ii, 366): the "bedrock" (217) conditions upon which our lives unfold.[17]

Having shown that the notion of "rules" proves unsatisfactory as an explanation for how language works, Cavell offers an alternative way of understanding the central thrust of the *Investigations*:

We learn and teach words in certain contexts, and then we are expected, and expect others, to be able to project them into further contexts. Nothing insures that this projection will take place (in particular, not the grasping of universals nor the grasping of books of rules), just as nothing insures that we will make, and understand, the same projections. That on the whole we do is a matter of our sharing routes of interest and feeling, modes of response, senses of humor and of significance and of fulfilment, of what is outrageous, what is similar to what else ... – all the whirl of organism Wittgenstein calls "forms of life." Human speech and activity, sanity and community, rest upon nothing more, but nothing less, than this. It is a vision as simple as it is difficult, and as difficult as it is (and because it is) terrifying. (*MWM* 52)

This passage offers an early formulation of what remains among the most distinctive features of Cavell's response to Wittgenstein: his focus on what *The Claim of Reason* (1979) calls "mutual attunement" or "agreement" between speakers as an explanation for how and why language works (*CR* 32). As Cavell writes in this later work, "The idea of agreement here is not that of coming to or arriving at an agreement on a given occasion, but of being in agreement throughout, being in harmony, like pitches or tones" (32). In the passage above, Cavell

[15] Toril Moi, *Revolution of the Ordinary: Literary Studies after Wittgenstein, Austin, and Cavell* (University of Chicago Press, 2017), 55–56.
[16] For more on Wittgenstein's development of the concept of "forms of life," see Juliet Floyd, "Chains of Life: Turing, *Lebensform*, and the Emergence of Wittgenstein's Later Style," *Nordic Review* 5/2 (2016), 7–89.
[17] Offering examples of such "very general facts" in *The Claim of Reason*, Cavell lists "the fact that the realization of intention requires action, that action requires movement, that movement involves consequences we had not intended, [and] that our knowledge (and ignorance) of ourselves and of others depends upon the way our minds are expressed (and distorted) in word and deed" (*CR* 110).

anticipates this understanding of "agreement" with his discussion of "sharing routes of interest and feeling." Humans tend to express sentiments and sensations in similar ways; if we experience pain, for example, our instinctive reaction is often to grimace or cry out. So if we see someone else behave in this way, we may find ourselves attuned to the fact that this person is in pain. However, Cavell also finds Wittgenstein's vision of language "terrifying," in the sense that "[n]othing insures" this attunement will persist indefinitely or apply to all cases. As Cavell notes later in "Availability," one of Wittgenstein's common answers to the question, "How do I know ... that others speak as I do?" is: "I do not" (*MWM* 67). While "forms of life" determine the parameters of our lives in language, they do not guarantee mutual comprehension or intelligibility.

In cases when "one human being" feels like "a complete enigma to another" (*PI* II, 325), Wittgenstein's later philosophy should – on Cavell's reading – encourage us to look carefully at the specific conditions of this person's life, both natural and cultural, in order to develop an understanding of how and why this person has lost, or failed to find, a sense of "agreement" with their interlocutors. It would be unsatisfying to explain this person's plight simply by saying that they are playing their own "language-game," governed by its own self-contained "rules": after all, if we've learned the language-games we know through our participation in a shared "form of life," then why do some feel more alienated or detached from this form of life than others? For answers to this question, it is helpful to turn to works of literary fiction – especially (though not exclusively) to works of modernism, which regularly give voice to the perspectives of one or more alienated speakers, each seemingly "locked into his or her private language," as Jameson puts it.[18] Whereas Lyotard mobilizes Wittgenstein in the service of his own postmodern project, Cavell's reading of the *Investigations* helps to establish the fundamental compatibility between Wittgenstein's philosophical vision and the concerns of literary modernism.

"A story of misunderstanding": Wittgenstein, Cavell, and *Winesburg, Ohio*

By way of illustrating what Cavell's reading of Wittgenstein has to offer (and its contrast with Lyotard's), let us look at how it helps to illuminate a particular literary text: Anderson's *Winesburg, Ohio*. I've chosen this

[18] Fredric R. Jameson, "Beyond the Cave: Demystifying the Ideology of Modernism," *Bulletin of the Midwest Modern Language Association* 8/1 (1975), 1–20 (at 19).

modernist short story cycle because it expresses a conception of language that might seem to anticipate Lyotard's theory of discrete, self-contained language-games, each with no necessary connection to underlying realities. In fact, however, I argue that *Winesburg* ultimately lends itself to a more Cavellian understanding of speakers who share a "form of life" but still struggle to attain "mutual attunement" with one another. Consisting of a series of vignettes, each focused on a different inhabitant of the titular town, *Winesburg* opens with a prologue, "The Book of the Grotesque," in which an elderly writer, someone who has "known people, many people ... in a peculiarly intimate way that was different from the way in which you and I know people," attempts to synthesize what he has learned from his years of observation.[19] The writer theorizes that the world is full of "truths," including "the truth of virginity and the truth of passion, the truth of wealth and of poverty," and that people have "snatched up" one or more of these truths for themselves (*WO* 9). The writer concludes that "the moment one of the people took one of the truths to himself, called it his truth, and tried to live his life by it, he became a grotesque, and the truth he embraced became a falsehood" (9).

The subsequent vignettes illustrate the writer's insight: in one way or another, all *Winesburg*'s characters have latched on to distorted, "grotesque" understandings of their place in the world and their relations with others. For example, "Respectability" focuses on Wash Williams: described by the narrator as an "ugly," "dirty" man (93), Wash tells the story of his wife's adultery and (what Wash saw as) his mother-in-law's meddlesome efforts to reunite the married couple. The dissolution of his marriage has driven Wash to the misogynistic – and implicitly grotesque – view that women have been put on earth "to prevent men making the world worth while" (96). A different episode, "Adventure," focuses on Alice Hindman, a woman who, at the age of sixteen, has a tryst with a man who subsequently leaves town. Alice makes this youthful experience into the defining event of her life, convincing herself that it would be "monstrous" to "belong" to any other man (87), and growing steadily older and more isolated as a result. "Adventure" shows Alice playing various language-games of her own design; for instance, while praying (one of the language-games Wittgenstein mentions in §23), she begins "whisper[ing] things she wanted to say to her lover" (*WO* 87).

Ultimately, however, *Winesburg* seeks not merely to illuminate the private purposes to which characters put their words, but also to highlight the "form of life" that underlies and determines their relationship to

---

[19] Sherwood Anderson, *Winesburg, Ohio*, ed. Glen A. Love (Oxford University Press, 1997), 8; hereafter cited parenthetically as *WO*.

language. On this point, let us consider "Godliness," the work's longest vignette, which begins with Jesse Bentley inheriting his family's farm after his brothers die in the Civil War. Determined to make the farm a success, Jesse acquires additional plots of land at low prices, purchases "new machines to cut down the cost of labor," and uses the profits to buy even more land (71). The narrator describes him as a "fanatic" (45), explaining that he "wanted to make the farm produce as no farm in his state had ever produced before," but he also "wanted something else" (46): "he wanted God to notice and to talk to him" (47).

Seeking to make this character's behavior legible to readers, the narrator explains that Jesse has been shaped by the values and beliefs of a bygone age:

It will perhaps be somewhat difficult for the men and women of a later day to understand Jesse Bentley. In the last fifty years a vast change has taken place in the lives of our people ... The coming of industrialization ... the shrill cries of millions of new voices that have come among us from over seas, the going and coming of trains, the growth of cities, the building of the interurban car lines that weave in and out of towns and past farmhouses, and now in these later days the coming of the automobiles has worked a tremendous change in the lives and in the habits of thought of our people of Mid-America. Books, badly imagined and written though they may be ... are in every household, magazines circulate by the millions of copies, newspapers are everywhere. In our day a farmer standing by the stove in the store in his village has his mind filled to overflowing with the words of other men ...

In Jesse Bentley's time and in the country districts of the whole Middle West in the years after the Civil War it was not so. Men labored too hard and were too tired to read ... As they worked in the fields, vague, half-formed thoughts took possession of them. They believed in God and in God's power to control their lives. (48–49)

In this sweeping passage, Anderson's narrator chronicles about fifty years of American history, describing how "industrialization" has created a more diverse, multiethnic, interconnected, and secular American populace. While this story of modernization is, in broad strokes, a familiar one, the particular aspect of this history to which the passage draws attention is the American people's increased saturation with *words*. As the narrator emphasizes, the increasingly widespread distribution of books, newspapers, and magazines means that even a farmer in "Mid-America" has "his mind filled to overflowing with the words of other men." By contrast, Jesse has been shaped by an earlier moment in history: he and his brothers had "clung to the old traditions and worked like driven animals," speaking only when necessary (43). Jesse's conception of the world has been shaped by a much smaller number of voices: he has been driven, almost exclusively, by his staunchly held religious beliefs and his powerful desire to distinguish himself from others. Though he has willingly, and shrewdly, modernized the operation of his farm, he has done so only as a means to an end, imagining that the success of his farming endeavors will make him worthy of a visitation from God.

Jesse's story demonstrates how the specific conditions of one's "form of life" shape one's sense of self. These conditions might be natural or environmental, such as the fertility of the land from which Jesse and his employees harvest their crops. They might be technological, such as the "new machines" that make this process more efficient. And they might be cultural, such as the increasingly diverse array of reading material to which modern American subjects have access. In this way, *Winesburg* indicates that even when its characters conceive of word–world relations in idiosyncratic ways, their views remain historically conditioned, determined by the interlocking sequence of language-games that these characters have learned, and been inclined, to play.

After initially describing the "contexts" (*MWM* 52) in which Jesse has learned to use words, "Godliness" extends this account of the relationship between language and the material conditions of modernity by shifting its focus to Jesse's daughter, Louise. Louise's history is, as the narrator explains, "a story of misunderstanding" (*WO* 63), which is to say that she has struggled to find any interlocutors with whom she shares "routes of interest and feeling" (*MWM* 52). Elaborating on this point, Anderson's narrator attests that "Before women such as Louise can be understood and their lives made livable, much will have to be done. Thoughtful books will have to be written and thoughtful lives lived" (*WO* 62). Whereas the lengthy passage quoted above emphasizes the major technological and cultural shifts brought about by modernization, these two sentences signal the way in which this modernization process remains incomplete. Louise may have access to more books than her father's generation did, but she still has been unable to find the words that will enable her to experience a sense of "community" (*MWM* 52).

As with its account of Alice Hindman in "Adventure," *Winesburg* emphasizes the degree to which patriarchal gender norms have determined Louise's persistent difficulty in being understood.[20] On the night

---

[20] As Peter Nagy writes, Anderson "recognizes individuals who have been wounded and deformed by the gender normative social order, especially women." Nagy, "The Woman in the Man: Male Modernism and Cross-Gender Identification in Sherwood Anderson's *Winesburg, Ohio*," *College Literature* 45/4 (2018), 773–800 (at 783). For more on the role of misunderstanding and communicative failure in *Winesburg*, see Glen A. Love, "*Winesburg, Ohio* and the Rhetoric of Silence," *American Literature* 40/1 (1968), 38–57; Rebecca Sanchez, "Shattering Communicative Norms: The Politics of Embodied Language in *Winesburg, Ohio*," *Modern Language Studies* 43/2 (2014), 25–39.

of her birth, Jesse calls upon God to grant him a son, and it is clear that Louise internalizes this familial and cultural preference for men. Many years later, after giving birth to a son herself, she expresses doubt as to "whether she wanted him or not," and when her husband reproaches her, she proclaims, "It is a man child and will get what it wants anyway ... Had it been a woman child there is nothing in the world I would not have done for it" (70). Through the narrator's account of the intervening years, we learn that in her youth Louise has been sent away from the Bentley farm to live with an acquaintance of her father who resides in Winesburg. This man, Hardy, is "an enthusiast on the subject of education" (62), and Louise proves a diligent student, "work[ing] constantly at her studies" and trying to answer "every question put to the class by the teacher" (63). Given *Winesburg*'s emphasis on books as a possible means of feeling understood, Louise's devotion to her studies suggests her desperate hope of coming across some words that would allow her to experience a sense of "mutual attunement" (*CR* 32) with others. In the meantime, she convinces herself that Hardy's son John is a kindred spirit and reaches out to him for companionship.

Unfortunately, Louise's dedication to her schoolwork notwithstanding, her form of life has not taught her any language-games that will allow her to convey the specificity and subtlety of her desires to John. She writes him a note in which, the narrator explains, "she tried to be quite definite about what she wanted. 'I want someone to love me, and I want to love someone,' she wrote" (*WO* 68). But her attempt at linguistic precision nonetheless misses its mark: "Louise Bentley took John Hardy to be her lover. That was not what she wanted but it was so the young man had interpreted her approach to him, and so anxious was she to achieve something else that she made no resistance" (69). Even after she and John are married, Louise continues trying "to make her husband understand the vague and intangible hunger that had led to the writing of the note ... but always without success. Filled with his own notions of love between men and women, he did not listen but began to kiss her upon the lips" (69–70). To her dismay, Louise finds that a man like John cannot understand a lonely woman's appeal for companionship as anything other than a request for sex (and, eventually, marriage). By the time Louise abandons her hopes of conveying the specificity of her emotional needs, it is already too late; she is an unhappy wife, en route to becoming an unhappy mother, constrained by the dearth of language-games her culture has developed for expanding the normative options available to human speakers like her.

★

Cavell concludes his "Availability" essay with a brief discussion of Wittgenstein's "literary style" (*MWM* 70). Cavell identifies the style of the *Investigations* as that of "confession" (71), in the mold of Augustine's famous work (which Wittgenstein opens his own book by quoting). As Cavell explains, a confession has an expressive quality that differentiates it from a more conventional work of philosophical argumentation: "In confessing you do not explain or justify, but describe how it is with you" (71). He goes on to observe that "Such writing has its risks": here, he compares Wittgenstein with Freud, noting that "both were obsessed with the idea, or fact, that they would be misunderstood" (72). The history of the *Investigations'* reception has borne out Cavell's sense that its story is – like that of Louise Bentley – "a story of misunderstanding" (*WO* 62); such misunderstandings are evident in both Pole's reading (which Cavell challenges) and Lyotard's (which I've sought to challenge here). At the same time, there's also a suggestion running across the work of Anderson, Wittgenstein, and Cavell that the "story of misunderstanding" need not be the full, or only, story. After all, despite criticizing the books of his own age as "badly imagined and written" (*WO* 48), Anderson, too, has written a book – perhaps in the hope that it might serve as a modest contribution to the project of making ordinary people's lives more "livable" (62). Along similar lines, Wittgenstein emphasizes that "new language-games ... come into existence, and others become obsolete and get forgotten" (*PI* 23). And we might understand Cavell in *Must We Mean* as seeking to initiate this process himself, by offering his readers a new way to understand Wittgenstein's project. Those of us invested in this project would do well to continue along the "routes of interest and feeling" Cavell has laid out (*MWM* 52).

6 Philosophic and Aesthetic Appeal
Stanley Cavell on the Irreducibility of the First Person in Aesthetics and in Philosophy

Arata Hamawaki

In "Aesthetic Problems of Modern Philosophy," Stanley Cavell proposed that the judgments that constitute the ordinary, and that are the subject matter of philosophy that proceeds from ordinary language – or "ordinary language philosophy," as it is commonly called – are to be modelled on aesthetic judgments. And the notion of aesthetic judgment that Cavell had in mind here is Kant's, in particular Kant's view of aesthetic judgment as expressing what he called a "universal voice" (or "subjective universality"). Cavell writes,

> Kant's "universal voice" is, with perhaps a slight shift of accent, what we hear recorded in the philosopher's claims about "what we say": such claims are at least as close to what Kant calls aesthetical judgments as they are to ordinary empirical hypotheses. Though the philosopher seems to claim, or depend upon, severer agreement than is carried by the aesthetic analogue, I wish to suggest that it is a claim or dependence of the *same kind*. (*MWM* 94, my emphasis)

What does Cavell mean by saying that their claims to agreement, or their dependence on agreement, is of the same "kind"? What is the "kind" of claim or dependence that he has in mind?

As is well known – if not well understood – for Kant an aesthetic judgment, like a theoretical judgment, makes a claim to universal agreement. That is what, according to him, distinguishes a judgment of the beautiful from what he called a judgment of the "agreeable." He says that with a judgment of the agreeable, such as "Canary wine is pleasant," "another man may correct his expression and remind him that he ought to say, 'It is pleasant to me.'" But, he goes on,

> the case is quite different with the beautiful. It would (on the contrary) be laughable if a man who imagined anything to his own taste thought to justify himself by saying: "This object (the house we see, the coat that person wears, the concert we hear, the poem submitted to our judgment) is beautiful for me." For he must not call it beautiful if it merely pleases him ...[1]

---

[1] Immanuel Kant, *Critique of the Power of Judgment*, ed. Paul Guyer, trans. Guyer and Eric Matthews (Cambridge University Press, 2000), 90 (§7, 5:213); hereafter cited parenthetically as *CPJ*. It should be obvious that the universal validity of a judgment

Cavell takes the difference that Kant registers between the agreeable and the beautiful to be what Cavell calls a "logical" difference:

> those of us who keep finding ourselves wanting to call such differences "logical" are, I think, responding to a sense of necessity we feel in them, together with a sense that necessity is, partly, a matter of the ways a judgment is supported, the ways in which conviction in it is produced: it is only by virtue of these recurrent patterns of support that a remark will count as – will be – aesthetic, or a mere matter of taste, or moral, propagandistic, religious, magical, scientific, philosophical ... (*MWM* 93)

We can call Kant's concept of a beautiful object a "critical" one, just as the concept of an object in general that he analyzes in the first *Critique* is a critical concept of an object. By that I mean that Kant understands what it is for something to be an object of thought, or of knowledge, something to which our thought seeks to conform, by analyzing the form of our judgments about them. We are not, then, to understand what an object is by, so to speak, looking out at the world and seeing what is there, by seeing what properties are instantiated in the object. Rather, the nature of the objects of our judgments is to be understood by exhibiting the form of the judgments we make about them. In this way Kant arrives at the conclusion that it belongs to the concept of "an object in general" that objects are, for example, substances governed by causal laws, and so on. Similarly, if we are to understand what it is for an object to be beautiful, we aren't, at least in the first instance, to look at the world for instruction; rather, we ought to begin by reflecting on the form of the judgments we make about the beautiful and to consider whether there is something distinctive about such judgments. It is implicit in this methodology that the beautiful is not a special domain or field of objects, the special content of a generic form of judgment, but is rather the object of a particular species of judgment, a species of judgment with its own logical form or grammar.[2] When Cavell says that the appeals of the ordinary language philosopher to "what we say when" is of "the same kind" as the claim to universal agreement in an aesthetic judgment, he is drawing attention to the logical form they have in common, and it is this commonality in their "logic" that for him serves as a clue to what these judgments are about – to the nature of their "objects" – and to why

---

does not have any implications about the extent of the agreement we can expect to find. It is conceivable that a universally valid judgment meet with very little agreement and that a private judgment meet with considerable, even universal, agreement.

[2] Kant took the same approach to action. Action isn't a special content of a generic form of judgment, but is rather the object of a distinctive species of judgment, practical judgment.

agreement and disagreement matters with respect to these judgments in the way that it does (*MWM* 96).

I will begin, then, by bringing out, and remarking on, what Cavell takes to be the features that constitute the logic of aesthetic judgment. And then I will turn to an all-too-brief characterization of the logical form of the judgments in ordinary language philosophy (OLP), its claims about "what we say when," or what, following Wittgenstein, Cavell calls its "eliciting of criteria." Finally, I will conclude with some conjectures about what can be learned from the "logical" affinities between these judgments, conjectures concerning what Cavell might have meant by calling them claims to agreement "of the same kind."

The Appeal of the Beautiful

Kant called the universal validity of aesthetic judgments "something remarkable, not indeed for the logician, but certainly for the transcendental philosopher" (*CPJ* §8, 5:213). What makes it remarkable is that the judgment of taste is not based on a concept, the sharing of which could explain why in making the judgment I demand universal agreement. As Frege later stressed, concepts are by their very nature shared. Unlike a headache, a perception, or an image, a concept is not owned: it makes no sense to speak of *my* concept or *your* concept, or perhaps even "our" concept. A concept isn't anyone's; it is impersonal.[3] This is essential to what a concept is because a concept determines what is true and false, determines what does and does not fall under it. If a concept is owned, then what determines what is true and false would be whatever is in the mind of an individual thinker. But then truth would depend on the one who thinks it – truth itself would be "owned": I would have my truth and you would have yours. And that is tantamount to destroying the very idea of truth.[4] The objectivity of truth mandates that what determines truth, namely, the concept, be essentially shared. However, according to Kant,

if one judges in accordance with concepts, then all representation of beauty is lost. Thus, there can also be no rule in accordance with which someone could be compelled to acknowledge something as beautiful. Whether a garment, a house, a flower is beautiful: no one allows himself to be talked into his judgment about

---

[3] For the classic formulation of this point, see Gottlob Frege, "The Thought: A Logical Inquiry," in *Philosophical Logic*, ed. P.F. Strawson (Oxford University Press, 1967), 17–38.

[4] Here is C.I. Lewis: "if there is nothing objective about propositions and concepts, then there is no such thing as truth and there can be no serious purpose in reflection and discussion." Lewis, *Mind and the World Order* (Mineola, NY: Dover, 1929), 70.

that by means of any grounds or fundamental principles. One wants to submit the object to his own eyes, just as if his satisfaction depended on sensation ... (*CPJ* §8, 5:215–16)

This too is a "logical" or "grammatical" feature of judgments of taste. Cavell's version of Kant's point goes like this:

It is essential to making an aesthetic judgment that at some point we be prepared to say in its support: don't you see, don't you hear, don't you dig? The best critic will know the best points. Because if you do not see something, without explanation, then there is nothing further to discuss. Which does not mean that the critic has no recourse: he can start training and instructing you and preaching at you – a direction in which criticism invariably will start to veer ... At some point, the critic will have to say: This is what I see. Reasons – at definite points, for definite reasons, in different circumstances – come to an end. (Cf. *Investigations*, §217.) (*MWM* 93)

That it is essential to the nature of an aesthetic judgment that it can bottom out in "This is what I see" echoes Kant's observation that there can be no rule in accordance with which "one could be compelled to acknowledge something as beautiful."[5] It is essential to a judgment of taste that it be arrived at "freely," that is, apart from compulsion or constraint by a rule.

Thus, unlike a perceptual judgment, aesthetic judgments are essentially indeterminate. Someone who has the concept "red" must know that "this" (some random thing) does, or doesn't, count as red. Now, undoubtedly, for all but the technical concepts employed in the sciences (concepts that Kant viewed as "constructible in intuition") there are "borderline" cases. But with the aesthetic, it is the central cases that are indeterminate, not just the borderline ones. In fact, where the judgment is determinate, the judgment would be, so to speak, borderline aesthetic: for example, imagine a stereotypically cheerful melody, or a picturesque scene on a postcard – in such cases anyone who has the relevant concepts would recognize their instances. As a dead metaphor is not a metaphor, so a determinate aesthetic judgment is not an aesthetic judgment – it is, as it were, a "dead" aesthetic judgment.[6]

---

[5] While I take Cavell's point of departure from Kant to be Kant's claim that aesthetic judgments are "subjectively universal" (the second moment of the Analytic of the Beautiful), Eli Friedlander, in Chapter 4, uses as his point of entry into Cavell Kant's claim that aesthetic judgment constitutes a "common sense." These are, of course, different but compatible points of orientation.

[6] This point tends to be missed by those who think of aesthetic judgment as the attribution of "aesthetic properties," for it is a strange concept of a property on which it is essentially indeterminate.

Nonetheless, it is important to see that Cavell isn't saying here that there aren't aesthetic reasons, that is, reasons that can be said to support aesthetic judgment; rather, he is saying that at a certain point reasons give out, and we are left with "don't you see ...?" The role that reasons play in aesthetic judgment seems, then, to be peculiar. As with a belief it makes sense to ask someone to provide reasons for an aesthetic judgment, but unlike a belief it is essential to an aesthetic judgment that the reasons give out. In the case of belief, were we to lack conclusive reasons in its support, that would be a contingent fact about our position with regard to answering a particular question – we need to conduct more experiments, devise better arguments, or get a better look.[7] But, according to Cavell, it is a feature of the *logical grammar* of aesthetic judgment that there cannot be conclusive reasons. This is peculiar because, as I said, this is not due to the fact that reasons are not in order – as they would not be in relation to, say, a headache or a bout of indigestion, or to sensory perception. An aesthetic judgment is after all a judgment, and not just a wail of pain or a squeal of pleasure, although they can surely express such feelings. And this isn't, I take it, because the gap between reasons and conviction is crossed by an irrational, blind leap of faith. Certainly, that isn't what Wittgenstein was implying in the context of the passage that Cavell directs us to. Cavell doesn't think that aesthetic judgments are irrational, but he does think that reasons "come to an end," but if so, how can they not be irrational? He doesn't think that they are perceptual judgments either, since in the aesthetic case a failure to see, or to hear, or to dig, may not be due to a sensory failure or inadequacy of perceptual position (such as: the lighting was poor). Aesthetic acuity isn't a perceptual faculty. And yet, as the passage indicates, we express success and failure by using sensory terms, and not only that, when I judge that something is beautiful, or is an awe-inspiring work of art, my experience may leave me with nothing else to think, just as when I perceive some unmistakable truth, such as that I am sitting here right now typing on my computer. Just as with a perceptual judgment, my experience *saddles* me with the judgment that this is beautiful. An aesthetic judgment isn't a demonstrable belief, or a perceptual judgment, or a blind leap of faith. It is "rational" but its rationality is not that of a theoretical – or a practical – judgment. What sort of rationality does it have?[8]

---

[7] Leibniz may have been wrong in holding that all truths are demonstrable (analytic) in the mind of God, but it doesn't seem that he was just speaking nonsense.

[8] It has been tempting to take issue with Kant's view that aesthetic judgments have universal purport. There are familiar techniques of accommodation, ways of blunting the audacity that Kant took to be a defining feature of a judgment of taste, ways, you might say, of domesticating these judgments. We might treat the psychological or

In a later essay, "Music Discomposed," Cavell develops the idea of the unprovability of aesthetic judgment in connection with his explorations on modernism in the arts. There, he defends the claim that it is definitive of modern art that it is haunted by an irremovable "threat of fraudulence." He writes there,

the only exposure of false art lies in recognizing something about the object itself, but something whose recognition requires exactly the same capacity as recognizing the genuine article. It is a capacity not insured by understanding the language in which it is composed, and yet we may not understand what is said; nor insured by the healthy functioning of the senses, though we may be told we do not see or that we fail to *hear* something; nor insured by the aptness of our logical powers, though what we may have missed was the object's consistency or the way one thing followed from another. (*MWM* 190)

We may think a work of art deeply moving and later discover that we were taken in by it: we may find on reflection that it is merely sentimental schlock. What kind of confusion is this? Is it like the error of thinking that a whale is a fish? Well, no, since in that case we could just be told what the difference is. Nor is it simply a mistake of perceptual judgment, like mistaking a decoy duck for a real duck, for that would be just a mistake, not a form of confusion. I take Cavell's distinction between the genuine and the fraudulent to be "of the same kind" as Kant's distinction between the beautiful and the agreeable. The beautiful and the genuine make *claims on* us, on our enjoyment of them, whereas the agreeable and the fraudulent can be said to pander to us, are simply narcissistic reflections of ourselves. We make a distinction in our aesthetic engagement between that which is genuinely deeply moving and that which merely gratifies us, and we can readily confound the one for the other. But were there a proof that could distinguish the one from the other, writes Cavell, "art and criticism of art would not have their special importance nor elicit their own forms of distrust and of gratitude. The problem of the critic, as of the artist, is not to discount his subjectivity, but to include it; not to overcome it in agreement, but to master it in exemplary ways" (*MWM* 94).[9]

sociological conditions under which a judgment of taste is made as determinative of its content, as is done by both expressivist and relativist views. Kant and Cavell seek to preserve the audacity of aesthetic judgment as essential to them.

9 Aristotle distinguished between a friendship of convenience and a friendship of virtue. How do we know which type of friendship we have? It could be said that it is internal to the sort of thing that a friendship is that there can be no proof. And this point could be extended to society: does our society reflect what Rousseau called "a general will," or is it just a Hobbesian group of individuals who have come together for mutual benefit? It is internal to what a society is that there can be no proof. For Cavell our relation to

When it comes to propositional knowledge, I can simply rule someone out as incompetent to pronounce on the matter, and if I hold someone as competent, I must regard her judgment as authoritative, unless I have some special reason to distrust her judgment on a particular occasion. It is essential to aesthetic judgment that there be no such thing as expertise – whatever a critic is, she is not an expert. This isn't, of course, to claim that we shouldn't make use of expert knowledge in judging a work of art: it is to say just that expert knowledge in this arena isn't determinative.[10] Were someone deficient in her ability to draw the relevant distinctions, to distinguish between the genuine and the fraudulent, the agreeable and the beautiful, that would compromise our relation to her. It wouldn't just be that I could no longer count on the person for reliable information; rather, I would not, in Cavell's favored phrase, share a "world" with her. As he writes in a different, though related, context, "I may realize we are not ready to walk certain places together" (*CR* 172).

Part of the problem we are encountering in understanding the role of reasons in aesthetic judgment is that we are prone to think of reasons as reasons for "thinking that…," where a proposition fills in the ellipsis. But for Cavell, and for Kant, the content of an aesthetic judgment isn't a proposition, and while they can be correct, error isn't factual error, even though they are judgments that are directed toward disclosure of the world. Not all disclosure of the world is a disclosure of facts about it. It is a feature of aesthetic judgment that in it one apprehends an object in its singularity rather than just a fact about it. All apprehension of a fact involves a general representation, even if the fact concerns a particular object, for it involves bringing the particular under a general concept. But that isn't the form of an aesthetic judgment – it rather involves appreciation of an object in its singularity, not as an instance of a general kind. It is a feature of aesthetic judgment that its object is apprehended as *calling for* articulation of its ground, even in cases where there is nothing more that one can say. And even where one can articulate the source of the thing's appeal, one feels that one is never done doing so. It isn't, then, that there aren't reasons for one's aesthetic judgment, or that the reasons

aesthetic objects belongs in this register. This is, I take it, part of what he means when he says, "in emphasizing the experiences of fraudulence and trust as essential to the experience of art, I am in effect claiming that the answer to the question 'What is art?' will in part be an answer which explains why it is we treat certain objects, or how we *can* treat certain objects, in ways normally reserved for treating persons" (*MWM* 189).

[10] In this respect aesthetic judgment is similar to practical judgment. We should, of course, make use of expert knowledge in determining what social policy to adopt, but it doesn't follow that our decision to adopt a social policy is a matter of expertise, for expertise can only bear on our knowledge of the means, not on our adoption of an end. Like the determination of an end, aesthetic judgment is everyone's business.

always fall short, so that one is left with at bottom an irrational leap of faith. It is that it belongs to the nature of one's attraction to the beautiful, as opposed to one's attraction to the merely agreeable, that one can never fully spell out the ground of one's attraction to it. That's why there is a bottoming out in "don't you see?"[11] An astute critic's descriptions don't figure *simply* as descriptions of a work of art, expressions of beliefs that the critic has about the work, although they are that in part. I want to say that a critic's descriptions of the work, or better, her elaborations in words of what is compelling in it, aim at making the object itself available to aesthetic appreciation, to make available what is appreciable *in* the object.[12] This implies that unlike perceptual confirmation of a belief, confirmation of the claims of the critic in one's experience isn't the end of the matter. Having confirmed a belief, we can move on to other questions, other beliefs. But there is a sense in which we are never done with making an object available for aesthetic appreciation.[13]

Because of the combination of features that characterizes an aesthetic judgment for both Kant and Cavell, they run a risk that is peculiar to them, the risk of what Cavell calls "isolation" or "alienation." As he puts it, "Art is often praised because it brings men together. But it also separates them" (*MWM* 193). The threat of isolation isn't just a function of having different beliefs, but about what Cavell calls inhabiting a

---

[11] Cavell writes in "The Avoidance of Love," "a critical position will finally rest upon calling a claim *obvious*" (*MWM* 311). That one may fail to see what is "obvious" is one factor that leads Cavell to call criticism itself "inherently immodest and melodramatic – not merely from its temptations to uninstructive superiority and to presumptuous fellow feeling (with audience and artist) but from the logic of its claims" (311), and why for him "recognition of a critical lapse is accompanied by its peculiar chagrin" (312). The question how can one fail to see the obvious is a central topic of Cavell's essay on Lear, and is one point on which aesthetic judgment and the statements of ordinary language philosophy converge.

[12] Eli Friedlander, in Chapter 4, suggests a promising way to go on from this point. He writes, "As we articulate our experience in being sensitively cued to the singularity of a work, our language is not just right, merely correct, but pitched *just right*. Its fit to the work reveals the latter to be a place of convergence for our concepts" (82).

[13] It might be objected that not all aesthetic judgments are like that, for example, negative aesthetic judgments such as the judgment that something is ugly or dumpy, or "Sibleyan" aesthetic judgments such as the melody is haunting. Frank Sibley, "Aesthetic Concepts," in *Approach to Aesthetics: Collected Papers on Philosophical Aesthetics*, ed. John Benson, Betty Redfern, and Jeremy Roxbee Cox (Oxford University Press, 2001), 1–24. Our capacity to engage with the beautiful isn't something "added on" to a more rudimentary aesthetic capacity that is exemplified in all aesthetic judgment – the least common denominator of aesthetic judgment – but rather displays the form that is internal to aesthetic judgment: it is a perfection of that capacity. If one accepts this point, one implicitly rejects the method of much recent philosophy, which assumes that general statements in philosophy can be refuted by providing counterexamples.

different "world." If you call something beautiful and I don't, I am bound to think: "how *can* you *call* that beautiful? How can *that* count as beautiful?" And your feeling could very well be: "how *can* you *fail* to see the beauty in it? It's so obvious." That is the sort of predicament that I take Cavell to be expressing when he says that it is internal to an aesthetic judgment that at some point we must have recourse to "don't you see, don't you hear, don't you dig?" Neither of us is perceptually deficient - we each perceive the same thing – but we don't agree in our judgment, and so, we don't understand one another. But this isn't something that can be remedied by getting clearer about our concepts: there may be no deficiency there either. And yet the difference between us is logical: the aesthetic gulf that divides us is a logical gulf.[14] What we have is an aesthetic version of the encounter with the logical alien of philosophical lore – only in the aesthetic case we may not be able simply to dismiss the other on grounds of unintelligibility.

Of course, a way to go here is to understand the disagreement as predicated on differences in psychological or sociological facts, to view the disagreement as an expression of a psychological or sociological gulf. But then we lose the idea that we make a *claim* on one another, and so lose the possibility that in aesthetic judgment we could be of *one* mind. If our agreement has a basis in psychological facts – whether empirical or "transcendental" – it would be at best a *matching* of minds not a *meeting* of them. Ever since at least Hume, it is commonly assumed that there are two ways in which we can fall into disagreement with another: the disagreement can be a disagreement with regard to a matter of fact or it can be a disagreement in our concepts ("a relation of ideas"), but we have seen that for Kant and Cavell aesthetic disagreement cannot be conceived along either of these lines. However, aesthetic disagreement does share a feature with conceptual disagreement, in that it seems to be a disagreement not just about whether something is beautiful or genuine, but about what counts as beautiful or genuine. It is a disagreement about the standard of the judgment itself.

In an aesthetic judgment the object itself is exhibited not just as an *instance* of a concept that we grasp independently of its application to the object, but as *exemplary* of the standard of aesthetic judgment itself. Aesthetic judgments aren't just *about* the world, but *display* the world,

---

[14] I have stressed that the disagreement is not disagreement on a proposition, but our finding that we do not in Cavell's words "share a world" – the world that is displayed in the work – or as he also puts it "a form of life." Friedlander in Chapter 4 makes the helpful and provocative point that "agreement" for Cavell is to be understood as "harmony" or "attunement" everywhere throughout the entire range of what we say, what he calls "affinities sensed, echoes over a wide range of meaning" (82).

the aesthetic world that is disclosed in the aesthetic object. To disagree in aesthetic judgment is to be isolated in one's own aesthetic world – a kind of *logical isolation*, but one for which there is no remedy simply in "defining your concepts." Criticism as Cavell conceives it is, then, a matter of making available the aesthetic world *in* the work, to overcome the threat of our mutual alienation.[15]

The Appeal to/of the Ordinary

Leaving our discussion of the nature of aesthetic judgment somewhat unresolved, let us briefly turn our attention to the sorts of claims made by OLP. Cavell writes, the philosopher appealing to everyday language turns to the reader not to convince

> him without proof but to get him to prove something, test something against himself. He is saying: Look and find out whether you can see what I see, wish to say what I wish to say. Of course he often seems to answer or beg his own question by posing it in plural form: "We say...; We want to say...; We can imagine..." (*MWM* 95–96)

Ordinary language philosophers aren't making empirical claims about certain groups of speakers, of which they happen to be members. They are rather "speaking for" others: hence, the use of "we." In his paper, "Must We Mean What We Say," Cavell distinguishes between the sentence, "When we ask whether an action is voluntary we imply that the action is fishy," which he calls "S," and the sentence, "'Is X voluntary?' implies that X is fishy," which he calls "T." He writes,

> but S and T, though they are true together and false together, are not everywhere interchangeable; the identical state of affairs is described by both, but a person who may be entitled to say T, may not be entitled to say S. Only a native speaker of English is entitled to the statement S, whereas a linguist describing English

---

[15] In "The Avoidance of Love" Cavell writes, "if philosophy can be thought of as the world of a particular culture brought to consciousness of itself, then one mode of criticism (call it philosophical criticism) can be thought of as the world of a particular work brought to consciousness of itself" (*MWM* 313). A new work is liable to transform one's grasp of aesthetic possibility. But the ensuing change is neither synthetic nor analytic, neither a change in belief nor a change in concept. We recognize in the new work what we always meant by "beautiful" but were not able to articulate. There is thus a continuity between different instances of judging that something is beautiful, but a continuity that cannot be grasped in the abstract, that isn't determined by a general concept. That's why you "have" to see the thing, for seeing it is liable not just to change what you believe, but to change what you understand by the concept "beautiful." In Chapter 4, Friedlander draws on the invocation by Cavell in "Aesthetic Problems of Modern Philosophy" of the Hegelian notion of *Aufhebung* to explore the idea that a work of art can open up a "new world," or "our world recognized anew" (84).

may, though he is not a native speaker of English, be entitled to T. What entitles him to T is his having gathered a certain amount and kind of evidence in its favor. But the person entitled to S is not entitled to that statement for the same reason. He needs no evidence for it … But there is nothing he needs, and there is no evidence (which it makes sense, in general, to say) he has: the question of evidence is irrelevant. (*MWM* 13–14)[16]

A standard reply to OLP, stemming from H. P. Grice's well-known critique, begins by noting that if there is an implication, it is pragmatic rather than semantic, an implication not of the meaning of the *word* 'voluntary,' but of what I mean when I use the word. Anticipating this line of attack, Cavell responds as follows:

call this implication of the utterance "pragmatic"; the fact remains that he wouldn't (couldn't) say what he did without implying what he did: he MUST MEAN that my clothes are peculiar. I am less interested now in the "mean" than I am in the "must." (After all, there is bound to be some reason why a number of philosophers are tempted to call a relation logical; "must" is logical.) But on this, the "pragmatic" formula throws no light whatever. (*MWM* 9)

It is a feature of logic that its principles are constraints that condition the possibility of understanding; someone who is unconstrained by *modus tollens* is someone who is incomprehensible, and so similarly someone who is unconstrained by the pragmatic implications of what he says is also incomprehensible. It might be said that a violation of constraints on logic (in the purely semantic sense) makes *what* someone says incomprehensible, whereas someone who violates pragmatic constraints (logic in the extended sense) makes *himself* incomprehensible. What OLP insists is that there *are* constraints – "necessities" – that govern both, and that since they are constraints on the comprehensibility either of *what* someone says or of the person *herself*, that is, of what a *person means* by what she says, the constraints count as "logical." Both are essential aspects of language in the sense that both must be assumed to be understood by

---

[16] Importantly, this isn't because we can't be wrong about what we are doing or about what we mean by what we say, "but only that it would be extraordinary if we were (often) … If I am wrong about what he does (they do), that may be no great surprise; but if I am wrong about what I (we) do, that is liable, where it is not comic, to be tragic" (*MWM* 14). As many philosophers have since pointed out, I am able straightaway to say what I am (intentionally) doing without basing my statement on the evidence of my behavior (as it would have to be for another person's statement about what I am, intentionally, doing). (Elizabeth Anscombe's *Intention* is the locus classicus of this view.) Since meaning something by a word is an intentional action, it follows that I am able straightaway to say what I mean by a word without a basis in observational evidence. Cavell is pointing out that the same is true for a native speaker's assertions about what "we" mean.

the participants in linguistic address. Neither is an optional part of linguistic communication. In order to communicate in language, it must not only be the case that your words are comprehensible but that *you yourself* are comprehensible in your words, that your words bear not only, so to speak, *their* meaning but *your* meaning, that you manage to mean coherently. Cavell writes,

> what needs to be argued now is that something does follow from the fact that a term is used in its usual way: it entitles you (or, using the term, you entitle others) to make certain inferences, draw certain conclusions. (This is part of what you say when you say that you are talking about the logic of ordinary language.) Learning what these implications are is part of learning the language; no less a part than learning its syntax, or learning what it is to which terms apply: they are an essential part of what we communicate when we talk ... We are, therefore, exactly as responsible for the specific implications of our utterances as we are for their explicit factual claims ... Misnaming and misdescribing are not the only mistakes we can make in talking. Nor is lying its only immorality. (*MWM* 11–12)

What I pragmatically imply by what I say is not something that is simply up to me, it is not something I can decide, nor is it determined by a convention, by rules that we have mutually agreed to abide by (there would be, as Cavell says elsewhere, too many such conventions): "intimate understanding is understanding that is implicit. Nor could everything we say (mean to communicate), in normal communication, be said explicitly – otherwise the only threat to communication would be acoustical" (*MWM* 12).

For the empirical linguist the relation between the general and the particular is no different from the relation between the general and the particular in the context of any inductive inference: features possessed by a sufficient sample of observed particulars entitle one to infer that those features obtain generally across the class of unobserved particulars of the same kind. For example, having noticed that every jazz performance I've attended starts late, I may infer that all jazz performances start late. Similarly, having observed that every speaker of English implies fishy by "voluntary?," the empirical linguist may infer that speakers of English imply fishy by "voluntary?" But the speaker herself cannot, at least in general (unless the situation is, as Cavell puts it, to burst into comedy or descend into tragedy), have that relation to what "we" say, or what "we" imply. It could be said, then, that "we" does not have the specific generality of "every jazz performance" or "every speaker of English" – the generality, it could be said, of a "general concept." It is the superficial resemblance of "we" and "every – or most – speakers of this language" that makes it look like ordinary language philosophers are making wildly unwarranted *inferences* from what they themselves mean to what we mean.[17] But in the use of language, in meaning what we do by our words, there is no *transition* from the particular to the general: to mean anything at all by my words, I must mean what we mean by them (there's that pivotal word "must" again). If I am authoritative about what *I* mean, that is only because I am authoritative about what we mean – my claim to authority in both cases has the same basis: the "I" is in the "we."[18]

A jazz performance that begins on time is just an exception to what is otherwise generally true – we don't have any difficulty comprehending the possibility of such an exception. However, someone who doesn't mean fishy by "voluntary?" isn't just an exception to a general rule, she is, at least at the outset, incomprehensible, we don't understand her. This is implied by Cavell's stress on the "necessity" of the dimension of meaning that is OLP's stock in trade. The kind of "necessity" that is involved in "what we *must* mean" is a form of necessity that is dependent on its being acknowledged by those who are constrained by it: the "we" is in the "I."[19] That the "I" is in the "We" and the "We" is in the "I" are together what constitutes the irreducibly first-person character of "we" as it figures in the appeals of the OLP to "what we say when." What *I* mean is dependent on what *we* mean; hence, the "I" is in the "we." And my claims about what we mean have validity only insofar as everyone – everyone who belongs to the "we" – acknowledges it; hence, the "we" is in the "I."

If one does not find confirmation from others then one discovers that one speaks only for oneself. In other words, while the risk we take on when we make a knowledge or truth claim is that we might be rebuffed by the world, that we might be mistaken, the risk we undertake in making a criterial judgment is that we might be rebuffed by others, that we might be isolated, found unintelligible. What we may find is not that we disagree about a matter of fact, but that we don't, in Cavell's phrase, "share a world." Thus, he writes,

---

[17] This is one of Benson Mates' primary objections to the procedures of OLP to which Cavell is responding in this paper.

[18] If there is anything that "we mean" by "voluntary," what we mean is not determined by facts about what native speakers would say they mean, by native speakers' dispositions, which is all that an empirical linguist is able to record, a result that she would sum up by the statement T. Rather, it is the other way around: there are facts that the empirical linguist can record, facts about what native speakers mean by a term only because the native speakers themselves are able to form judgments in the first person plural about meaning, that is, judgments that are not determined by empirical dispositions, or at least not generally.

[19] See G.W.F. Hegel, *Phenomenology of Spirit*, trans. Terry Pinkard (Cambridge University Press, 2018), "B. Self-Consciousness," §177, 108. This is what I take Cavell to mean by, "the clue to the sort of statement S is lies in appreciating the fact that the 'we,' while plural, is first person" (*MWM* 14).

the philosophical appeal to what we say, and the search for our criteria on the basis of which we say what we say, are claims to community. And the claim to community is always a search for the basis upon which it can or has been established. I have nothing more to go on than my conviction that I make sense. It may prove to be the case that I am wrong, that my conviction isolates me, from all others, from myself. (*CR*20)

You can, importantly for Cavell, become alienated from yourself – that is something that can happen when you philosophize.

The World Is My World, Our World

I observed at the outset that Cavell follows Kant in conceiving of the logical form of judgment as a guide to understanding the nature of the object of judgment. In the case of aesthetic judgment Cavell, like Kant, is opposing the view that the difference between art and non-art is like the difference between a gas and a liquid or between a fish and a mammal. The latter aren't logical differences, but merely conceptual ones. But our concept of a work of art is an object of a judgment with a distinct logical form. The distinction between action and mere event is a logical distinction as well; as is the distinction between person and non-person; and the same goes for the distinction between art and non-art. It almost immediately follows that there cannot be a proof of something's being a work of art – or being a person – for there can be proofs of something's being an F only where the distinction between F and non-F is a conceptual distinction not a logical one. Disagreement with regard to a logical distinction is not a matter of differing with respect to a belief, with respect to whether something is an F or a G, where those are distinct concepts that divide up the logical space of a species of judgment. It is a matter of not sharing a "world." What Cavell calls the truth of skepticism is that our relation to the world isn't just concept-mediated, a matter of belief, but a logical relation – mediated by forms of judgment. This is why our relation to the world as a whole cannot even in principle be based on proof, and is that in relation to which the demand for certainty is out of place. That's not to say that it is based on probable belief: for Cavell an appeal to fallibilism as a response to the skeptic's search for certainty remains as much in the clutches of skepticism as its infallibilist counterpart. The idea that disagreement in aesthetic judgment and in the OLP's appeal to "what we say when" is "logical," thus haunted by the threat of "isolation," is, I take it, an expression of what Cavell called "the truth of skepticism": the idea that our relation to the world and to others "in general" is not one of knowing (see *MWM* 324).

In an oft-quoted passage from "Aesthetic Problems," Cavell writes,

we know the efforts of such philosophers as Frege and Husserl to undo the "psychologizing" of logic (like Kant's undoing Hume's psychologizing of knowledge): now, the shortest way I might describe such a book as the *Philosophical Investigations* is to say that it attempts to undo the psychologizing of psychology, to show the necessity controlling our application of psychological and behavioral categories; even, one could say, show the necessities in human action and passion themselves. And at the same time it seems to turn all of philosophy into psychology – matters of what we call things, how we treat them, what their role is in our lives. (*MWM* 91)

Frege, of course, insisted on distinguishing between what is thought in any act of thinking, the content of thought, which he conceived of as having a propositional form, and the thinking of it. A thought is what can be common to different acts of thinking, whether of one's own or of another. It is thus essentially public, essentially shareable, unowned. By contrast the thinking of a thought is necessarily someone's, necessarily owned, and so in that sense private. Frege depsychologized logic, by excluding the psychological from it. The logical must bear no trace of the psychological, for if that were not so, there would be nothing that could be true or false – and so no judgment, no belief, no propositional attitude, as thoughts have subsequently come to be called. There would be, in Thomas Ricketts' memorable words, merely "mooing."[20] The first person is consequently banished from the logical order, for a first-person thought is constituted by the thinking of it.

However, as crucial as it is to separate the logical from the psychological, as Frege insisted that we must do, the very attempt to do so runs the threat of "psychologizing" the psychological. Psychologizing the psychological is a matter of psychologizing the first person, or "subjectivizing" the subjective. In the context of OLP, psychologizing the psychological is a matter of conflating the remarks of the ordinary language philosopher with those of the empirical linguist. It is a matter of failing to see that "we" is irreducibly first-personal, that the ordinary language philosopher's remarks do not, as Cavell says, adapting Kant, "'postulate' that 'we,' you and I and she, say and want and imagine and feel and suffer together" (*MWM* 96). The "exhortation" in the OLP's appeals are as Cavell puts it, "not to belief, but to self-scrutiny" (71). They are claims to agreement, claims to community, for which there can be no basis in evidence. In the context of aesthetic judgments,

---

[20] Thomas Ricketts, "Objectivity and Objecthood: Frege's Metaphysics of Judgment," in *Frege Synthesized: Essays on the Philosophical and Foundational Work of Gottlob Frege*, ed. Leila Haaparanta and Jaakko Hintikka (Dordrecht: D. Reidel, 1986), 65–95.

psychologizing the psychological is to treat their "subjectivity" as a matter of the reflection of standing psychological facts, which is how their "subjectivity" is conceived of by expressivism and relativism.[21] I have tried in this chapter to show why for Cavell, psychologizing the first person is tantamount to obliterating the very idea of aesthetic judgment and with it the idea of OLP. And a way to read Cavell here is that if we make room in logical space for a conception of aesthetic judgment, we have thereby made room in logical space for the ordinary language philosopher's appeals to "what we say when." But if we have made room for both, then we have made room for a new way of inheriting what Kant called "transcendental philosophy," which is how Cavell conceived of the import of the work of OLP generally.

For Kant and Wittgenstein, as for Cavell, philosophical statements, like aesthetic statements, are essentially first-personal – are mine to make.[22] And the risk we bear in making them is not the risk of error but the risk of alienation and exposure, the risk of isolation – the discovery that I speak only for myself. What we may find is not that we disagree about a matter of fact, but that we do not "share a world."[23] To use Kant's language, such judgments have, or purport to have, necessary universal "subjective valid-ity." And, according to Cavell, it is only against the background of neces-sities of this "subjective" kind that there can be propositions, something on which there can be agreement and disagreement. You might say that it is only against the backdrop of such subjectively universal necessities that propositions have their life, so that it is so much as possible for us to have propositional attitudes. Contra Frege, the domain of the logical cannot be insulated against the first person.

Kant famously said, "it must be possible for the 'I think' to accompany all of my representations" (B131).[24] The 'I think' here is, in Kant's

---

[21] That may be obvious enough; what is perhaps less obvious is that the "realist" shares this conception of the subjective with her opponent in the familiar dialectic: hence, in the eagerness to respect something like Kant's distinction between the agreeable and the beautiful, her assimilation of aesthetic judgments to theoretical judgments. We can see Cavell as exposing the natural conviction that the two sides of the familiar dialectic – the subjectivist side and the realist side – are contradictories as a transcendental illusion.

[22] In this paragraph I have drawn material from my paper, "Undoing the Psychologizing of the Psychological," *Conversations: A Cavellian Journal*, Special Issue, 7 (2019), 87–91.

[23] Unlike matters of fact, the "world" is mine, or ours: it is expressed in "claims of community." In Chapter 4 (77–86), Friedlander, in a thought-provoking discussion, invokes Wittgenstein's beguiling remark, "the world is my world" in interpreting Cavell's remark that the OLP confronts "the culture with itself along the lines in which it meets in me" (*CR* 125), a matter I discussed earlier in bringing in Hegel's idea that the "I" is in the "We" and the "We" is in the "I."

[24] Immanuel Kant, *Critique of Pure Reason*, trans. Norman Kemp Smith (Basingstoke: Macmillan, 2003).

terms, "pure" or "transcendental." The transcendental "I think" is distinguished from the empirical "I think" in that while the empirical "I think" represents a particular thinker and her state of thinking what she thinks, the transcendental "I think" represents the unity of thought that is the condition of my thoughts agreeing, or disagreeing, with one another, or for that matter the condition of my thoughts agreeing or disagreeing with yours: it is, as Kant puts it, that which "in all consciousness is one and the same" and "cannot be accompanied by any further representation" (B132). For Cavell the OLP's what "we say" is a descendant of Kant's "I think," and so belongs in the transcendental register (*MWM* 13). However, for Kant the "I think" constitutes the unity of the proposition, the unity of a possible content of thought, or as he puts it "the relation between representation and object." And he argues (in the Transcendental Deduction) that it is only if the faculty by which objects are given to us in intuition (sensibility) and the faculty by which we think objects through concepts (the understanding) are bound together in an essential, indissoluble unity that thought is possible. But OLP's appeals to what "we say," while transcendental, concern the possibility of recognizing an *act* of *saying* as a coherent act of speech. Thus, if OLP's appeals to what "we say" are to have a transcendental standing, are to condition the possibility of the relation between representation and object, it must be supposed that *what* we say is dependent on the coherence of what we *say*. That is, it is only inside (transcendental) OLP's claims to community that there can be agreement and disagreement of a factual nature. The unity of an *act* of saying must be distinguished from the unity of *what* is said, a unity that is provided by concepts, even by transcendental concepts such as Kant's categories. But in order for there to be a recognizable unity to *what* one says, there must be a recognizable unity to one's *saying* (meaning) what one says. If there isn't, we don't in Cavell's sense "share a world." The "world" that we share, or fail to share, in this sense is *shown in* what "we say" and is not an *object* of what one says: my relation to the world in general is not one of knowing. We have seen that Kant says something nearly identical about aesthetic judgment when he says that it isn't based on a concept and yet, unlike a judgment of the agreeable, makes a claim to universal validity. If we disagree in an aesthetic judgment, the disagreement is substantive even though it is not a disagreement in the application of a concept: we fail to understand one another, we don't share the same "world." We might think of aesthetic judgments as made from the perspective of a possible future community, pressing the form of life we share in new directions. And we might think of the judgments of OLP as measuring the community of mind we already have. But the possibility of each is contained in the possibililty of the other. It is essential to both sorts of judgment that they turn toward others to see if others recognize themselves in them and point to the common root from which the theoretical and the practical orders spring and from which they cannot liberate themselves, the pivot on which "the whirl of organism" whirls.

The philosopher's remarks, as the critic's, may not only be met with disagreement but, worse, with complete indifference,[25] – since unlike the sciences, neither has a guaranteed audience, but this does not render them dependent on individual fancy or whim. Far from it, as Cavell wrote, "philosophy, like art, is, and should be, powerless to prove its relevance; and that says something about the kind of relevance it wishes to have. All the philosopher, this kind of philosopher, can do is to express ... his world, and attract our undivided attention to our own" (*MWM* 96).

---

[25] What Kant in the (first edition) Preface of the first *Critique* called "the mother of chaos and night." Kant, *Critique of Pure Reason*, Ax, 8.

7 Reading Into It or Hearing It Out?: Cavell on Modernism and the Art Critic's Hermeneutical Risk

Robert Engelman

> To fully understand this language and to grasp its details implies, in general, being able to recognize the beginning, middle, and end of every melody, to hear the simultaneity of voices not as chance phenomena but as harmonies and harmonic progressions, and to perceive the small and large relationships and contrasts as such; in short, being able to follow a piece of music as one follows the words of a poem written in a language that one knows perfectly.
>
> Alban Berg, "Why Is Schoenberg's Music So Difficult to Understand?"[1]

Introduction

Alban Berg claimed that to understand Schoenberg's music, one must hear its elements – its harmonies, harmonic progressions, etc. – as musical, as intentionally organized tones rather than mere jumbles of sound, even when tonality is not their organizing principle. If one cannot perceive Schoenberg's music's elements as musical elements, one cannot understand his music. In Berg's words, the listener or critic is tasked with "testing the intelligibility of Schoenberg's means of compositional expression."[2] However, because the *intelligibility* of Schoenberg's music is at issue, the problem Schoenberg's music poses to the critic entails a problem for Schoenberg's music itself. For if Schoenberg's atonal work fails to exhibit intentionally organized tones, it seems that it is not music. Worse yet, if it seems to lack any intentional organization that renders its elements meaningful, it does not even appear to be art. As Schoenberg's

I would like to thank Matthew Congdon, Eric Ritter, and Chelsea Wegrzyniak for their insightful comments on earlier drafts of this piece, as well as for stimulating conversation concerning Cavell's work. I would also like to thank Idit Dobbs-Weinstein for discussing *Endgame* with me on numerous occasions. Finally, warm thanks to those who provided me with feedback at the Continuing Cavell conference in Boston and the ASA Rocky Mountain conference in Santa Fe.
[1] Alban Berg, "Why Is Schoenberg's Music So Difficult to Understand?" in *Pro Mundo – Pro Domo: The Writings of Alban Berg*, ed. and trans. Bryan R. Simms (Oxford University Press, 2014), 183–94 (at 183–84).
[2] *Ibid.*, 184.

student and fellow avant-garde composer, perhaps Berg was unable to appreciate the threat of failing to make music or art implicit in the interpretive challenges he recognized in Schoenberg's music. But things are otherwise with Stanley Cavell, who exhibited a deep sensitivity to this threat and its relation to modernism more generally. In *Must We Mean What We Say?* he provocatively called it "the threat of fraudulence" (*MWM* 176). He regarded this threat as pertinent to the critic as much as to the artwork because of the ambiguity in not understanding a putative work, "whether it is the art or its audience which is on trial" (*MWM* 176).

Throughout *Must We Mean*, Cavell accounts for what I will call "the artwork's problematic" and "the critic's problematic," the intertwined problem-spaces in which to become what they are, artworks and art critics must subject themselves to the fundamental risk of being mere "art looks"[3] and "imposters," respectively (*MWM* 190). Cavell held that no outward mark differentiates a reading from a misreading, and that by posing highly obscure works to critics, modernism exacerbates this problem in a way that makes it perspicuous. Accordingly, I argue that Cavell diagnosed the art critic's problematic as a condition in which the distinction between finding meaning in and imposing meaning upon a putative artwork – or, in terms of ordinary language, between *reading into it* and *hearing it out* – is "non-criterial" (*PP* 92). The critic must do things that look like imposing meaning upon a work to find and illuminate its meaning, which is especially apparent when a work's meaning is not plain or direct, as is often the case with modernist works. In other words, modernism reveals that hearing an artwork out involves activities that threateningly resemble reading into it. Moreover, Cavell thought that the critic must emphatically accept the risk of reading into a work, and that attempts to avoid this risk both fail and introduce new risks.

In section 1, I sketch out Cavell's account of the artwork's problematic as pertaining to the artwork's need to achieve its "voice" to truly be an artwork. Section 2 accounts for Cavell's diagnosis of the critic's problematic and his subsequent prescription for the critic. Finally, because, in Cavell's words, "modernism only makes explicit and bare what has always been true of art" and arts criticism, I conclude by considering how his prescription might hold for us today, whether or not we are still moderns (*MWM* 189). Here, however, I am not concerned with how it might hold for us as critics, but how it might help us live with one another

---

[3] J.M. Bernstein, "Aesthetics, Modernism, Literature: Cavell's Transformations of Philosophy," in *Stanley Cavell*, ed. Richard Eldridge (New York: Cambridge University Press, 2003), 107–42 (at 128).

in our increasingly diverse, multicultural world; after all, Cavell did liken artworks to human beings (*MWM* 197–98).

The Artwork's Problematic

Modernity is commonly taken to have destabilized traditions by undermining past sources of authority as sources of authority – even precedent, the past itself. Metaphysical, moral, and aesthetic authorities suffer the same fate: true, good, and beautiful things can no longer be measured by an unquestionable standard, because whatever (or whoever) has vindicated any such standard as universally binding has lost the authority to do so. When God's existence became an object of rational proof, whether by those given to religion (Aquinas) or science (Descartes), the word of God lost its absolute sway. What once seemed certain and necessary has been exposed as questionable and contingent, such that what we once justified on the basis of such supposed certainties requires new kinds of justification.

"Modernism," in Jay Bernstein's words, "is what happens to art under conditions of modernity."[4] When genres (e.g., sonata form) and basic organizing principles of artforms (e.g., tonality) are revealed to be merely conventional and contingent, following their strictures guarantees neither arthood nor what Cavell called "the first fact of works of art": that artworks are "meant," i.e., that they exhibit intentional organization, meaning, and comprehensibility *as artworks* (*MWM* 227–28). To exhibit this fact, artworks must exhibit some fidelity to an artform's conventions. But modernism makes it obvious that abiding by conventions is insufficient. Arthood requires objects to differentiate themselves from an artform's antecedent conventions and past instances – otherwise, they are not artworks, but "fraudulent" (*MWM* 189). The problem is that an otherwise putative artwork might defy an artform's conventions to the point that it fails to *mean* and hence to be an artwork.

Cavell provided a basic expression of the artwork's problematic ("the artistic problem") in "Ending the Waiting Game":

in modernist arts the achievement of the autonomy of the object is a *problem* – the artistic problem. Autonomy is no longer provided by the conventions of an art, for the modernist artist has continuously to question the conventions upon which his art has depended. (*MWM* 116)

Cavell claimed that artistic conventions provided artworks with autonomy prior to modernism, but "autonomy" cannot mean what it typically

---

[4] *Ibid.*, 117.

means in art-talk, freedom from functionality, because pre-modernist conventions did not free art from functionality, but reinforced the functions art was meant to serve. For example, the conventions of a march (the easily transportable instruments, the pronounced downbeat, the even time signature) tailored music to military service. So if anything, pre-modernist conventions rendered art functionally heteronomous, and by the time modernism began to take hold in the nineteenth century, convention supported freedom from function in large measure.

I want to suggest that Cavell's abovementioned invocation of "autonomy" is both Kantian and Emersonian. However, it has less to do with Kant's notion of autonomy as self-legislation (though this is precisely what Cavell had in mind when referring to the autonomy of *artforms*; see *MWM* 320), and more with Kant's notion of *Mündigkeit*, autonomy as the free expression of one's independently formed thoughts.[5] In Cavellian terms, *Mündigkeit* is the achievement of one's own voice. To be *unmündig* is to form thoughts in a way that does not render them genuinely one's own; Emerson would call it a failure to form "self-derived" thoughts.[6] Achieving *Mündigkeit* requires making "*public* use of one's reason ... before the entire public of the *world of readers*."[7] With this, Kant introduced the need to make one's thoughts intelligible to the public, or "the world."[8] Insofar as one freely expresses oneself, one is tasked with publicizing the personal, rendering it intelligible to others; otherwise, one fails to *express* or to recognizably demonstrate that one has expressed oneself. In Emerson's words, one "must employ the symbols in use in his day" to recognizably express oneself, without lapsing into merely repeating one's inherited idiom.[9] As such, *Mündigkeit* describes a condition in tension: to be *mündig* is to achieve one's own voice, but the independence of one's voice is constrained by the need to make oneself intelligible to others (cf. *MWM* 187).

Having a voice, or being autonomous, is necessary for arthood, as it pertains to the "first fact" of artworks: that they mean. Non-autonomous

---

[5] Immanuel Kant, "An Answer to the Question: What is Enlightenment?" in *Practical Philosophy*, ed. and trans. Mary J. Gregor (New York: Cambridge University Press, 1996), 11–22 (at 19). For a similar discussion of the idea that an artwork's autonomy can be understood in terms of Kantian *Mündigkeit*, see Gordon Finlayson, "Beethoven, Adorno and the Dialectics of Freedom," in *Aesthetic and Artistic Autonomy*, ed. Owen Hulatt (New York: Bloomsbury, 2013), 147–70.
[6] Ralph Waldo Emerson, "Self Reliance," in *The Collected Works of Ralph Waldo Emerson*, vol. II: *Essays: First Series*, ed. Alfred R. Ferguson and Jean Ferguson Carr (Cambridge, MA: Belknap Press, 1979), 35.
[7] Kant, "What is Enlightenment?," 18. Of course, Kant's use of the term "reader" resonates with Cavell's treatment of arts criticism as a kind of reading.
[8] *Ibid.*, 19.   [9] Ralph Waldo Emerson, "Art," in *Collected Works*, vol. II, 210.

objects are not artworks. But as we have seen, achieving autonomy is a problem, especially in the age of modernism. When Cavell claimed that conventions supplied artworks with autonomy prior to modernism, he meant that artworks could rely heavily on a tradition's conventions for their voices (*MWM* 116). Of course, pre-modernist artworks could not simply mime a tradition's past iterations, flatly recapitulate its conventions, and still achieve autonomy and hence arthood. But the demand for an artwork to be irreducible to other artworks and antecedent conventions, to be more than a mere version or exercise, was comparably mild. Once conventions have come to seem utterly impersonal – nothing but "slogans, sponsored messages, ideologies," and the like – voice requires further differentiation from previous artworks and conventions (*MWM* 201). But again, convention cannot be rejected outright and arthood maintained, because the conditions of voicehood (or at least those of determining a voice's presence, or rendering a voice intelligible) include convention. In short, for artworks, the "entire enterprise of action and communication has become problematic" (*MWM* 201). In light of this condition, the alternatives are either to accept "silence" or "attempt to re-invent convention" (*MWM* 202). However, attempts to reinvent convention and thereby achieve a voice are fraught with difficulty. In Cavell's words, they "are most likely to fail even to seem to communicate," let alone exhibit genuine voicehood (*MWM* 202).

Now we can properly see what the artwork's problematic consists in. The artwork's achievement of autonomy amounts to achieving its voice. To be *the artwork's voice*, this voice must be at once "personal" and publicly available (*MWM* 202). To achieve its voice and thereby be an artwork, an artwork must depart from traditional, generally accessible forms of expression, which entails moving toward an obscure, esoteric or hermetic manner of meaning. But an artwork must also maintain the conventions of an artform to be an artwork. These requirements pull artworks in opposing directions, and artworks must satisfy both without overdoing either. If a work remains too close to a tradition, it becomes merely conventional – "pure mechanism" – and thereby fails to achieve its voice (*MWM* 205). On the other hand, if an artwork diverges too far from a tradition, it falls into "the wrong silence" and thereby fails to achieve its *voice* (*MWM* 175).[10] Voicehood requires that artworks aim away from existing conventions, but in so doing, works risk undercutting their voices and arthood. However, if a work does not aim away from existing conventions, it also undercuts its voice and arthood; it might not

---

[10] Wittgenstein's remarks on private language loom largely here.

fall silent, but it will *surely* not speak in a voice of its own. To achieve arthood, then, the risk of failing to achieve arthood must be emphatically accepted by accepting the threat of succumbing to a thing-like silence.

Cavell identified *indirectness* as a reasonably common modernist strategy for navigating this problematic (*MWM* 179). The hope entailed by this strategy is that through the obscurity engendered by indirectness, artworks can be both unique and, albeit with some difficulty, intelligible. However, obscurity renders an artwork's voice harder to discern as a voice, let alone as meaning or "saying" anything in particular. The critic's task of illuminating a work's meaning then becomes one of finding, in Cavell's words, what, "contrary to appearance, and in spite of all, speaks" (*MWM* 179).[11] When an otherwise putative artwork seems voiceless, the critic is faced with the possibility of not simply misreading an artwork, but of misidentifying something as art – of not simply mistaking the meaning, but of attributing meaning to the meaningless, voice to the voiceless. Of course, misreading is not unique to modernism, but when modernism challenges one's ability to interpret a work and reveals a qualitatively more extreme kind of misreading, the critic's condition becomes more perspicuous.

The Critic's Problematic

To understand Cavell's diagnosis of the critic's problematic, it helps to briefly take stock of some of the key facets of arts criticism for Cavell. The opening paragraph to "Ending the Waiting Game" is instructive:

Various keys to [*Endgame*'s] interpretation are in place: "Endgame" is a term of chess; the name Hamm is shared by Noah's cursed son, it titles a kind of actor, it starts recalling Hamlet. But no interpretation I have seen details the textual evidence for these relations nor shows how the play's meaning opens with them. Without this, we will have a general impression of the play, one something like this: Beckett's perception is of a "meaningless universe" and language in his plays "serves to express the breakdown, the disintegration of language" – by, one gathers, itself undergoing disintegration. Such descriptions

---

[11] This passage from the end of "Kierkegaard's *On Authority and Revelation*" contains a further move worth briefly mentioning. Cavell suggests that indirectness too has become conventional, that "every indirectness is dime-a-dozen, and any weirdness can be assembled and imitated on demand" (*MWM* 179). Old conventions have been largely bucked, but what once seemed unconventional has become standard fare. (Perhaps this marks the onset of "late modernism.") This suggests that at a certain point, it is not only unclear whether a work strays too far from or remains too close to tradition, but insofar as obscurity or radicalism has become a tradition of its own (strange as that might sound), it is also unclear how to differentiate between straying from and remaining close to tradition.

are usual in the discussions of Beckett I am aware of, but are they anything more than impositions from an impression of fashionable philosophy? (*MWM* 115)

There are six basic theses describing the art critic's activity and problematic that we can tease out of this passage:

1. The critic identifies "keys" to interpreting an artwork that are located in the work, and these keys are elements of the work (e.g., its title, a character's name).
2. Keys are taken to indicate particular "relations" the artwork bears to other things (e.g., *Endgame*'s title and chess, Hamm's name and the story of Noah).
3. "Evidence" is needed to vindicate the relations these keys suggest.
4. An artwork's meaning "opens" when one traces the significance of the relations indicated by the keys one identifies.
5. Failing to accept the tasks involved in the first three theses leaves one with only a "general impression" of the work.
6. Interpretations and "descriptions" of an artwork might turn out to be mere "impositions," and sometimes these impositions are based on "impressions" of things other than the work.

Although these theses and categories (keys, relations, evidence) are central to arts criticism, they do not quite convey the art critic's task. Fortunately, Cavell expressed this task (the "first critical problem") shortly after the paragraph quoted above: in the case of *Endgame*, the critic must "discover how Beckett's objects mean at all" (*MWM* 116). In more general terms, Cavell took the criticism of artworks to be the "assessment of their objects" or elements (*MWM* 185). This assessment of elements and discovery of "how [they] mean" aims at discovering what "can illuminate" them and in turn the work's meaning more broadly (*MWM* 117). Specifically, illuminating an artwork's elements involves identifying some of them as keys to interpreting the work; however, because it is not given in advance which elements in the work are keys to interpretation, they require "critical determination" (*MWM* 189). In determining keys to interpretation, the critic defines "which objects are and which are not relevant to his response" to the work (*MWM* 208). Moreover, these keys suggest relations (to aesthetic traditions, other artworks, historical events, etc.) for which the critic must find evidence (see *MWM* 104). In collecting this evidence, the critic looks to illuminate the work's meaning in light of the manner in which the work relates to the relata she identifies. But, for Cavell, evidence for one's claims or convictions about a work just is experience of a work that vindicates one's claims or convictions about that work, seeing or feeling the work's elements as meaningful in light of (or, as illuminated by) one's interpretive claims (see *MWM* 87).

Cavell's account of arts criticism faces up to challenges related to the hermeneutic circle, where, as Friedrich Schleiermacher put it, *"the particular can only be understood from out of the whole"* and the whole in light of the particulars.[12] Schleiermacher claimed that the critic must begin with *"a cursory reading"* of a work to "find the leading ideas according to which the other ideas must be assessed."[13] This accords with how Cavell's interpretation of *Endgame* begins, with two "convictions" about the play, which function as working hypotheses (*MWM* 117). However, modernism problematizes this use of a cursory reading, because what the critic would have general convictions about – Schleiermacher's "tendency," Cavell's "intentionality" (*MWM* 228) – tends to be "deliberately hidden," or as Cavell would say, indirect.[14] Moreover, because the work's elements have meaning in light of the relations the critic must make apparent, they are not transparently given but are about as obscure or clear as the critic's general sense of the work.

Endgame exemplifies this modernist problematization of the critic's activity. At least explicitly, everything is stripped-down. There is no clear indication of who the characters are, where they are, or how they got there.[15] As such, it is unclear what *Endgame*'s elements are, what broader dimensions of the play they contribute to, and, consequently, why they appear as they do (*MWM* 182). To interpret the play, the critic must thereby pose "Why?" questions concerning the elements and their place within the play, questions that invite the work to speak for itself. Seeking answers to these questions – listening for the work's voice – "directs you further into the work" (*MWM* 227). But because the work's elements are not transparently given to the critic and often suggest relations to things other than the work, it is unclear what "going further into the work" means or requires. Moreover, because the problematization of going further into the work arises from features that vary between works (viz. the elements' transparency), a general procedure for going further into some work cannot be fully determined in advance. And if "going further into the work" generally means something like "examining the work

---

[12] Friedrich Schleiermacher, *Hermeneutics and Criticism*, ed. and trans. Andrew Bowie (Cambridge University Press, 1998), 27. Admittedly, Cavell was coy in discussing the hermeneutic circle. He generally avoided the term, and instead employed expressions like "the cinematic circle" (*WV* xiv) and discussed the possibility that "theory and evidence become a closed and vicious circle" (*MWM* 216).

[13] Schleiermacher, *Hermeneutics and Criticism*, 27.   [14] *Ibid.*, 109.

[15] Hence Cavell's questions at the outset of his reading of *Endgame*: "Who are these people? Where are they, and how did they get there?" (*MWM* 117).

more carefully," it will nearly always require the critic to look outside the work as well (see *MWM* 227).

Cavell's exploration of *Endgame*'s elements and the possible relations therein exemplifies this roving way of investigating a work to make its meaning available. Cavell identified Hamm's name as a key to interpreting *Endgame*, and thus tasked himself with answering why Hamm is named "Hamm" and why his name *matters* in the play. For Cavell, one relation that Hamm's name implies is with the story of Noah, as one of Noah's sons shares the name. But Cavell needed to further substantiate that Hamm's name implies a relation to the story of Noah that is more than a happy accident or one-off flourish (cf. *MWM* 235). Or better, he needed to see how the story of Noah might illuminate *Endgame* in a way that shows the story's relevance to *Endgame*; if it does, Cavell is vindicated in his manner of regarding Hamm's name as a key to interpretation. His approach is somewhat speculative, positioning *Endgame*'s elements in accordance with the story of Noah and subsequently examining whether or not the details cohere:

> That Hamm and Clov want (so to speak) the world to end is obvious enough, but an understanding of the way they imagine its end, the reason it must end, the terms in which it can be brought to an end, are given by placing these characters this way: The shelter they are in is the ark, the family is Noah's, and the time is sometime after the Flood. (*MWM* 137)

Cavell's claim is that reading *Endgame* through the story of Noah helps us to make sense of the play where it might otherwise seem obscure, where it is otherwise hard to determine what is happening. But my aim here is not to assess whether Cavell's reading of *Endgame* actually illuminates the play. Rather, I want to treat this reading as exemplifying Cavell's understanding of how the critic's problematic conditions the practice of arts criticism, and how the critic might respond to it. That said, Cavell is not the only serious reader of *Endgame* to relate Hamm's name to Noah's son's – Theodor Adorno did so as well.[16] But Cavell took the significance of Noah's tale to *Endgame* much further than Adorno, indeed, about as far as it could possibly go, claiming that "the entire action of the play is determined by the action of that tale" (*MWM* 138).

There are four important points to note here. First, it is not so obvious that Beckett's play relates to Noah's tale. Hamm's name is the most explicit it gets, but it is not that explicit – its spelling differs from the

---

[16] See Theodor W. Adorno, "Trying to Understand *Endgame*," in *Notes to Literature*, vol. I, ed. Rolf Tiedemann, trans. Shierry Weber Nicholsen (New York: Columbia University Press, 1991), 267.

typical way in which Noah's son's name is rendered in English (Ham).[17]
Second, Cavell did not simply claim that *Endgame* refers to Noah's tale
via Hamm's name, but that Noah's tale thoroughly determines the play.
In a certain sense, Cavell claimed that the tale is there to be seen in the
action of the play, even though Noah's tale and *Endgame* are obviously
not identical. Third, in claiming that there is a particular relatum that
shapes the work to which it relates, the critic is plainly required to look
outside of the work in addition to inside of it. One cannot identify an
allusion in a work without looking to the object of allusion, and the need
to defer to that object intensifies the more one attributes importance to it.
Cavell had to say more about Noah's tale to vindicate his strong claim
about its relevance to *Endgame* than if he had simply noted a likeness
between Hamm and Ham. Finally, while the invocation of what is
"inside" and "outside" of a work might initially seem unproblematic,
we know in advance neither what is inside nor, consequently, what
outside things are pertinent to what is inside.

Now the critic's problematic can come properly into view. Quite
plainly, the critic's oscillation between part and whole, as well as between
the work and the relata she identifies, might result in reading into the
work: imposing alien meaning that obscures rather than illuminates the
work. The claims that emerge from these oscillations (e.g., that the story
of Noah determines *the entire action* of Beckett's play) invite doubt by
suggesting that the critic is overemphasizing certain elements and taking
her associations too seriously. These claims rest on less-than-obvious
appeals (e.g., that "Hamm" is a reference to the story of Noah) and tend
to involve connecting dots within the work as well as between the work
and its supposed relata. In general, such dot-connecting suggests that
one is reading into something, making more of it than is warranted. The
problem is that the process that raises suspicions about reading into a
work is necessary to hear a work out (cf. *MWM* 190–91). In other words,
what it takes to hear an artwork out involves activities that threateningly
resemble reading into it, like making claims about a work on the basis of
the critic's associations and emphasizing some elements over others. The
critic's process of guiding the work to share its voice looks alarmingly like
speaking over the work.

Again, this is even more the case in modernism, where works' voices
tend to be highly obscure. All that distinguishes a significant yet
obscurely expressed allusion from a chance likeness or shallow flourish

---

[17] Cavell identified "*hidden literality*" as an important method of indirectness in *Endgame*
(*MWM* 119), but my point here is that, literally, Hamm does not share a name with
Noah's son.

of cleverness is how one traces its significance to the work, and there one is open to error. What the critic claims to know about the work from its elements is "only known by feeling, or in feeling" – but of course, feeling does not preclude doubt (*MWM* 192). To that point, Cavell conceded that he might have been hallucinating when he claimed to "hear" a relation to the Sermon on the Mount in an exchange between Clov and Hamm (*MWM* 121). One might strengthen conviction in a feeling by continuing to read the work in light of one's feeling or by seeing whether others (can) share it, but this might be no more than deluding oneself or others (*MWM* 212).

No criterion can *ultimately* distinguish reading from misreading, an interpretation from a misinterpretation, or finding meaning from imposing it. And yet we must distinguish between apt and inapt interpretations. This describes the "frustrations inherent" in arts criticism; the critic, Cavell said,

> is part detective, part lawyer, part judge, in a country in which crimes and deeds of glory look alike, and in which the public not only, therefore, confuses one with the other, but does not know that one or the other has been committed; not because the news has not got out, but because what counts as the one or the other cannot be defined until it happens; and when it has happened there is no sure way he can get the news out; and no way at all without risking something like a glory or a crime of his own. (*MWM* 191)

I am not merely suggesting that arts criticism is a fallible enterprise; good criticism – hearing a work out – necessarily resembles fraudulent criticism – reading into a work – because the difference between the two is non-criterial. One must see whether or not the critic illuminates the work by experiencing the work for oneself and testing one's reading against the critic's. But with the possibility of shared insight and genuine clarity comes the threat of shared delusion and false clarity.

As with the artwork's problematic, Cavell thought that the critic should emphatically accept the risk of reading into a work in order to hear it out. Almost paradoxically, refusing to accept the risk – and thereby refusing to accept the likeness between reading into and hearing out a work – further subjects the critic to it. We can see this in Cavell's critique of New Criticism and in what we might call the "absurdist reading" of *Endgame* that Cavell sketched out in "Ending the Waiting Game." While Cavell followed the New Critics in granting a kind of sovereignty to the individual work, and had no objection to close reading in principle, he took their manner of close reading to be over-restrictive. New Criticism brackets out everything other than the putative work, but by doing so it creates two problems for itself. First, because the work (especially the modernist work) is not transparently given to the critic, the New Critic might bracket out in advance constitutive elements of the work (e.g., the story of Noah in *Endgame*). By taking concentration on the work to mean bracketing out everything that is not obviously part of it (the artist's intention, the audience's response, other phenomena), the New Critic ends up with only a "general impression" (*MWM* 115) of the work from which she can at best develop a "confined interpretation" (*DK* 231).[18] New Criticism mistakes covering one's ears to the echoes and resonances of a work's voice for concentrating on the work, and consequently reads too narrowly and vaguely. Second, in reading too narrowly and vaguely, the New Critic also risks misreading in the form of what one might call "muffled hearing." In muting a work's resonances with other things, one hears too little in a way that increases the possibility of imposing meaning upon the work. Imagine trying to transcribe a conversation with earplugs in: perhaps the earplugs help block out what you don't need to hear, but they do so by impairing your hearing of everything, including what you obviously need to hear (i.e., everything the New Critic does not bracket out). As such, the New Critic's attempt to avoid the risk of reading into a work fails and introduces an additional risk – vague reading or under-reading. In denying the conditions of arts criticism, especially the subjectivity involved in it, the New Critic falls into an impoverished experience of the work from which she can only develop an impoverished or even distorted reading.

What does it mean to accept the risk of mistaking reading into a work for hearing it out? What did Cavell prescribe for the critic? In Cavell's words, accepting this risk means that the critic does not "discount" her subjectivity – e.g., the associations she is led to make, the points of interest she develops – but instead seeks to "include it" and "master it in exemplary ways" by continually testing her reading against the work, other readers, and other readings (*MWM* 94). This prescription entails that the critic can intimately respond to a work while seeming itinerant, and that a roving interpretation is not necessarily a distracted or deluded one. The nature of an interpretation's itinerance can arise out of a careful engagement with the work, which does not exclude subjectivity, but requires the subject to imaginatively listen to the work's voice so as to piece its world together for herself, examining how the work can occupy the center of a grander context that comes into view through her engagement with the work (see *MWM* 215). As Cavell wrote in *Disowning Knowledge*, the critic should go "only where, and wherever" the work

---

[18] See William K. Wimsatt, Jr. and M.C. Beardsley, "The Intentional Fallacy," *Sewanee Review* 54/3 (July–September 1946), 468–88; see also William K. Wimsatt, Jr. and M.C. Beardsley, "The Affective Fallacy," *Sewanee Review* 57/1 (Winter 1949), 31–55.

leads her, and must accept her way of responding to the work and hone her responsiveness to it; Cavell called this complete fidelity to one's experience of the work "my manner" of interpretation – personal to both Cavell and critics who accept his general approach (*DK* xiv).

Conclusion

Whether or not we are still moderns, how might Cavell's work on criticism matter for us in the present? I would like to address this question not in terms of our standing as art critics, but as citizens of an increasingly multicultural world. As our world becomes increasingly multicultural, we increasingly encounter unfamiliar people who bear unfamiliar relations to unfamiliar forms of life, which heightens the challenge of hearing others out. Cavell explicitly likened our ways of regarding artworks to our ways of relating to other human beings:

> But objects of art not merely interest and absorb, they move us; we are not merely involved with them, but concerned with them, and care about them; we treat them in special ways, invest them with a value which normal people otherwise reserve only for other people – and with the same kind of scorn and outrage. They mean something to us, not just the way statements do, but the way people do. (*MWM* 197–98)

Cavell anthropomorphized artworks throughout *Must We Mean*. Illuminating an artwork's meaning is a matter of illuminating its intentionality – *not* what the artist meant or attempted to mean by making the work, but what *the work means* through its purposive form or its meaningful nexus of elements (see *MWM* 198). An artwork *speaks* to us, and Cavell's manner of interpreting an artwork is akin to "interviewing" it: identifying important details in it, posing questions in light of those details, and looking to the work for answers while drawing upon one's own resources to render the work's answers available (*MWM* 237).

Cavell's lesson for us arises from how seriously he took modernism to have problematized authority. Just as an artwork cannot be understood solely by reference to what its tradition or maker says it should be, we cannot be understood just by reference to our forms of life or our families. Insofar as we achieve a kind of autonomy, it is not simply the case that our forms of life and families determine who we are; we may allow them to determine us by forming intentional relationships to them, but we might just as well forge formative relationships elsewhere. As such, our general impressions of one another must be provisional if we really want to hear each other out. We have to be "willing to rethink" one another and, more controversially, discount nothing in our experiences of others on the basis of our own anticipated failures (e.g., prejudices) or those we might suppose of others (e.g., that they are withholding something from us) (*DK* 244). Cavell's discussions of arts criticism in *Must We Mean What We Say?* guide us away from false sources and hopes of *Sicherheit* and illuminate the open possibility of accepting the risks involved in actively listening to others without the safeguard of pretense. Cavell's treatment of the art critic's problematic surely exhibits traces of modernist heroism, but the courage Cavell exemplified and advanced in this respect does not pertain to creating meaning in a meaningless world by imposing our literary will. Instead, it pertains to putting ourselves out there as active listeners, overcoming our general impressions of others and of our proximity to or distance from them, and seeing if we might find or create shared meaning together.

8   Must We Sing What We Mean?:
"Music Discomposed" and Philosophy Composed

Vincent Colapietro

> Understanding a sentence is much more akin to understanding a theme in
> music than one may think. What I mean is that understanding a sentence
> lies nearer than one thinks to what is ordinarily called understanding a
> musical theme.
>
> Wittgenstein, Philosophical Investigations, §527[1]

> 'Lu ral lu ral lu!' [not quite scat but it fits the occasion. These nonsense
> syllables] may be more impressively sung than very respectable wisdom
> talked. It is well-timed, as wisdom is not always.
>
> H.D. Thoreau, journal entry dated February 6, 1841[2]

Introduction: A Student of Composition

Please listen to the Hot Five, featuring a young Louis Armstrong, playing
"West End Blues."[3] In the words of an African proverb, the Spirit does
not descend without song or, in a slightly different version, the Spirit
does not descend without music. So, allow this piece to be an invocation
of the Spirit of this occasion. I will come back to it later in my discussion,
but for the moment let it stand as a text without commentary.

One way of identifying my task on this occasion is this: I am endeavor-
ing to put to rest, once and for all, a slanderous rumor regarding Stanley
Cavell. After graduating from UCLA, he went to Juilliard to study
musical composition (this is not the slanderous part of the rumor) and
he spent a great deal of time playing hooky, reading psychoanalysis and
philosophy but also going to the movies (we are still at a distance from the
slander I desire to eradicate) (*LDIK*). Rather quickly, rumor would have

---

[1] Ludwig Wittgenstein, *Philosophical Investigations*, trans. Elizabeth Anscombe (New York:
Macmillan, 1953).
[2] H.D. Thoreau, *The Heart of Thoreau's Journals*, ed. Odell Shepard (New York: Dover, 1961).
[3] Louis Armstrong, "West End Blues," 78 rpm recording, June 28, 1928. For a recording
of this piece, go to www.youtube.com/watch?v=4WPCBieSESI. See also Gary Giddens,
Visions of Jazz: The First Century (Oxford University Press, 1998); Giddens and Scott
DeVeaux, *Jazz* (New York: W.W. Norton, 2009).

it, Stanley Cavell jettisoned his aspiration to become a composer. Therein lies the calumny. It is, I realize, no news to those who have spent time with his writings, but I want to state the obvious: Stanley Cavell never abandoned composition. Though it is more of a stretch, I am in my more reckless moments inclined to insist he never abandoned playing alto sax in a swing band, even if in trading black brothers for overwhelmingly white academics as his bandmates meant much of what he heard and read as a philosopher didn't mean a thing because it didn't have that swing. What is misleading here is that his sax looks like a pen or keyboard. But don't be fooled. The utterly *un*musical modes of philosophizing in too many Anglophone circles throughout most of the twentieth century make the rather plodding playing of Louis Armstrong's bandmates in the Red Hot Five sound like Count Basie's band, with its incomparable swing, that is, with its visceral, cerebral, unabashedly assertive, and intensely self-aversive *sound*. In brief, too much of Anglophone philosophy during the period in question makes Armstrong's bandmates sound as though they swung.

In a footnote to the title essay of the book being celebrated in this volume, Cavell notes: "Wittgenstein's role in combating the idea of privacy (whether of the meaning of what is said or what is done), and in emphasizing the functions and contexts of language, scarcely needs to be mentioned." But it "might be worth pointing out that these teachings are fundamental to American pragmatism; but then we must keep in mind how their arguments sound, and admit that *in philosophy it is the sound which makes all the difference*" (*MWM* 36, n. 31, emphasis added).[4] In the same breath, he takes a step toward the acknowledgment of an affinity with pragmatism and notes a difference that truly makes a difference (in philosophy, the sound makes all the difference) (*CHU*). The work of acknowledgment is no more quickly accomplished or straightforwardly executed than that of mourning. There is implicit in this claim regarding the differential sounds of philosophical authors, traditions, and texts an acknowledgment of voice, above all, the singular voice not only of those implicated in the dramas of everyday life but also the embodied speakers (hence, gendered, racialized subjects) who have no other recourse than to ordinary language, *even* in their efforts to craft an ideal or artificial language, also in their efforts to speak in their singular voices.

"Music Discomposed" and Philosophy Composed

Only a student of musical composition is likely to have been able to write "Music Discomposed" and its companion piece "A Matter of Meaning

---

[4] Also quoted in Stanley Cavell, *Emerson's Transcendental Etudes*, ed. David Justin Hodge (Stanford University Press, 2003).

It."[5] These might seem to be merely occasional pieces, included in *Must We Mean* only to round off the volume. They are occasional pieces, but not merely such. "Music Discomposed" was composed by stitching together two papers. One "was read as the opening paper of a symposium held at the sixth annual Oberlin Colloquium in Philosophy in April 1965" (*MWM* xi). "Most of the material in sections V, VI, and VII [of "Music Discomposed"] ... was presented as part of a symposium called 'Composition, Improvisation and Chance,' held at a joint meeting of the American Musicological Society, the Society for Ethnomusicology, and the College Music Society, at the University of California, Berkeley, December 1960" (xiv). Of the ten sections of "Music Discomposed," then, seven (I–IV and VIII–X) were drawn from material presented at Oberlin in 1965, three (V, VI, and VII) at the symposium at Berkeley five years earlier. This material is finely integrated, deftly composed, so "Music Discomposed" is unquestionably an integral whole. On the occasion of those parts read at Oberlin, Monroe Beardsley and Joseph Margolis commented on Cavell's presentation. Cavell's paper and these responses were shortly thereafter made available in "the Proceedings of that Colloquium ... [a volume entitled] *Art, Mind, and Religion*" (xiv). Cavell's own response to Beardsley and Margolis, "A Matter of Meaning It," "while not read at the Oberlin Colloquium," was included in the Proceedings.

Three points especially merit emphasis. First, "Music Discomposed" and "A Matter of Meaning It" should be read together. Second, while occasional pieces, ones written for specific occasions, they unquestionably transcend their origin. They resound as forcefully today as they did 55 or 60 years ago. Third, and finally, they are thematically linked to the other essays in *Must We Mean* at least by their focus on writing or composition. These two essays are as much about how (especially in the wake of modernism) to write philosophically about art in general as they are about either how to compose music after Arnold Schoenberg or how to write about atonal and other innovative forms of musical composition in the teeth of the polemics being issued in such journals as *Die Reihe* (inaugurated in 1955) and *Perspectives of New Music* (1962) (*MWM* 185). Cavell is especially concerned with the way certain polemical forms of writing, accompanying the appearance of the "new music," close off both critical reflection and a candid appeal to one's own musical experience (including the experience of listeners). The experience of listeners, tied to the question of audience, cannot be gainsaid. As worthy of serious regard as they are, the manifestos and pronouncements of the composers and their champions cannot be taken at face value. This is why Cavell's engagement

---

[5] Given the scope of this chapter, however, I will focus primarily on "Music Discomposed."

with the writings of Ernst Krenek (1900–91), a Czech composer who wrote a number of books (including *Music Here and Now*, 1939, and *Horizons Circled: Reflections on My Music*, 1974) and articles such as "A Composer's Influence" (*Perspectives of New Music*, 3/1) and the one in *Die Reihe* (1960) quoted at length by Cavell, is so central to "Music Discomposed." A passage from one of Krenek's articles ("Extents and Limits of Serial Techniques" in *Die Reihe*, 1960), quoted at length by Cavell (*MWM* 195), is truly pivotal. Though these are my words, Krenek presents, in Cavell's judgment, contemporary composers with a false disjunctive (either "inspiration" or "impersonal mechanism"). In light of the later Cavell, we might identify the younger Cavell opposing Krenek in terms of Emersonian "self-trust." This is not how Cavell in 1965 puts it in those sections of "Music Discomposed," but can there be any question that this is how he would have put it in his later writings? In any event, Krenek is calling for anyone committed to composing today "to *distrust* his inspiration" (*MWM* 195, emphasis added). While appreciative of the need for self-aversive thought, Cavell is also attentive to the other side of this – the equal need for self-trust (trust solid and secure enough to subject itself to rigorous and continual testing).

To repeat, these two essays by Cavell are, at least, as much about how to write about music as they are about how to compose music. His principal focus is not Schoenberg but Krenek and, then, not Krenek as a musical composer but as a polemical author expressing himself in books and articles. His orienting disposition is to win a hearing for listeners, amid the din generated by such authors in defense of their compositions. In Cavell's judgment, Krenek's fantasy is that of "physics" (or an impersonal mechanism) substituting for "the real satisfaction of knowledge" (204). The operation of such a mechanism precludes improvisation, whereas "improvisation implies shared conventions" (204). While "the fantasy of physics" here underwrites another fantasy ("you can create a living community at a moment's notice"), the exacting task of musical composition, ultimately rooted in the improvisational capacity of *auditory* artists, is linked to a tremendous "body of recollection, tradition, training, and experience" (195) in which, on Cavell's account, composers, performers, and listeners are rooted. This is the living community of musical practices, though one time and again threatened by its successes or, at least, innovations (188). Resting one's hope on such a mechanism of "composition" expresses, in his judgment, "contempt" for the artistic or creative process. It also expresses contempt for or, at least, indifference to *the experience of listening*. For this hope drives one to call "something musically organized [music] ... on grounds unrelated to any which in which it is, or is meant to be, heard" (*MWM* 204–05).

If our cultural condition is one in which musical composers are con-
temptuous of or, at best, indifferent to how their means of composition
might be related to the experience of listening, then all the more is it one
in which the *sound* of the human voice in the writings of, say, professional
philosophers can only seem to be an impertinence. Part of what is
distinctive about Cavell is that he insists upon the sound of that voice,
in philosophy no less than in music. He is far from oblivious to "the
human effort to escape our humanness," to transcend our finitude in one
decisive bound, but he seems to agree with Wallace Stevens about what
constitutes "acutest speech" ("To speak humanly from the height or
from the depth / Of human things"[6]). Such speech not only speaks
from the height and the depths of the everyday world of human beings
(cf. *CHU* 13). It also speaks humanly: its "*utterance*[s] (outer-ance[s])
(*MWM* 228) are audible voicings. Again, this goes for philosophy no less
than music. And it, decidedly, goes for music!

What Cavell asserts in *Philosophy the Day After Tomorrow* (2005) seems
to be what, in effect (i.e., *not* in so many words), is at play in his response
to Krenek. "Experience missed, in certain forms in which philosophy has
interested itself in this condition, is a theme developing itself through
various of my intellectual turns in recent years" (*PDAT* 10). But this was
true not only in recent years. This theme is evident in "Music
Discomposed." Experience can be missed in various ways,[7] not least of
all by being ceded. Cavell is quite explicit about this: "If I am to possess
my own experience I cannot afford to cede it to my culture as that culture
stands. I must find ways to insist upon it, if I find it unheard, ways to let
the culture confront itself in me, driving me some distance to distraction"
(*PDAT* 82). I must insist upon my own experience and not cede that
experience to the authoritative voices that would browbeat me out of the
experiential appeals on which all humane criticism is based. Of course,
this experience must itself be interrogated: it must be tested, time and
again. It however must not be ceded to "my culture as that culture [now]
stands"; above all, it must not be jettisoned because the intimating
sophistications of a polemical author, allegedly speaking on behalf of
my culture, can engender radical self-doubt.[8] The future of music
depends on the ability of listeners to evolve into audiences who are not

---

[6] *The Collected Poems of Wallace Stevens* (New York: Vintage, 1990), 300.
[7] "We had," T.S. Eliot writes in "The Dry Salvages," "the experience, but missed the
   meaning, / And approach to the meaning restores the experience / In a different form,
   beyond any meaning / We can assign to happiness." Eliot, *Four Quartets* (New York:
   Harcourt, Brace, 1943), 39.
[8] See also Vincent Colapietro, "Experience Ceded and Negated," *Journal of Speculative
   Philosophy* 22/2 (2008), 118–26.

intimidated by the "new." Such listeners neither dismiss it out of hand nor immediately grant it the status claimed for it by its defenders and polemicists. Such listeners – *listen*. They do so patiently, thoughtfully, carefully, honestly, imaginatively, allowing the new music to challenge their accustomed modes of sensitivity but also self-trusting enough to challenge the claims (pretensions?) of avant-garde composers. They listen and they do so in a manner exhibiting trust, trust not so much in their present capacity to hear as their musical educability, the possibility of their experience becoming more nuanced, discerning, and susceptible to a wider range of musical intimations.

In the end, the work of art must stand on its own feet. For this reason, the sheer amount of polemical paraphernalia disposes a thinker such as Cavell to be somewhat dubious. What is going on here? Why the need to spend so many words to defend serial or atonal music? Why do composers feel so compelled to compose polemical writings to accompany their musical compositions? Do they no longer trust a critical mass of intelligent listeners to begin, perhaps quickly, to acquire new ears? In his characteristic manner, Cavell slyly observes the focus is on composers, not performers or listeners. The writing in such journals as *Die Reihe* and *Perspectives of New Music* is focused "on composer[s] and [their] problems" (*MWM* 186). Indeed, "a great many of the articles are produced by the composers themselves, sometimes directly about, sometimes indirectly, their own music" (186). Taking note of an observation made by Paul Oskar Kristeller, Cavell contrasts this to "writing about the arts produced from Plato to Kant": the categories and indeed styles of these writings are "from the spectator's or amateur's point of view" (186). In terms of music, this means from the listener's angle of engagement.

In "Music Discomposed," Cavell explores the topic of composition in the context of a modernist ethos driving militantly toward atonality. What can hardly escape notice is that, while his treatment of composition primarily focuses on *musical* composition, especially the composition of music in which chance, improvisation, and radical skepticism regarding shared conventions play a critical role, he is attentive to the broader implications of his seemingly narrowly focused reflections. For his treatment of such composition manifestly carries implications for other forms of composition, including of course the linguistic composition of philosophical texts. In this respect, it ties in with one of the overarching texts of the various essays gathered in *Must We Mean*, that of writing (see especially "The Availability of Wittgenstein's Later Philosophy").

Cavell was uncompromisingly committed to the *experiential* and not merely the philosophical recovery of experience. It would be more

accurate to say, for this is what I mean (Hegel: what I meant to mean[9]),
he worked tirelessly to make the philosophical recovery of experience to
be nothing less than an experiential recovery, at once deeply personal and
widely relevant. Even at a purely philosophical level, most historical
versions of empiricism have been, to use Walter Kaufmann's witty coinage, *empiricide*. No theorist can kill experience as quickly as an empiricist
(think of the a prioristic molds into which professed empiricists have
poured the data of experience).[10] For his purpose, Cavell was right to
find pragmatism lacking, though he appreciated the extent to which the
function and contexts of language, so central to Wittgenstein's approach,
were no less central to, say, Peirce's, Dewey's, and Mead's. How the
writings of the pragmatists sounded and resounded in his ears, however,
counted heavily against them, even when he was sympathetic to the
points being pressed.[11]

Virtually all of the traditional distinctions – to highlight but a handful,
subjectivity and objectivity, passivity and activity, heteronomy and
autonomy, self and other, reason and madness, tradition and creativity –
are rendered in a single stroke *experientially* problematic. At the same
time, however, they are, in countless contexts for various functions,
critical. However elusive are the criteria for drawing these distinctions,
the task is not hopeless. The necessity, even urgency, to draw these or
analogous distinctions cannot be gainsaid, while the criteria for carrying
out the task prove (to repeat) elusive but not hopelessly so. In the face of
such challenges, the *sound* of a supremely confident voice almost certainly sounds *fraudulent*, while that of a skeptically inflected voice is likely
to win, provisionally at least, our confidence (for the sound of this voice
indicates that our struggles have been this individual's as well).[12]

On the one hand, the lubricity (to use Emerson's word in
"Experience") of a world imagined to exist beyond the touch of words
poses one set of problems, problems to be dissolved. On the other hand,
the *airy-nothings* of words themselves, imagined to exist at a distance
from the world, great or exceedingly slight (actually, the measure of the
distance does not matter at all, only imagining that there *is* a distance),

[9] G.W.F. Hegel, *Phenomenology of Spirit*, trans. A.V. Miller (Oxford: Clarendon Press, 1977).
[10] See John Dewey, "The Need for a Recovery of Philosophy," in *John Dewey: The Middle Works, 1899–1924*, ed. Jo Ann Boydston, vol. x (Carbondale: Southern Illinois University Press, 1980).
[11] See *CHU* 13; Stanley Cavell, "What's the Use of Calling Emerson a Pragmatist?" in *The Revival of Pragmatism: New Essays on Social Thought, Law, and Culture*, ed. Morris Dickstein (Durham, NC: Duke University Press, 1998), 72–80.
[12] See Timothy Gould, *Hearing Things: Voice and Method in the Writing of Stanley Cavell* (University of Chicago Press, 1998).

these airy-nothings uttered in complete abstraction from the quotidian world pose another set of problems, also to be dissolved. Words can be imperceptibly wrested from the worlds. Please allow for a self-interruption: our feminist sisters have taught us, more effectively than the classical pragmatists, to stress *the plurality of worlds* and if we do not get it – and it often does not seem we have – that is not on them, it is on us: they have been tireless, acute, and eloquent in their insistence upon this plurality.[13] Words wrested from the worlds in which they are actually uttered and, thus, are actually binding, wounding, annihilative, solicitous to the point of being not unlike a mother's enveloping embrace, also elevating to the height of being taken up in an uncle's hands and thrown up into the air and, in the ascent, having the *experience* of flight – words having these and countless other effects – words wrested from worlds and their effects are indeed airy-nothings. But, alas, they are not anything we could possibly *mean* by a word. My words bear nothing less than the weight of the world, my world, but not merely my world, just as our worlds ineluctably – fatefully – employ my and our words in the inescapable dramas of everyday life. I – but not I alone, I often in solitude, but again even then not utterly alone or ripped from relationships to others – I am responsible for holding worlds and words together, though the pressures, promptings, and propensities on both sides aid me incalculably in keeping my word, in meaning what I say. If there is *grace* anywhere (and I am strongly disposed to insist there is), it is these pressures, promptings, and propensities of worlds-and-words. That I am able to speak at all and, beyond this, that I am able to keep my word or, at the most rudimentary level, that I am able simply to make sense (that I am able to do *any* of this) is aided immensely by the words and gestures, the embraces and encouragement of my interlocutors. The vortices of worlds and words allow me to hold myself together, and when I am at my most admirable, to stretch myself from, say, a promise made to that promise kept, from a word said to *that* word meant with its full force and contemporary urgency.

When my worlds and words come apart, that means that I have already come undone, possibly to the point where I am gliding (to use Emerson's figure) ghost-like through nature. Stanley Cavell could not be more explicit about the locus: *I* am the scandal of skepticism. I am responsible for unhinging worlds and words; that makes me responsible for rejoining them. In this, I must assume nothing less than cosmic responsibility (responsibility for the world in which I live), on the one hand, and an

---

[13] See Adam Phillips, *On Flirtation: Psychoanalytic Essays on the Uncommitted Life* (Cambridge, MA: Harvard University Press, 1994), 40, 68.

unmeasurable responsibility for my linguistic inheritance and indeed for my specific deployment of this inheritance on some unique occasion (and all occasions are unique). Rather total heaviosity. Here I return to an anecdote of Cathleen Cavell's, shared at the same conference at which I delivered an earlier version of this chapter. Given such a weight to bear, is it in the least surprising that the folks in the storage house marked a box of books with the words: *Must I Moan What I Sigh?* I am inclined however to think "Mourn" would have been more apt than "Moan." But even this must be qualified, for in this and later books Cavell carries out grief-work in a way that opens possibilities of childlike awe and even joyful embrace.

In any event, I do *not* hear moans and sighs, though I discern countless traces of the work of mourning. Moreover, Cavell's voice is in my mind's ear of course audibly Wittgensteinian and Emersonian, Austinian and musical, but it is no less Jewish. As dangerous as it is to say such things, his wisdom is a distinctively Jewish wisdom, as were Freud's and Derrida's. One of the most important respects in which this is so concerns Cavell's commitment to repair a broken world and, on a more intimate level, to repair fissured psyches (better: to assist them in repairing themselves). The torn fabric has to be sewn back together.

Another respect in which echoes of the rabbis are audible in his writings, at least in my ears, bears directly upon the book being celebrated in this collection. His questions, including the very title of this book, are intimately related to those of the old rabbis, especially, Do they hear the words coming out of their own mouths? Better: Do *we* – do we – hear the words coming out of *our* mouths? Do we know adequately for the purpose of what we are requesting, or demanding, or desiring (pick whatever performative you like) – do we know adequately for whatever it is we are *doing* with these words on this occasion what these words mean here and now, addressed to this sentient, vulnerable being? Of greatest moment, can we acknowledge – can we even simply begin to entertain the possibility of acknowledging – that our words, on this occasion, addressed to these flesh-and-blood others mean more than we realize? And do we have the courage to own up to and the intelligence simply to ascertain some range of this wider, deeper meaning?

Turning from the Jewish rabbis, we might recall a philosophical "teacher" whose wisdom could be deep-cutting, if his prose was all too often an abomination. Consider Hegel's observation: to the extent that we are in flight from something, that thing remains in control of us. On this occasion, however, it is another bit of his wisdom to which I would like to call your attention. We find out, time and again, in light of our own experience what we *meant to mean* stands at odds with what we consciously intended. At this juncture, we must go back over what we meant to be and try to make it more explicit, more perspicuous, and more opportune (temporarily spot-on). This is Hegel's counsel, with slight modifications. Do we have the resolve, the courage, and the patience *to go back over* what we said and revise it in light of what experience has taught us we meant to mean? Hegel's way of putting this is not Cavell's but the kinship between his and the author of *Must We Mean What We Say?* is discernible, better, audible.

All titles are implicit promises, while most texts are broken ones. Did I mean what I submitted to the editors as the title of this chapter? Alas, my title is constrained by the grammar of promising, however tacit, and far more disconcerting, my text has up to this point *evaded* the titular performative: I have in effect *vowed* to speak to a topic and have left it unaddressed. So, allow me to try to keep the promise of my title – Must We Sing What We Mean? No.

I however imagine it is incumbent upon me to expand a bit on this emphatic negative. In deliberately trying or directly striving to make our words sing, we would only succeed in making our texts *sound* labored or precious or mannered or all of these and more. The biting pertinence of a traditional adage invites recollection here: in trying to make an impression, poetic, literary, or otherwise, in trying to make an impression, we are bound to make a trying impression. Whenever philosophers too willfully and self-consciously style themselves poets, this ends, *at best*, in self-congratulatory cleverness and, at worst, in other-negating monotony.

But words – sometimes even our own, both because of and despite ourselves, because of our care, and patience, and craft, and indeed because of our abandonment of self and craft – to repeat, words, even our own, sometimes – *do* sing and the event of their having done so is to be accepted as a gift, that is, *acknowledged* with humility and gratitude, joy and hope. While we ought not to strive too willfully to make our words sing, we ought to avail ourselves to the *sounds* of our own speaking and writing – to open ourselves to and, of far greater difficulty, to *remain* open to *just* how they sound, especially in the face of likely ridicule and inevitable doubts. This is, after all, Cavell's manner of composition, manifestly akin to that of Ellington and Mingus, Charlie Parker and Miles Davis. (Have you seen the footage of Davis improving the score for Louis Malle's first film? That's for another occasion.) Cavell listens with the utmost care to the sound of his own words and revises them as a result of what he hears; and, then, does so again. His soundings are occasions for revisions, though the ocular metaphor buried in this word works to some extent against what I *mean* to say.

If our words do not occasionally sing, if language and worlds in either their lovers' quarrels or felicitous remarriages do *not* sing in and through us, then a diagnosis, in a way belated, is necessary. For if our words are flat and dull, dead and deadening, something has gone dead *in us*. And we need to find out just what has gone dead (what has died in us). So, to repeat, our direct striving to craft the loftiest utterances, poetically stunning sentences, needs to be abandoned and we must simply (simply!) make ourselves *available* for the world or language or the remarriage of language with the world or, even in the context of such remarriage, the lovers' quarrel of the world. We must simply make ourselves available, so our ordinary language and everyday world might sing in and through our words, phrases, and sentences.

It is pertinent to recall at this juncture a rather surprising assertion by Emerson, at the very end of his essay on "Montaigne; or, the Skeptic": let us learn to bear the disappearance of things we were wont to reverence without losing our capacity for reverence; (here is the surprising part) let us learn that we are here, not to work but to be worked upon.[14] I find the lines of the contemporary poet A.R. Ammons helpful in making sense out of Emerson's startling claim: Ammons confessed, he was not looking for "the shape" of reality, far less for an opportunity to *impose* a shape upon it, rather he wanted to be "as being available / to any shape that may be summoning itself / through me / from the self not mine but ours."[15] We must make ourselves available for the music of the world to sing in and through us. At a more rudimentary level, we must simply facilitate processes in which life answers to life and, as a result, vitality is intensified, deepened, expanded.

Whatever worlds of words we compose, the *site* of our composition is inescapably the everyday world in its irreducibly plural character. And the wisdom of the rabbis is clear regarding the state of *this* world: at best, it is in need of repair and, more likely, we are living amid ruins. So, the question becomes: How are we to rebuild the quotidian world and how are we to repair our broken selves? Please do not doubt that the touch of words can be magical, because their sound can be consoling and exhilarating, heartening and enlivening (that is, words can give us heart and reflame our lives).

If the *site* of our efforts is obvious, even if we often enough fail to acknowledge it fully, our *motivation* for doing so is no less so, though,

---

[14] See Ralph Waldo Emerson, *Essays and Lectures*, ed. Joel Porte (New York: Library of America, 1983), 709.

[15] A.R. Ammons, "Poetics," in *The Complete Poems of A.R. Ammons*, vol. I, ed. Robert M. West (New York: W.W. Norton, 2017), 465.

again, we might fail to acknowledge *this* adequately. "The work of the philosopher consists," Wittgenstein reminds us, "in assembling reminders for a particular purpose."[16] What do we most need to remind ourselves of regarding our drive to repair and rebuild our world?

"Strange as it may seem today to say, the aim of life is," Henry Miller suggests, "to live, and to live means to be aware, joyously, drunkenly, serenely, divinely aware. In the state of this god-like awareness one sings; in this realm[,] the world exists as poem."[17]

Two other Harvard professors who died roughly a century ago were in fact neighbors. When one or the other was away from home, they carried on their incessant conversation by letters. These missives would often contain trivial details regarding their shared neighborhood (both lived on Irving Street in Cambridge, very close to one another; their houses bear historical markers). One or the other might, for example, report how Estlin, who lived close to William James and even closer to Josiah Royce, was coming into his own. When he fully came into his own, e. e. cummings would write a number of poems in which the words do indeed sing. Allow me to recall here the concluding stanza of one of his most famous poems, "in the time of daffodils," since it bears on the topics we are considering:

> and in a mystery to be
> (when time from time shall set us free)
> forgetting me, remember me[18]

The mystery resides in "to be" (not least of all, *to be* heard and thereby to be a self) and, for us, this is enacted and, when fortunate, achieved *in time*. To have the time of our lives however requires that there be moments and occasions "when time from time shall set us free." Tied to such moments or occasions, the remembrance of those we have heard in their unforgettable singularity and perhaps also in their exacting presence inevitably involves forms of forgetting. For our encounters with some individuals are, at once, requests by them to be forgotten ("What is important are," a teacher might say to students, "not my words but the words and worlds to which mine point, helping making available what otherwise might be missed or, worse, scoffed at") and a hope to be remembered ("forgetting me, remember me").

[16] Wittgenstein, *Philosophical Investigations*, §127.
[17] Henry Miller, "Creative Death," in *The Wisdom of the Heart* (New York: New Directions, 1941), 3–12.
[18] e.e. cummings, *Complete Poems, 1904–1962* (New York: Liveright, 1994).

On this occasion, Cavell's own words, his works, his abiding but no longer perceptible or palpable presence seem to insist, without a trace of vanity or even pathos: "forgetting me, remember me." It is not an exaggeration to say that he signed almost every word he uttered or wrote with incomparable integrity and arresting eloquence. He *meant* what he said and wrote, even (better: *especially*) when the implications of his utterances carried him to surprising and disconcerting places. There is and always will be in my mind's ear the unforgettable sound of his singular voice. His commitment to singularity risked unintelligibility, but his commitment to intelligibility insured that this voice whenever it was heard, whatever the occasion, speaking to whoever happened to be within earshot – to repeat, his commitment to intelligibility insured he would work indefatigably to make himself comprehensible. But he asked and occasionally demanded that his voice be heard in its irreducible singularity. Some mistook this for vanity or arrogance. But it was, in truth, an insistence, a demand, more than anything else, an invitation rooted in both radical self-affirmation and the deepest humility.

Conclusion: Singular Voices and Shared Practices

Despite their numerous and fundamental differences, philosophy can be (though more often than not, it is not) – still it can be – akin to jazz in this crucial respect: philosophy can be a communal celebration of the singular voice and, ideally, a cumulative series of singular enactments of a hard-won solidarity.[19] This can be unmistakably heard on "West End Blues." Armstrong's musical voice rises far above the ones in the Hot Five. His solo is truly a transcendent moment, marking the way forward for countless musicians who heard how music could be improvised (i.e., *composed* extemporaneously). In addition, it can be clearly heard in the writings of Stanley Cavell, from "Must We Mean What We Say?" (1957) to his very last compositions. And please make no mistake: his writings are compositions attuned to the ear of the reader.

While we should not consciously or directly strive to sing what we mean, even when what we intend to say is exalted or in some other respect of utmost significance, we must be alert to our own deadness, alive to the countless ways in which our words and deeds, evasions and erasures, the ceding of our experience to our culture and the often all too facile denunciation of our cultural inheritance (we must be alive to how

---

[19] See Vincent Colapietro, "Voice and the Interrogation of Philosophy: Inheritance, and Abandonment, and Jazz," in *Stanley Cavell and the Education of Grownups*, ed. Naoko Saito and Paul Standish (New York: Fordham University Press, 2012), 133–47.

all this, all too often) *eviscerates our lives*. The experiential recovery of experience cannot but be an enlivening reclamation of our lives. Jonathan Lear, another philosopher who has been deeply influenced by psychoanalysis (he is in fact a trained psychoanalyst), suggests, "Plato, who did so much to bring philosophy to life, was ever wary of the myriad ways it can go dead. He also tried to warn us of the many sham activities that called themselves 'philosophy'."[20] In brief, Plato was alive to all the ways philosophy can go dead. This is no doubt true and indeed important.

But Stanley Cavell was also alive to how philosophy and *much else* can suffer this fate. And the human psyche in its complex fragility and remarkable resilience was to figure most prominently in this *much else*, to be counted among the important things that can go dead. Regarding how a philosophical account of the world in which we are so fatefully entangled (in a word, how our *philosophies*) can go dead, but also how they can be revived and reclaimed, Stanley Cavell's voice was one of fluency inflected with hesitancy, of self-affirmation conjoined with self-aversion, one of bold assertion tied to nuanced qualification, and a voice prone to protracted pauses, not all of which were unabashed. He was a fiercely gentle man whose doubts, including self-doubts, made him appreciative of what he called the scandal of skepticism. For him, skepticism is not a doctrine to be refuted, but a process to be worked through, time and again.

Stanley Cavell not only played for keeps but kept his word, by giving it – and he gave his word by *meaning* it as much as anyone who ever took his word to be his bond. All of this is, paradoxically, audible in the words on the page. For me and, no doubt, many of my readers, the *sound* of those words has made a difference in our lives beyond what, at least, my words can express. That unbridgeable chasm is also part of meaning, as the spaces between sounds no less than the sounds themselves are integral to music.

In a letter, Henry James noted: "No theory is kind that cheats us of seeing."[21] To which I am inclined to add: no theory is kind that cheats us of *hearing*. Put positively, any theory enabling us to acquire more discerning ears, truly to hear the words on the page and the singular voice in the shared words out of which utterances and texts are composed, is generous and welcome.[22]

---

[20] Jonathan Lear, *Freud* (New York: Routledge, 2005), 222.
[21] *Letters of Henry James*, ed. Percy Lubbock (New York: Charles Scribner's Sons, 1920), 174 (Letter to R.L Stevenson, January 12, 1891).
[22] See also Gould, *Hearing Things*.

Part III

Tragedy and the Self

9   Philosophy as Autobiography
From *Must We Mean What We Say?* to *Little Did
I Know*

Naoko Saito

Introduction: Voice in Philosophy

There are multiple entries into the breadth of Cavell's work. And yet one
of the crucial concepts that is sustained from the early to the later writings
is that of "voice" – voice in philosophy. It is true that voice comes to be
foregrounded in his later autobiographical writings, but, as Veena Das
has put this, "The repression of voice and hence of confession, of
autobiography, in philosophy is an abiding theme of Cavell's work ...
Cavell sees the banishing of the human voice in the register of the
philosophical as a suspicion of all that is ordinary, as the fantasy of some
kind of purified medium outside of language that was available to us."[1]
The purpose of this chapter is to show that voice is a significant feature
not only of his autobiographical writings but also of his ordinary language
philosophy as a whole and, especially, that it is incipient in his earliest
work, *Must We Mean What We Say?* (1969). Autobiography is surely a
matter of speaking in one's voice. And yet if we read *Must We Mean* along
with *A Pitch of Philosophy* (1994) and *Little Did I Know* (2010), we come
to realize that Cavell's autobiographical writing involves not only self-
education – as is typically associated with the idea of voice – but also a
radical re-placement of the subject of philosophy. Cavell's philosophy as
autobiography is inseparable from the larger endeavor of his ordinary
language philosophy in reconfiguring what we mean by philosophy.
Philosophy involves the transformation of the way we see the world. In
this chapter, I shall try to elucidate how such a radical reconfiguration of
philosophy germinated in *Must We Mean* and how, later, it came to be
materialized, illustrated, and enacted in *A Pitch of Philosophy* and *Little
Did I Know*.

In the following, I shall move to a rereading of Cavell's philosophy as
autobiography, centering on an idea of "tonality" in philosophy,

---

[1] Veena Das, *Life and Words: Violence and the Descent into the Ordinary* (Berkeley: University
of California Press, 2007), 6.

developed in relation to Cavell by Paul Standish. To evince and further develop this alternative line of reading, I shall consider Cavell's essay "Aesthetic Problems of Modern Philosophy." This will serve to show some crucial features of his ordinary language philosophy and how it prepares the ground for his development of the idea of voice in philosophy as autobiography. In the latter part of the chapter, I shall move on to his later autobiographical writings, *Pitch* and *Little*. Attention to *Must We Mean* enables a more "Cavellian" reading of *Little Did I Know*. With *Must We Mean* as a guide, these later writings can be seen to reveal better the breadth and depth of his ordinary language philosophy. While *Little Did I Know* may be thought by some (Colapietro) to be somewhat self-indulgent in relation to the past, philosophy as autobiography turns out to be a matter of finding one's self and yet much more than that. In conclusion, I shall summarize what I try to show of the ways that Cavell's early and later works reinforce one another, realizing an understanding of the nature of voice in a manner that should matter to each of us and to philosophy. The territory Cavell explores is philosophical and therapeutic, but it is not narcissistic. *Must We Mean* shows the philosophical origins of the grand endeavor of Cavell's exploration of these themes.

The Question of Tonality

Paul Standish's response to Ken Wain, "Momentous Occasions: Philosophy and Autobiography in Richard Rorty, Stanley Cavell, and Kenneth Wain" provides some intimation of a way beyond the limits in Wain's misreading of Cavell.[2] Aspects of this misreading are not unfamiliar. The first limit lies in the unintended lapse into a sort of foundationalism. Second, there is Wain's use of the term "universal" in a conventional way. Third, there is the apparent inheriting of the Rortian division between the private and the public. Standish's response provides an alternative entry into the realm of philosophy as autobiography. Quoting from Cornel West, Standish writes that "The question of tone is particularly pertinent to what might count as distinctively American philosophy" ("MO" 286). While appreciating Rorty's contribution in turning tonality and style of writing into a different style of philosophy, Standish tries to show that Rorty's resigned and ironical tone may deflect

---

[2] Paul Standish, "Momentous Occasions: Philosophy and Autobiography in Richard Rorty, Stanley Cavell, and Kenneth Wain," in *My Teaching, My Philosophy: Kenneth Wain and the Lifelong Engagement with Education*, ed. John Baldacchino, Simone Galea, and Duncan P. Mercieca (New York: Peter Lang, 2014), 285–302; hereafter cited parenthetically as "MO."

us from serious engagement with philosophy – amplified by the kind of "blockage" created by Rorty's division between one's public responsibility in social justice and one's private, literary endeavor. It is here that Standish contrasts Rorty to Cavell, in whose writing he finds hope of a more thorough sensitization to tone in philosophy – a matter of style that Standish alleges to be inseparable from the content of philosophy.

To elucidate this point, Standish introduces us to Cavell's ordinary language philosophy, in which the first-person plural formulation of "When we say ..., we mean ..." links our private voice to the language community of the "we" ("MO" 291). "That this is first person reflects the way that the procedure depends upon our ear or voice" (291). "That the expression is plural ... shows that this is never a purely 'subjective' matter, never a merely private judgment, for it is a seeking after objectivity, an affirmation of community" (292). In the language community, one has to test his or her own voice in the face of the other; this is a "projection of our words, in an ongoing aspiration towards the common" (293). Standish here emphasizes the ongoing process of projection, not a retrospective recounting of one's own past; and hence, the universal, if there be such a thing, is to be understood as something always still to be achieved. Standish is attuned also, in keeping with the commitments of Cavell, to "Measures of exposure and vulnerability [as] means of access to the nature of the wrestling of philosophers" (294). This is an indication of the precariousness and instability of the self, which defies our aspiration toward the authentic, secure core of the self. This is related to Cavell's serious take on the issue of skepticism in philosophy – regarding our knowledge of an external world and, more essentially for Cavell, our knowledge of other minds. These are dimensions that Standish thinks are missing from Rorty's private irony and his flat rejection of metaphysics.

Tonality is a sort of hub around which Cavell's idea of philosophy as autobiography, his ordinary language philosophy, and his Emersonian perfectionism meet one another. It is inseparable from what Cavell means by voice in philosophy. The perspective of tonality also makes us reconsider the meaning of writing in the first person singular. What kind of voice is called for in order to achieve universality, and what kind of universality would that be? What is the style of "personal" writing through which philosophy's universal force is reinforced or, better, released, not lessened? And, conversely, what is the nature of a concept of the universal sufficient to release the self from its self-contained narrative? To respond to these questions, and to show that finding one's voice is more than a matter of self-discovery and self-edification, we need to go back to some crucial tenets of Cavell's ordinary language philosophy.

"Aesthetic Problems of Modern Philosophy"

The Spirit of the Age is not easy to place, ontologically or empirically; and it is idle to suggest that creative effort must express its age, either because that cannot fail to happen, or because a new effort can create a new age. Still, one knows what it means when an art historian says, thinking of the succession of plastic styles, "not everything is possible in every period." And that is equally true for every person and every philosophy. But then one is never sure what is possible until it happens; and when it happens it may produce a sense of revolution, of the past escaped and our problem solved – even when we also know that one man's solution is another man's problem. (*MWM* 73)

A further guidepost for an alternative reading of Cavell's philosophy as autobiography in the manner that Standish describes can be found in "Aesthetic Problems of Modern Philosophy." In this essay, Cavell attempts to explore an alternative way of doing philosophy (of dealing with philosophical problems), based upon the resemblance between aesthetic judgment, Wittgenstein, and ordinary language philosophy. He tries to make the medium of philosophy "a significant problem for aesthetics" (*MWM* 74). The target in the first part of this essay is a false conception of aesthetic criticism. He begins with a debate among art critics concerning the paraphraseability of metaphors and idioms (including those in poetry) and the views of language that accompany this. The debate turns on assumptions about the "cores" and "essences" of a poem "that are not reached by the paraphrase" (76–77), and it relates to the quest for revealing its true meaning. The quest for such definitiveness in pointing to the object, and the kind of reductivism that accompanies this, Cavell says, can been seen in philosophy (77). Such a metaphorical expression as "Juliet is the sun" is for sure paraphraseable, but this phrase is not a true or false claim (80). An idiom such as "The mind is brushed by sparrow wings" cannot be paraphrased. The expression itself is obscure. It evokes an atmosphere – "describing more or less elaborately a particular day or evening, a certain place and mood and gesture, in whose presence the line in question comes to seem a natural expression, the only expression" (81). Whether paraphraseable or not, both metaphor and idiom are, Cavell writes, meaningful, a claim that again illustrates his anti-essentialist and anti-reductionalist view of language.

Cavell considers also the parallel case in music in respect of the distinction between tonality and atonality. Thus, in making the remark, somewhat provocatively, that "atonal music is really tonal" (*MWM* 83), his point is that we would do better to describe in detail the particular ways in which we are and are not engaged in hearing the details of a particular difficult musical work rather than deciding according to some formula or definition that it is or is not tonal. With an allusion to Wittgenstein's observation that "the *speaking* of language is part of an activity, or of a form of life" (*Investigations*, §23), Cavell makes the claim that the "language of tonality is part of a particular form of life" – "particular ways of being trained to perform [music] and to listen to it" (84). In a later essay in *Must We Mean*, "Music Discomposed," it becomes apparent that what Cavell means by tonality is something different from formal tonal structure. Tonality is more closely related to taste, taste in aesthetic judgment, on the part both of artists and of their audience, in virtue of its "partialness" (*MWM* 206). For us to trust our taste and to express it involves a risk: we must take a chance. We stake ourselves in expression, stake ourselves in what we mean. "The task of the modern artist, as of the modern man, is to find something he can be sincere and serious in: something he can mean. And he may not at all" (212). To find the right tone, in the right moment, and through the right medium, is something in which one's aesthetic judgment is at stake. Thus sensing an atmosphere and being attuned to things – the tone of voice, the tone of text – is a significant aspect of doing philosophy for Cavell, and as we shall see in more detail later, it is the crucial component of philosophy as autobiography.

Furthermore, Cavell shows in this essay that philosophy is not a matter of problem-solving. Rather it is a matter of "resolution" – a Wittgensteinian process of bringing back philosophy into our form of life, "putting our souls back into our bodies" (*MWM* 84). Cavell calls this the resolution of a (traditional) philosophical problem and "the goal" of Wittgenstein's particular mode of criticism (84–85). Later Wittgenstein makes it clear that the problems of life and the problems of philosophy are "solved only when they disappear and answers are arrived at only when there are no longer questions – when, as it were, our accounts have cancelled them" (*MWM* 85). Resolution of a problem takes place when "perspicuous representation" is made possible – when one can see the world holistically and see things clearly in the round (85). This process is not along a path that is linear or smooth: it is intermittent and continual. For Wittgenstein and for Cavell, psychoanalytic therapy is inseparable from the method of philosophy. Such a method extends and expands: it involves an open-ended set of techniques, encountering new problems in new ways. Again, this therapeutic drive comes to be seen as an essential component of philosophy as autobiography. When the resolution takes place in one's life,

there is no longer any question or problem which your words would match. You have reached conviction, but not about a proposition; and consistency, but not in a theory. You are different, what you recognize as problems are different, your world is different ... And this is the sense, the only sense, in which what a work of art means cannot be said. Believing it is seeing it. (*MWM* 86)

When a therapeutic moment comes in your life, it visits you as a matter of *conviction*: the way you look at the world is transformed. "[T]he claim to severe philosophical advance entails a reconception of the subject, a specific sense of revolution" (*MWM* 86). Cavell reconfigures "the form of account"; it alters "the way we look at things" (86). Autobiographical writing for Cavell, as we shall see later, is exactly a testament to these alternative forms of accounting for one's life, a continual shifting in the way the world is seen.

In the second part of the essay, Cavell delves in more detail into the nature of aesthetic judgment and how it informs his ordinary language philosophy. Aesthetic judgment models the claims of ordinary language philosophy, its "characteristic appeal to what 'we' say and mean, or cannot or must say or mean" (86). Aesthetic judgment is a judgment without a governing rule or conclusiveness, and yet this does not mean that it lacks rationality. Referring to Kant, Cavell says that aesthetic judgment is conditioned by our being subjective and by our taste (88): "The problem of the critic, as of the artist, is not to discount his subjectivity, but to include it; not to overcome it in agreement, but to master it in exemplary ways" (94). Paul Standish points out that the "denial of subjectivity" is often taken to be a mark of philosophy, accompanied by unfailing objectivity, and that this also implies a "repression of aesthetics."[3] Cavell's endeavor of reconstruction in philosophy is to reclaim the subject in philosophy, subjectivity as a matter of voice. Cavell connects this subjective element of aesthetic judgment with the "'psychologizing' of logic" and with Wittgenstein's undoing of the "psychologizing of psychology" (*MWM* 91). (Wittgenstein weakens the line between psychology and logic, and he psychologizes the world.) As Standish explains this, Cavell's ordinary language philosophy is supported by Wittgenstein's endeavor of depsychologizing psychology and its attempt to overcome any one-tracked, metaphysical dichotomization of the inner and the outer, on which rest also false views of the subjective and the objective.[4] A proper appreciation of aesthetics provides a way beyond a false dichotomy between the subjective and the objective: "aesthetics is a mode of 'depsychologising' psychology, or retrieving the

---

[3] Paul Standish, "Public and Private: Aesthetics, Education, and Depsychologising Psychology," in *Biteki no mono: no kyoikuteki eikyo ni kansuru rironnteki bunkahikakuteki kenkyu* (*A Theoretical and Cultural-Comparative Study on Educational Influences of the Aesthetic*), ed. Y. Imai, Final Report (Tokyo: Society for the Promotion of Science, 2005), 23.

[4] Paul Standish, "'Nothing but sounds, ink-marks' – Is Nothing Hidden? Must Everything Be Transparent?" in *Yearbook of the Danish Philosophy Association* 51/1 (2018), 71–91.

psychological life from the effects of psychology."[5] That it is subjective
does not mean that it is simply individualistic or that it lacks logic. Rather
it implies that psychology is there in the way the world is: subjectivity
already structures the world. Paradoxical though it may seem, subjectivity and taste are conditions for the achieving of universality: meaning
what we say, and saying what we mean, is a move in the achieving of "the
universal voice" (*MWM* 89) – my aesthetic judgment is an appeal to
other people, for all people. Here again Cavell says: "Kant's 'universal
voice' is, with perhaps a slight shift of accent, what we hear recorded in
the philosopher's claims about 'what we say'" (94). This is the fated
arrogance of philosophy – a matter of belief that "if we could articulate
[what we should say when] fully we would have spoken for all men, found
the necessities common to us all" (96). The sense of necessity declared
here is inextricable from the "matter of the ways a judgment is supported,
the ways in which conviction in it is produced" (93).

Cavell concludes this essay by emphasizing three features of ordinary
language philosophy that have common ground with aesthetic judgment.
First, the philosophical claim to voice what we say is not a matter of
argument and counter-argument but of how other people hear what rings
true to me: my voice effects a refinement of examples that themselves
become data. Moreover, it is not being suggested that evidence of how
others use an expression should make me, as ordinary language philosopher, simply withdraw my own sense of its meaning and use: the
response from others has its greatest bearing when it succeeds in producing new cases or deepening examples that show me that I would not say
what I have said "we" say (*MWM* 95). Hence, second, disagreement is
crucial in the procedures of ordinary language philosophy. Here disagreement is not a matter of counter-argument or of "disconfirming":
"it is as much a datum for philosophizing as agreement is" (95). Third,
Cavell says that "ordinary language philosophy is about whatever ordinary language is about" (95). This implies that ordinary language philosophy, unlike linguistics, is concerned with the means of our thought and
world, what makes the world possible. We cannot detach ourselves from
language. There is no limit to the range of ordinary language. It is
endlessly extendable, always beyond our control. These are the features
that apply to language in general.

In all these three related aspects of ordinary language philosophy, what
is important is to test one's voice, the voice of the "I," to risk it, in the face
of others, as the voice of the "we." The ordinary language philosopher

[5] Standish, "Public and Private," 25.

says: "Look and find out whether you can see what I see, wish to say what I wish to say" (*MWM* 95–96). All he can do is to "express, as fully as he can, his world, and attract our undivided attention to our own" (96). Standish explains this dimension of Cavell's ordinary language philosophy as follows: "In expressing my judgement, I am, as it were, *speaking for you*, not to override you but to find objectivity with you, with the aspiration to a kind of universality. Objectivity in the realm of the aesthetic depends crucially on this public discourse."[6] Standish also indicates that in this passage of creating public discourse, the objectivity to be achieved is not known beforehand. "The *polis* depends upon the articulation that its members can achieve; this is the kind of objectivity that the idea of the *polis* admits."[7] The inseparability of the aesthetic and ordinary language philosophy is thus characterized by the mutual testing of the voice of the "I" (as that of the "we"). This is, I shall argue in the latter half of this chapter, exactly what Cavell enacted in his autobiographical writings.

From *A Pitch of Philosophy* to *Little Did I Know*

Revisiting *A Pitch of Philosophy*:

A formative idea in planning these lectures was to pose the question whether, or how, philosophy's arrogance is linked to its ambivalence toward the autobiographical, as if something internal to the importance of philosophy tempts it to self-importance. (PP 3)

I propose here to talk about philosophy in connection with something I call the voice, by which I mean to talk at once about the tone of philosophy and about my right to take that tone; and to conduct my talking, to some unspecified extent, anecdotally, which is more or less to say, autobiographically. (PP 3–4)

In most books, the *I*, or first person, is omitted; in this it will be retained; that, in respect to egotism, is the main difference. We commonly do not remember that it is, after all, always the first person that is speaking. I should not talk so much about myself if there were anybody else whom I knew as well. Unfortunately, I am confined to this theme by the narrowness of my experience. Moreover, I, on my side, require of every writer, first or last, a simple and sincere account of his own life, and not merely what he has heard of other men's lives; some such account as he would send to his kindred from a distant land.[8]

Let us now examine how the crucial aspects of Cavell's ordinary language philosophy and its inseparability from aesthetics are developed

---

[6] *Ibid.*, 24.   [7] *Ibid.*

[8] *Walden and Other Writings of Henry David Thoreau*, ed. Brooks Atkinson (New York: Modern Library, 1992), 3.

later in his autobiographical writings and how they are illustrated, given substance, and enacted in these writings.

The first chapter in *A Pitch of Philosophy*, "Philosophy and the Arrogation of Voice," is a good starting point. The chapter begins with the passage quoted above about the intricate relationship between philosophy's quest for universality, on the one hand, and the autobiographical element of voice, on the other hand. This enigmatic passage is gradually unpacked by the autobiographical account of Cavell's youth, his relation to his father and mother, and of how he underwent a change of career, from being a musician to a philosopher. And with these detailed descriptions of his past, Cavell demonstrates what he considers to be "philosophy as autobiography" (*PP* 44) or "philosophical autobiographies" (3). But there are some distinctive features to the idea of philosophy as autobiography. What makes Cavell's writing more than personal narrative, and what makes it philosophical (and universal)?

In line with Thoreau's words, Cavell's philosophy is first-person. The "I" in his writing is not, however, the voice of egotism. In illustration, Cavell quotes from Emerson's "Self-Reliance" the episode of the "nonchalant boy" who, apparently in an "irresponsible" air, judges in his own voice the world to be "good, bad, interesting, silly, eloquent, troublesome" (*PP* 34); and Emerson's remark: "He would utter opinions on all passing affairs, which being seen to be not private but necessary, would ink like darts into the ear of men, and put them in fear" (quoted in *PP* 34). Cavell interprets this scene as an illustration of the voice of "neutrality" – the voice through which you remember "who or what you are before you are known to the world, accountable" (*PP* 34), before you become "fixated, finalized" (35). This echoes Emerson's idea of representativeness: it is each of us, as "I," who has a responsibility to represent humanity. Though the term "neutrality" is not identical to "universality," the idea here resounds with the aforementioned remark of Emerson's: "The deeper he dives into his privatest, secretest presentiment, to his wonder he finds this is the most acceptable, most public, and universally true." And in this episode of the nonchalant boy, Cavell makes it explicit that "neutrality *as an achievement* is of one in recounting one's past" (*PP* 34, my italics). Neutrality is a matter of "becoming what you are" by recounting your past. This is anything but identifying the authentic source of yourself in a retrospective way: it is a projective experiment involving the testing of your words in the language community. Cavell calls this the act of "autobiographizing, signing the world" (34).

In Cavell's case, this autobiographizing has an element of the "work of mourning" (*PP* 36), as a therapeutic endeavor to be born again, to regain "my right to exist, to have a birth," a birth from his father and mother. (Here he connects the clinical with the critical, *PP* 8, 31.) This is an act simultaneously of "stealing" and of "inheriting" the words of his parents, of "translating" their language (38) – or, to borrow Thoreau's phrase, an act in the acquisition of the "father tongue" (40). The father tongue is not a dead, distant language (as it is surprisingly translated in the Japanese version of *A Pitch of Philosophy*, *PP* 74), but a continuous endeavor of enriching and translating the mother tongue, to create moments of rebirth. Finding one's voice cannot simply be a negation of the past: it becomes a question of how you can return the axe you borrow with a sharpened edge, as Thoreau says. You find your own voice, in this state of neutrality, through a "discontinuous reconstitution of what has been said, a recounting of the past, autobiographizing, deriving words for yourself" (*PP* 41).

Thus Cavell's autobiographical writing does not simply record the events of his past but illustrates and substantiates the Emersonian (and Kantian) theme of achieving neutrality, commonness and universality, of achieving it by beginning with the subjective voice of the "I." Founding, if there is any, is finding, which is to say, "finding together through the projection of our words, in an ongoing aspiration toward the common" (Standish, "MO" 293). If there is any "proof" of the degree of universality, it is only given through such testing and projecting of our language in the eyes of others. The private here is anything but a matter of self-possession: rather it is a way toward self-transcendence, to release ourselves from our "desire to grasp" (*LDIK* 533).

Questions may still be raised concerning the nature and style of philosophical autobiography. If a philosopher writes about his own past, would his writing therefore qualify as philosophical autobiography? To answer these questions I would like, in the next section, to examine Cavell's own autobiographical writing and see in what ways it might qualify as philosophy as autobiography: how far is it a demonstration of his own Emersonian thesis about the relationship between the private and the universal (the neutral), and between philosophy and autobiography? How far does it reveal the nature of the "arrogance" that Cavell claims to be linked to philosophy's ambivalence toward the autobiographical?

Little Did I Know: The Unknowability of the Self

My bargain with myself from the beginning has been to write here of the past essentially from memory, and to articulate memories, however unpromising in appearance, whenever I could, with some idea of how just these events and images have led to, or shaped, a reasonable life nevertheless also devoted to a certain ambition for philosophical writing, or what is meant as such. (*LDIK*516)

The solution of the problem of life is seen in the vanishing of the problem (Wittgenstein, 6.521). (*MWM* 85)

In a way, *Little Did I Know* most thoroughly demonstrates – indeed performs – the connection between the aesthetic judgment and OLP. In its subtle and narrative description of his life and thought, Cavell conveys what might be called the inner landscape of his life, that of his subjective self. If we read this work in a Cavellian way (which is to say, by following the procedures of his ordinary language philosophy that germinated in *Must We Mean*) and, in the process, experience vicariously the passage of his life, we can see most concretely the terrain that the perspective of this "I" unfolds; and we can hear its distinctive first-person tonality. This "I" is intertwined with the "we," revealing a landscape of the subjective self that is not narcissistic or self-contained but is to be tested and opened to others – to the public, to the universal. Eventually it gives us a hint about how the overcoming of the metaphysical dichotomization of the subjective and the objective, the inner and the outer, is to be achieved through Cavell's testament of his voice.

Little Did I Know is in a sense a provocative project in that Cavell not only claims to combine autobiography with philosophy, but also himself practices philosophy *as* autobiography. Indeed, in this book, Cavell describes and discloses events from his own past in amazing detail. A reader sometimes needs to be patient in the process of reading this book, sometimes being at a loss as to what she can learn from it, questioning the point of reading the narrative of a single philosopher's life. How is it to be distinguished from a self-explanatory account of a personal life? No wonder if a reader can misread this as a writing on self-discovery and self-reflection.

In a sense, *Little Did I Know* is a demonstration of what was announced in *A Pitch of Philosophy*. There are some distinctive features of the book – in respect especially to the tonality of the text. Many particular episodes seem on the surface to be accidental, and yet as the story moves on, some of them turn out to be, as it were, fatal. The path of one's life is not linear, and the problems of life cannot be fully solved. The book is characterized by inconsistency, uncertainty, and unpredictability, and yet, overall there is a coherence. The life he describes is one of reconciliation with situations, partial and faltering, of course. A reader hears the occasional tone of boredom from the text but then the moment of a turning, which, it seems, testifies to "the ordinariness of the extraordinary" (*LDIK* 374). The text consists of a strange mixture of, or is written on the border between, the insignificant and the significant, the personal and the philosophical. Cavell was uncertain of himself as a child and as a youth, even as an adult, but writing this autobiography here and now, in his early eighties, is of the order of a process of salvation of the soul, or, in Cavell's own words, "a transcendental rescue in, or from, our words" (523). The book contains none of that familiar, conventional autobiographical style, where the writer looks back on his past with partial regret but mostly in self-satisfaction, and with a tone of self-exoneration. This autobiography has more to do with the "therapeutic impulse" of ancient philosophy, "leading the soul up and out of a cave or deeper into a dark wood, in both cases eventually toward light" (514).

As the double structure of the book helps to show, writing autobiography is not simply a matter of tracing memories. And as the very title of the book *Little Did I Know* intimates, when Cavell says that he wishes "to articulate memories," he does not mean to write with certainty about what happened in the past, or about who he was or had been. The text is characterized by a tone of uncertainty and precariousness. It is written not for "argumentation" – that is, in order to prove something – but for "conviction" (*LDIK* 344). *Little Did I Know* certainly illustrates and performs the writing style that was hinted at in *Must We Mean*. This is the very style that demonstrates "philosophy as the achievement of the unpolemical" (*PP* 22). In other words, it is not written in order retrospectively to secure his identity, or to ascertain the correctness of his memory. The present self and the past self call upon each other, as if to be in dialogue, to project the self toward its future: there is no continuity of identity as is typically presumed in autobiography. The prevailing tone is that of "disruption" (*LDIK* 522). Rather than being written on the basis of a routine assumption of perception ("conventional, unquestioned, serving merely to recall, not to reconsider"), this particular memoir is written for "liberation" (518). I do not think that it can quite be said that it is written in the spirit of the Emerson who affirms: "I simply experiment, an endless seeker with no Past on my back,"[9] but the book is mindful of the need for "learning to walk away" (*LDIK* 499).

How does *Little Did I Know* then help the reader answer the question concerning what makes Cavell's writing more than personal narrative, and what makes it philosophical (universal)? Toward the end of the book, Cavell revisits the example of Emerson's nonchalant boy, with its idea of neutrality to be achieved as the mark of objectivity (*LDIK* 531).

[9] *The Essential Writings of Ralph Waldo Emerson*, ed. Brooks Atkinson (New York: Modern Library, 2000), 260.

We observed the Kantian element of subjectivity and universality in *Must We Mean*. In contrast to the Kantian idea of objectivity and universality, Cavell restates in this book that Emerson's universality is "never ... guaranteed a priori by the conditions of there being a knowable world of things, but proposes a task for each of us in each utterance" (531). If there is anything to be called neutral or universal, it is gained through "onward thinking," by "the self as on a path" (499).

The tone of uncertainty and unknowability is paradoxical, especially if the term "autobiography" is associated with the notion of autonomy, a concept affiliated with security and rationality. The self (or the selves) of Cavell that appears in the text – not only in the past, but even now when he is writing the text – is far from what is imagined in philosophy as the autonomous self: it is more vulnerable, insecure, and yet more receptive to the voice of multiple others (including the other selves within himself). Thus, he achieves the replacement of the subject of philosophy as he announced in *Must We Mean*.

Writing philosophy as autobiography is the experimental process of learning to live with skepticism (*LDIK* 528) – with the "terror of inexpressiveness" (452) and with a "horror of understanding" (525). What motivates Cavell's writing is the fated human condition of "denial" of the other and "interest in the world withdrawn to the point of chronic boredom, lost in lovelessness" (514). In response to this skeptical condition, and in order to regain our sense of bearing in the world, we cannot resort to the "a priori, the necessary and universal" beyond language. He writes:

Analytical philosophers do not preoccupy themselves professionally with, for example, my relation to my power of speech, with speech as confrontation, hence with the ineluctably moral fact of assertion, with my declaring my standing in disturbing the world with each of my words; nor with my mortality, my knowledge that I am finite, that my words must, in each prompting to utterance, come to or be brought to an end. This cannot be a matter merely of style, any more than it is a matter of style that analytical philosophy does not habitually veer toward an interest in theology. (*LDIK* 537)

Little Did I Know in this sense is a testament of his lifelong resistance to the impersonality of philosophy[10] and to his identification of aesthetic judgment as the crucial component of his ordinary language philosophy. It is his expression of his "unappeasable wish or need to say 'we,'" showing that "the matter of 'speaking for' is never an epistemological certainty but something like a moral claim, an arrogation of right, which

---

[10] See Standish, "Public and Private," 23.

others may grant or question or refuse" (432). The book as a whole can then be reconsidered as a trial of this private voice of the "I" in the eyes of the "we": it records assiduous and unresigned efforts of "making myself comprehensible to those of good enough will" in the face of "public incomprehensibility" (443). In testing his voice of the "I" in the eye of the other, he risks the chance of his voice not being heard or understood. Here a division between the private and the public is impossible: the achievement of the public is already initiated in the private.

Finding Perfect Pitch: The Autobiographical Passage from *Must We Mean* to *Little Did I Know*

Coming back to *Must We Mean* after undergoing the reading of *Little Did I Know*, we now realize that Cavell's whole endeavor is to reconstruct philosophy radically. *Must We Mean* serves the crucial role, along this autobiographical path, of originating such a view. We now see that philosophy as autobiography is not simply a matter of the subjective self and is more than a matter of self-education. I raised at the start the question of how Cavell's autobiographical writing, with its distinctive tonality, can be rescued from familiar misreadings, and I asked what might demonstrate that kind of autobiography to be inseparable from philosophy. In response, the tonality of *Little Did I Know* has shown that Cavell's autobiographical writing involves not only self-education, but also a calling into question of what we call "philosophy." It shows us what kind of commitment to the universal philosophy needs and why the subjective element is crucial in this. The question of his own personal voice is inseparable from the voice of Emersonian philosophy that has been suppressed in America. It is, by contrast, institutionalized philosophy itself that has suppressed Emerson's voice, with its fated arrogance – arrogance in its claims of universality, on the one hand, and arrogance produced by its denial of the other, and repression of the personal voice, on the other. The role of philosophy is to remember the voice that has been suppressed: "If there is such a task as remembering the present, the task is philosophy's – as if we chronically forget to live" (*LDIK* 519). Regaining the tonality of one's voice, the voice of the "I," in philosophy, is a justification of its place in the language community of philosophers, whom Cavell wants to call his "we." Cavell's autobiographical search for himself, the self that is yet to come, is a part of the assiduous process of "philosophy's self-criticism" (500).

Cavell's philosophy as autobiography is not intended merely for "self-education" in the private realm, as Rorty says, though it is surely initiated by each self: rather, the process of autobiographizing the world is always and already on the way to the creation of the public; it is a participation in the language community. Hence, the process is already that of *achieving* universality. And, hence, it staunchly resists the dominant narrative turn, in which the focus is given to the self, the inner self, and the true self retrospectively. Cavell's philosophy as autobiography demonstrates his anti-foundationalist view of the self. It enables us to resist what has become the ideology of narrative, which becomes obsessive in its quest for identity and continuity. Contingency is there at the heart of self-discovery and in the process of meaning-making. For Cavell, unlike Rorty, creativity and reengagement with language are to be understood as already started in early childhood; and conversely, adults, grownups, will continue to have their fatal relationship with the native, the mother tongue. It is not exactly that the mother tongue comes first, and then the father tongue later. The education of the mother tongue already involves the education of the father tongue. As a more provocative implication for education, Cavell's philosophy as autobiography will side with the education of the "nonchalant boy." This is the exemplar of the child whose voice is to represent humanity – echoing Emerson's words, quoted by Cavell: "I stand here for humanity" (*LDIK* 538). This is the kind of character that can bear up under the weight of, and, hence, with the pain of, fulfilling his responsibility to contribute his voice to the world and hence, learning to bear up under pain, in silence (541) – that is to say, learning to speak unpolemically. To learn to speak here is to "discover the possession of a virtue" (543) – the virtue of silence, receptivity, and acknowledgment. This is different from child-centered education in which the freedom of children is foregrounded. The utterance of the words "I think" is already embedded in the voice of the "we" – the "we" that is yet to come. This is the unflagging position throughout Cavell's career, originally proposed in *Must We Mean*.

In the light of Cavell's demonstration of philosophy as autobiography, the central focus of the education of voice is to inspire students to find their "perfect pitch" (*PP* 47, 48) – achieving universality here and now. They do not fully conform to given criteria, and yet it is from within such criteria that they bring forth their words. Cavell acknowledges the fact that the "feature of perfect pitch," as one of the conditions of philosophy as autobiography, is "apt to be the hardest to recognize, and the most variously or privately ratified" (47). And yet, once it is hit upon, it is a mark of "taking steps, walking on, on one's own" and the "attestation of one's autonomous power of perception" (47). The sense of "autonomous" here is, of course, different from that of rational autonomy in the liberal tradition: rather it is the acknowledgment of the singularity and separateness of one's power of existence. This is a therapeutic procedure and adds to Cavell's philosophy a dimension of philosophy as therapy. It is manifested with the conviction that "my morality, my knowledge that I am finite, that my words must, in each prompting to utterance, come to or be brought to an end" (*LDIK* 537). In ordinary language philosophy, it is already and always found in educative conversation, as he initially suggested in *Must We Mean*, and then found again in his own recounting of episodes from experience, excerpts from memory (*LDIK* 491). *Little Did I Know* itself is a book written in search of and testing perfect pitch, to the resonances of which we can attune ourselves. Little did he know in 1969 that he would find such a voice forty years later.

10 The Finer Weapon
Cavell, Philosophy, and Praise

Victor J. Krebs

> We stake our hopes thus on indirectness ... for the Criticism of the future ...
> May it not then be but a question, for the fullness of time, of the finer
> weapon, the sharper point, the stronger arm, the more extended lunge?
>
> Henry James[1]

Prelude

Must We Mean What We Say? is a book of essays, but we might just as
well think of it as a tray of robust seedlings that will grow strong to
become the luscious flora bequeathed to American philosophy by one
of the deepest and most original minds in the second half of the twentieth
century. These eclectic essays stretch from ordinary language and
meaning – with Austin and Wittgenstein – to aesthetics and tragedy
and revelation – with Beckett, Shakespeare, and Kierkegaard – to
knowledge and the problem of other minds. The book accurately pre-
ambles the singular and prolific path Stanley Cavell has trodden, and the
astounding range of subjects where he has left his unmistakable mark.

The urgency of the book's title, "Must we mean what we say?," already
signals the ethical (and poetic, even sometimes religious) tone that runs
through the book and will pervade Cavell's thinking throughout his life.
While Wittgenstein had characterized philosophy as a battle "against the
bewitchment of our intelligence by means of language," for Cavell the
battle is also (with and) against *desire*, that bewitches us and loses
our way, causing us to speak without knowing or meaning what
we say.[2] Our main adversary, he points out, is "self-obscurity"
(*LDIK* 515); our underlying quest, therefore, self-knowledge, or – more

Thanks to Byron Davies and Gordon Bearn for suggestions and improvements.

[1] Henry James, quoted in *PDAT* 96 (originally from the Introduction to Shakespeare's
Tempest, ed. Sydney Lee (New York: Harper, 1906–07).
[2] Ludwig Wittgenstein, *Philosophical Investigations*, rev. 4th edn, trans. G.E.M. Anscombe,
P.M.S. Hacker, and Joachim Schulte, ed. Hacker (Malden, MA: Wiley-Blackwell, 2009),
§109; hereafter cited parenthetically as *PI*.

precisely – Emersonian perfectionism's "unattained but attainable self" (*CW* 13). Engagement with language becomes a task, as Cavell puts it, that will involve risks and, "if not costs, blood" (*PDAT* 187). As these essays begin to show, in his hands, thinking philosophically will become existential and passionate.

"Outside the womb"

> But you grow if you stand still in the greatest doubt, and therefore steadfastness in great doubt is a veritable flower of life.
>
> Carl G. Jung, *The Red Book*[3]

As Cavell explains in his Foreword, these essays are driven by a new awareness in modernist culture, about the need for each discipline to reassess its identity and question the very criteria that ground it. In his words: "The essential fact of ... the modern lies in the relation between the present practice of an enterprise and the history of that enterprise, in the fact that this relation has become problematic" (*MWM* xxxiii). Specifically for philosophy, that confrontation with the past involves rethinking its relation to literature and to literary criticism. "My wish," he writes in *Philosophy the Day after Tomorrow*, is "to reinvest the ground of philosophy with the concern for the conditions of possibility of the aesthetic" (*PDAT* 83). His interest will range, as we see in *Must We Mean*, from literature all the way to art criticism and music. Not much later, he will bring film into philosophy, as the latest of the great arts, in *The World Viewed*.

In the modern, Cavell observes in *Philosophy the Day after Tomorrow*, history can no longer be seen as something we have merely left behind. The future, Benjamin would say, is "locked in undiscovered aspects of the past" (*PDAT* 85). So the past must be acknowledged and integrated into one's own consciousness of the present. Modernist philosophy will thus acquire a personal inflection for Cavell, since, as he says, "the past" is now precisely what the present needs to come to terms with, before it can discern or come to see what it is for itself. In his own words, it "refers to one's own past, to what is past, or what has passed, *within oneself*. One could say that in the modernist situation 'past' loses its temporal accent and means anything 'not present.' Meaning what one says becomes a matter of *making oneself present to oneself*" (*MWM* xxxiii, my italics). It is no longer tradition that matters but the way it can evolve in the present

---

[3] Carl G. Jung, *The Red Book: Liber Novus*, ed. Sonu Shamdasani (New York: W.W. Norton, 2009), 301.

practice. The resistance on the part of professional philosophy to acknowledge this modernist shift – we might want to say philosophy's return to itself (or to the self) of philosophy – is a failing that Cavell redresses by following his own intuition, that what he was doing was indeed still philosophy, even if its doubts and dangers seemed perhaps unrecognizable as such. Rather than a reason to leave it behind (as so many others around him had done, when faced with institutional disapproval of their singular sensibilities), their dissonance with his philosophy is, for Cavell, instead, a reason to pursue it, even if (or precisely because) it means having to stand steadfast in its greatest doubt. In a veritable asceticism of the intellect, unmoored from all received criteria, Cavell finds a path toward a kind of insight that would be impossible in any other way. As he once said, it is "in that dissonance where the gold is, and when you find a thread, then you hope that at the end of that thread there will be a gate opened for you."[4] One could see these essays as the first step in following that hope.

But the personal inflection in Cavell's writing comes also, or is rather reinforced, with Austin, from whom he discovered the ethical import of the appeal to ordinary language, when he saw how easy it was to not know one's own words in speaking; "whether I am," he reflects, "for example, expressing a desire or an intention or a decision or revealing a fantasy or echoing an opinion or repeating a rumor or accepting a commitment" (Caracas Seminar [CS] Lecture 1). In taking up this Austinian task of appealing to ordinary language in order to come to know what one is saying, philosophy – Cavell points out – "accepts in a new way [its] ancient challenge to know oneself" (Caracas Seminar [CS] Lecture 1).

If he learned the ethical and personal import of the appeal to ordinary language from Austin, with Wittgenstein Cavell learned of its clinical or therapeutic character. It is the pathological need in philosophy to "repress the human voice" (as he describes its main problem) that concerns him, and Wittgenstein is the only one he has found, who brings the human voice back to philosophy by leading words back "from their metaphysical to their ordinary use" (*Philosophical Investigations* §116). As Cavell wrote in the Foreword to *Must We Mean*: "I might express my particular sense of indebtedness to the teaching of Austin and Wittgenstein by saying that it is from them that I learned of the possibility of making my difficulties about philosophy into topics within philosophy itself" (*MWM* xxxvi). But on this point, again, he found himself at odds with the analytic philosophers of the time. They were not only deaf to the

---

[4] Stanley Cavell, Caracas Seminar, 1998 (unpublished), Lecture 1; hereafter cited parenthetically as CS.

emerging cultural demands that animated Cavell's modernist quest, they seemed also intent on obliterating anything that could challenge their narrow strictures, or fail to follow their particular understanding of the philosophical practice. Their unwillingness to listen to anyone speaking from outside the criteria consolidated in their scientistic conception of philosophy was, as Cavell reports, responsible for much "unhappy love" (*MWM* xxxvi) in the profession.

Cavell's essays were ahead of their time, and they were, at that point, perhaps just as inaccessible for philosophy as Beethoven's later sketches had been for the music of his time. These had had to be jotted, in Cavell's mind, "just for saving, just to await [their] company" (*MWM* 201) "both because," as he added ten years later in *The Claim of Reason*, "not all ideas are ready for use upon their appearance (because not ready ever in any but their right company), and also because not all are usable in their initial appearance, but must first, as it were, grow outside the womb" (*CR* 5). Thus orphaned before birth, Cavell's seedlings had to fend for themselves, for "Nothing we now have to say, no *personal* utterance," he declared, "has its meaning conveyed in the conventions and formulas we now share" (*MWM* 201). They had to recover or forge the conditions of their own intelligibility, not in their allegiance or kinship with what was present, but through their very estrangement, in terms primarily of an absence made good in them.

Idiosyncrasies

Don't be more to yourself than the pedestal
in which you raise the statue of your being
Everything else impoverishes, because it is poor
Fernando Pessoa[5]

In its identification with science, analytic philosophy sought to keep out personal interest, affect – subjectivity at large – as incompatible with its search for knowledge. For that reason Cavell's continuous appeal to self-experience in his writings struck (and still strikes) some as an intrusion "easily taken as concrete evidence of disciplinary transgression, a notable lack of self-control, an unchecked tendency to self-indulgence."[6] But the personal nature of Cavell's writings was not just a narcissistic idiosyncrasy of the author, as the charge implies, but a matter of essential import

[5] "Não sê mais para ti que o pedestal / No qual ergas a státua do teu ser / Tudo mais empobrece, porque é pobre." Fernando Pessoa, *Poesia completa de Ricardo Reis* (Sao Paulo: Editora Schwarcz, 2000), 93.
[6] Áine Mahon, "Fraudulence, Obscurity and Exposure: The Autobiographical Anxieties of Stanley Cavell," in *The Philosophy of Autobiography*, ed. Christopher Cowley (University of Chicago Press, 2015), 217–36 (at 218).

for the purpose of his texts, and for the particular conception of philosophy he is vindicating:

I don't mean to be merely transgressive, I'm not interested in random change, but I have to follow where I find myself intelligible to myself, where I make sense to myself, and that is to express my dissatisfaction … I look in the culture that I am a part of for signs that express a genuine space, not exactly for hopefulness, but for the expression of pleasure, for the expression of understanding, and for the expression of commitment … When we live in a cacophony, where there is a chaos of claims, our responsibility is to find where our desire is and is not satisfied. (CS press conference, November 15)

In turning to his own experience and following it despite the derision that it encountered amongst professional philosophers, Cavell was responding to a personal imperative.

He rebukes his analytic colleagues, for having made philosophical criticism a self-absorbed, defensive, and ruthless practice, and having rather "forgotten how to praise or forgotten its value" (*MWM* xxxv). Though it is understandable that they be intent on hedging philosophy from the pre-Enlightenment vices that may be spawned from subjectivity – animism, superstition, idolatry, fanaticism, vagueness or ambiguity, etc. – Cavell believes there must be more to philosophy than merely battling against them. As he explained it three decades later in the Seminar he taught in Caracas: "What I want from Philosophy is a criticism of the Enlightenment itself, some sense of what can be overdone or misdirected in these very goals, however admirable, of rationality. I am interested, that is to say, in the misuses of rationality, as itself the cause of, also, modern grief and modern danger" (CS Lecture 2, Q&A). Cavell's work may be seen as an argument in favor not just of the positive, complementary value of subjectivity and affect in general, but of its indispensability for the philosophical task as he conceives it. It is by turning inward – by trusting, indeed loving himself enough – that Cavell will forge, in virtue of his faithfulness, the kind of thinking and the mode of philosophical criticism he seeks: "My interest, it could be said, lies in finding out what my beliefs mean, and learning the particular ground they occupy. This is not the same as providing evidence for them. One could say it is a matter of making them evident" (*MWM* 241). Considering the charge of self-indulgence frequently raised against him, it is perhaps pertinent to distinguish, with Jacques Derrida, between a (bad) narcissism that closes us, and a (good) narcissism that can, instead, make us open to the other: "There is not narcissism and non-narcissism; there are narcissisms that are more or less comprehensive, generous, open, extended. What is called non-narcissism is in general but the economy of a much more welcoming and hospitable narcissism, one that is much more open to experience of the other as other."[7] In making his beliefs evident, rather than "rendering evidence for them," Cavell's welcoming and hospitable narcissism opens room for dialogue with others, whereas the professional philosopher, refusing to listen to them, except through the filter of his own scientistic criteria, remains narcissistically locked, sealed off from the other. Forgetful of praise, Cavell said, he refuses consent and so "threatens something about your existence, threatens to render you speechless about what is most important to you" (CS Lecture 3, Q&A).

The analytic philosopher makes impossible the modernist self-reflection and the search for mutual acknowledgment that drive Cavell's thinking. As he elaborates again in *Philosophy the Day after Tomorrow*, "acceptance becomes appreciation (a mode of praise), and appreciation figures consent [... which is] a show of a readiness for change" (107). Despite the absence of acceptance and appreciation, even the lack of consent, Cavell has the courage to assume his singularity. Even though personal subjectivity may become an impediment to scientific knowledge, it is rather a means to what he seeks in philosophical thinking. What he is intent on is not rational knowledge but his own reinterpretation of it as "acknowledgment." In a time of "slogans, ideologies, psychological warfare, mass projects" – as Cavell describes the present day – the philosophy of ordinary language becomes all important, and its grounding, personal and subjective:

where words have lost touch with their sources or objects, and in a phonographic culture where music is for dreaming, or for kissing, or for taking a shower, or for having your teeth drilled, our choices seem to be those of silence, or nihilism (the denial of the value of shared meaning altogether), or statements so personal as to form the possibility of communication without the support of convention – perhaps to become the source of new convention. (*MWM* 201–02)

Cavell falls neither into the cynicism of his colleagues nor the despair of his fellow-students, who left the profession convinced there was no place for them. Rather than abandon his philosophical intuition because of the uncongeniality of his colleagues, he took it instead as a reason to speak for oneself, from oneself.

Passionate Utterance

My joy comes from the uniqueness of my emotion. My exultation comes from not having felt the presence of life before. I have never felt it.

César Vallejo[8]

---

[7] Jacques Derrida, *Points: Interviews, 1974–1994* (Stanford University Press, 1995), 199.

[8] "Mi gozo viene de lo inédito de mi emoción. Mi exultación viene de que antes no sentí la presencia de la vida. No la he sentido nunca." César Vallejo, *Obra poética completa* (Caracas: Biblioteca Ayacucho, 1985), 116–17.

And where there had been
at most a makeshift hut to receive the music,
a shelter nailed up of their darkest longing,
with an entryway that shuddered in the wind –
you built a temple deep inside their hearing.
                    Rainer Maria Rilke, "Sonnets to Orpheus"[9]

In posing the question: "must we mean what we say?," Cavell was honoring his revered teacher John L. Austin whose ordinary language philosophy he would broaden and deepen in his own thinking. Although Austin had always privileged promising over all other utterances, "as if an 'I promise' implicitly lines every act of speech, of intelligibility, as it were a condition of speech as such,"[10] for Cavell we are much more than merely "promising" creatures. We are also (and perhaps primarily) beings of passion – poetic, musical, tragic. Our debt to words is not just that of honesty and truthfulness, as it is with a simple promise; not just the accordance with conventions and social agreements. Speaking, for Cavell, demands the permanent effort to make oneself intelligible to the other, seeking both understanding and acknowledgment amidst the intense complexity and unpredictability of the erotic, that lines all our utterances.

Not only does Austin, as Cavell puts it, "lift the non-descriptive or non-constative gestures of speech to renewed philosophical interest and respectability" (*PDAT* 159); he also opens up a space where we can analyze our obliviousness to our own desires and limitations, and become aware of how we chronically get lost. In Cavell's words, we can learn to live "with the sign of our finitude."[11]

But despite his originality, Austin was not willing to take on "the issue of passion or expression in speech." Cavell comments:

Well, it's easy to say we are lost, but to determine *how* are we lost, is a further philosophical task, and that's where Wittgenstein goes beyond Austin. Austin does not want us to look into the abyss. He wants to prevent us from getting close to the temptation to throw ourselves into it. He is an Enlightenment character. But for Wittgenstein, how we *get* lost is as important to him as it is to any theologian. Lost! It's perdition, it's damnation! And lost is for Wittgenstein where philosophy begins. (CS Lecture 3, Q&A)

Austin's reticence seemed to suggest that "the passional side of utterance is more or less a detachable issue" (*PDAT* 163), something Cavell will

---

[9] Rainer Maria Rilke, "The Sonnets to Orpheus," in *The Selected Poetry of Rainer Maria Rilke*, trans. Stephen Mitchell (New York: Vintage, 1989), 225–55.

[10] Stanley Cavell, Foreword to Shoshana Felman, *The Scandal of the Speaking Body: Don Juan with J.L. Austin, or Seduction in Two Languages* (Stanford University Press, 2002), xiii.

[11] Stanley Cavell, personal communication, 1999.

reproach him for and attempt to rectify. Indeed, to propose a theory of language that rescues the performative dimension of speech and yet takes the expression of desire as merely incidental, is not only absurd but symptomatic of a commitment to the very prejudices of the Enlightenment – to what is "overdone or misdirected" in its goals of rationality – that Cavell wished to leave behind.

The moral he drew from Austin's work on the performative was that, as he said, we are "in every moment and beyond any measure recognizable to us, affecting others (and ourselves) with our words, and therefore with our silence; drawing blood from as far as they are able to reach, namely, in a word, everywhere" (CS Interview). Austin however had given up on the attempt to map the perlocutionary effects as he had mapped the illocutionary forces of speech because, as he put it, "*Any*, or almost any, perlocutionary act is liable to be brought off ... by the issuing ... of any utterance whatsoever" (*PDAT* 173). But it is precisely for that reason that Cavell considers passionate utterances to merit "as scrupulous an attention to the world of fact as the performative does," as he puts it in his lecture "The Trials of Praise" (CS Lecture 2). As he explains:

A performative utterance is an offer of participation in the order of law. And perhaps we can say: A passionate utterance is an invitation to improvisation in the disorders of desire ... From the roots of speech ... two paths spring: that of the responsibilities of implication; and that of the rights of desire. (*PDAT* 185)

Cavell's theory of passionate utterance seeks to complete the unfinished path opened by his teacher, adding to his mapping of the responsibilities of implication the determination of the rights of desire:

Both performative and passionate utterances are modes of address in which our relation to another is staked; But with passionate utterances – if I say, for example, "But you promised," or more simply, "You coward," or "I hate you" – my passion demands a response from you here and now and in kind, that is, one undefinable by convention, one in which you recognize that our future is staked. (CS Lecture 2)

Even though personal subjectivity may become an obstacle for scientific knowledge, it is all the contrary with acknowledgment. But until this reconception of philosophy's objective is itself accepted, we may simply need to prepare the ground for a later reception. As Cavell wrote at the end of "A Matter of Meaning It," what we need is "not the re-assembly of community, but personal relationship unsponsored by that community; not the overcoming of our isolation, but the sharing of that isolation – not to save the world out of love, but to save love for the world, until it is responsive again" (*MWM* 229).

Thinking as Praise

It would be foolish to attribute the crisis into which we have led to thought and not to the fact of having tried to base our life on it.

Rafael Cadenas[12]

Ah, love, let us be true to one another!

Stanley Cavell (*MWM* 229)

As he wrote in his autobiography, Cavell had lived with the "incessant perception, or imagination, of ... a world bent on denial, interest in the world withdrawn to the point of chronic boredom, lost in lovelessness" (*LDIK* 514). Lovelessness seems like an accurate characterization of the philosopher's condition, in a world where the insistence on the pursuit of objective knowledge came hand in hand with the marginalization of the affective dimension of experience. But it merely reflects or is a sequel of an original blind spot, as Cavell points out, in the empiricism that grounds the analytic conception of philosophy. Recalling what Emerson points out in his essay "Experience," Cavell remarks that when the impressions of perception are taken as detached from attraction or desire, where there is no concern for why anything makes an impression on us, philosophy cannot but conceive knowledge as a matter of conquest and possession rather than as a function of attraction and desire. Refusing "the rightful draw of our attraction, our capacity to receive the world" (*TNYUA* 88), as Cavell puts it, makes the world, instead of interesting and self-affirming, a place of "chronic boredom" (*LDIK* 514).

With Nature no longer seen as a master from whom to derive wisdom but, as Newton once said, as a hostile witness from whom to rip out the secrets it denies us, the search for knowledge becomes a form of violence, a "clutching [of] things" in order to know them, that Emerson considered "the most unhandsome part of our human condition" (*TNYUA* 86). It ignores – and ultimately shatters – "the specifically human form of attractiveness ... the rightful call we have upon one another, and that it and the world make upon one another" (86–87). "Lost in lovelessness," as Cavell says, philosophy requires indeed "the guidance of a therapeutic sort [that is] associated with the work of psychoanalysis" (*MWM* xix).

For Cavell, Melanie Klein's emphasis on the radical necessity, in human flourishing, of the capacity for gratitude or praise, and her description of the dynamics between gratitude and envy, shed light on

---

[12] "Sería insensato atribuir la crisis en la que hemos desembocado al pensamiento y no al hecho de haber pretendido fundar nuestra vida sobre él." Rafael Cadenas, *Realidad y literatura* (Caracas: Equinoccio, 1979), 91.

the emotional withdrawal and denial of analytic philosophy and its forget-fulness of praise. As for the developing child, for the philosopher "grati-tude becomes a gesture of reparation" for the separateness that stands between him and the world. The exclusion of praise that Cavell chastised his colleagues for, is expression of their refusal of the vulnerability neces-sary for self-questioning as well as a disavowal of limitation, that turns knowledge aggressive and vindictive. "Cursing the world, precisely for its not providing you a cause of praise, hence being left with a doubt that its behavior is caused by your having cursed it with a tainted love" is the logic of what concerns Cavell in skepticism (*PDAT* 109).

Cavell's response to the skepticism of his colleagues involves a conver-sion, a return to the world with affective attachment and commitment. The task is aimed at countering "our efforts to evade [desire's] tasks of creativity by disparaging our present powers and opportunities." Meaning what one says (and saying what one means) becomes a matter of acknowledging and recognizing one's own interest and desire, or as Cavell puts it, of "making one's sense present to oneself" (*MWM* xxxiii). What this critic wants, or needs, is a possession of data and descriptions and diagnoses so clear and common that apart from them neither agreement nor disagreement would be possible – not as if the problem is for opposed positions to be reconciled, but for the halves of the mind to go back together. (*MWM* 241)

Seeking to engage rather than defeat the other, the task of philosophical criticism is a shared burden, not toward the establishment of some single truth, but toward mutual understanding. For, as Cavell stresses, "In the mood of passionate exchange there is no final word, no uptake or turn down, until the line is drawn, or withdrawal is affected, perhaps in turn to be revoked" (*PDAT* 83).

Toward a Criticism of the Future

> I mean Negative Capability, that is, when a man is capable of being in uncertainties, mysteries, doubts, without any irritable reaching after fact and reason.
>
> John Keats[13]

"Thinking is not a power of knowledge but a capacity for acknowledg-ment – an avowal of vulnerability, of finitude, and mortality – a labor of love," writes Cavell in "The Trials of Praise" (CS Lecture 2). This conception of thinking is diametrically opposed to the philosophical attitude expressed in the image of knowing as penetrating phenomena

[13] Quoted in Li Ou, *Keats and Negative Capability* (London: Continuum, 2009), ix.

(as in Wittgenstein's comment in *Investigations* §90: "We feel as if we had to *penetrate* phenomena"), which involves the fantasy of there being "something hidden behind the thing," that has to be "brought to light," or "completely clarified," supposedly as we should retrieve secrets from a hostile witness.

The violence behind that image of retrieval is symptomatic, as we saw with Melanie Klein, of the refusal to accept separateness or (in the particular case of philosophy) the impossibility of indubitable knowledge. What Cavell described as the modernist intuition that inspired his work – that one's own history needs to be revisited, that "no moment of the past may be assumed without explicit assumption" (*PDAT* 99) – involves necessarily confronting and questioning its identity and self-image as a scientific enterprise.

In the *Investigations*, when at the end of all our efforts at grounding or justification we reach bedrock, and "the spade is turned" (§217), Wittgenstein may be taken to suggest that what is needed, rather than to plunge forward toward the object, is to retreat from it; not attempting to possess it, but to let it rather approach us, reflect upon us as on a black mirror where our aggression is willingly turned on our self. It involves a discipline of (both inner and outer) listening and receptiveness, attention and care. Philosophy becomes an effort "not to get anywhere else, but to find itself, where it is" (*PDAT* 98).

There is a movement behind the conscious thoughts articulated in our words, a vitality that runs through our concepts, that is silently active in our encounter with the world and with others, that can gradually generate clarity and understanding. In other words, intuitions are there to become tuitions, as Emerson would say. It is with patience and a disposition for mortification – in the sense in which Benjamin thought of the labor of brooding needed to bring a work to its idea, confronting loss and absence and limitation – that the type of criticism Cavell is proposing for philosophy becomes possible. As he writes in the Foreword of *Must We Mean*,

I understand the presence of notable, surprising anticipations to suggest something more specific about the way, or space within which, I work, which I can put negatively as occurring within the knowledge that I never get things right, or let's rather say, see them through, the first time, causing my efforts perpetually to leave things so that they can be, and ask to be, returned to. Put positively, it is the knowledge that philosophical ideas reveal their good only in stages, and it is not clear whether a later stage will seem to be going forward or turning around or stopping, learning to find oneself at a loss. (*MWM* xvii)

Coda

Rather than possession and control, or what Emerson calls "manipular efforts," the thrust required by Cavell's turn "is stronger in another strength" than that of penetration; in particular, it is effected "in the ability to be patient, to suffer"; what is needed is the cultivation of something like John Keats' "negative capability," which he defines as the capacity "of being in uncertainties, mysteries, doubts, without any irritable reaching after fact and reason"; or in the words with which James describes the kind of future criticism he envisioned, the capacity "to be differently, more strongly, more finely, struck" (CS Interview 2). Indeed, as Cavell writes, "this fineness it is that communicates the virus of suggestion, anything more than the minimum of which spoils the operation" (*PDAT* 96).

"Penetration" is no longer getting through the object in order to grasp its essence but something more akin to circling it or incubating it, until it germinates and catches on like a fever or an epidemic. It is also how Cavell sometimes described what he expected from his own writing, functioning as, we could say, "the finer weapon, the sharper point, the stronger arm, the more extended lunge" that can perform the task. Philosophy transforms thus its violent power of penetration into "a conduct of gratitude ... a specification or test of tribute" (CS Lecture 2), a reparation that makes praise again possible. Hence the importance of considering the grammar of emotion, of sharpening our sense for the logic of passionate utterances.

Philosophical criticism "need not be uncomprehending, nor always entered out of enmity" (*MWM* xxxv), as Cavell wanted to remind his analytical colleagues. Though still sharp and questioning, it can be more empathic, more welcoming and caring. But its dangers and its complexities are moral: self-deception, the resistance to one's own desire, the fear of one's own mind – in other words, Cavell's "trials of praise."

11 On Cavell's "Kierkegaard's *On Authority and Revelation*" – with Constant Reference to Austen

Kelly Jolley

One of Samuel Johnson's best mottoes reminds his reader about reminders: "Men more frequently require to be reminded than informed."[1] It is hard to hear this in the *heightened* sense that, I am sure, Johnson intended. That is, it is hard to hear this as if it were not a peculiar, backhanded compliment: We, most of us anyway, already know what we need to know, we just forget it sometimes – as though Johnson had in mind *items of information* like phone numbers and addresses, and was pointing out that we sometimes forget them.

Now, no doubt, we do forget phone numbers and addresses. But Johnson does not, and it should seem clear that he could not, have meant *that*. Why? Because, for one thing, we do have to be informed of phone numbers and addresses: our having been previously informed is a condition of our (later) being rightly said to have forgotten or to be reminded.

"What's his number again? It's gone clean out of my head." – "Oh, c'mon, I told you it twice before, it's…" That is not the sort of exchange Johnson had in mind.

And that it is not helps to show what I have in mind by a *heightened sense*: Johnson does something special with his words, the words here, something that our very familiarity with "reminded" and "informed" can hide from us. The words seem so shopworn, so exposed, that they may seem incapable of

---

[1] Samuel Johnson, *The Rambler*, no. 2, Saturday, March 24, 1749, in *The Works of Samuel Johnson, LL.D.*, vol. I (London: Henry G. Bohn, 1850), 3–4. Johnson's remark, in context, can be seen as first and foremost a reminder to himself: specifically, a reminder to himself as he "commences author" of *The Rambler*, but, generally, to himself as a human being, and so as prone to *forget* (the crucial word of the essay's opening paragraph) the practical knowledge he possesses but often fails to acknowledge. For more on Jane Austen and Samuel Johnson, a good beginning is Mary Lascelles' chapter "Reading and Response" in her remarkable *Jane Austen and Her Art* (Oxford University Press, 1939), 41–85. Lascelles notes Austen's acceptance of Johnson's "practical wisdom," and the "exceptionally caressing tone" of her references to "my dear Dr. Johnson" in her letters.

heightened use, a heightened sense, their colors too faded to arrest attention. But they can be reactivated; they can be made capable of heightened senses; Johnson finds his way to doing it in his *Rambler* essay.

To understand the heightened sense in which Johnson meant the words, we have to consider the word that, as it were, stands behind them – knowledge. If we are informed, we come to know. If we are reminded, we once knew. Johnson's motto is itself a reminder about knowledge, namely that it comes in kinds: that some knowledge is not the product of being informed, that such knowledge can go dead for us or become in various ways inaccessible – and the name for one of those ways is "forgetting." But that means there are also kinds of forgetting: but, that, surely is an old lesson in philosophy, one Plato tried to teach us, or remind us of long ago, as he sought a language adequate to the effect of Socrates' *elenchus* on the mind, a language adequate to the peculiar bewilderment in which Socratic conversation often began and, almost as often, ended.

Johnson is not reminding us of our propensity to forget things of which we have been informed. He is reminding us of our need to be reminded of things of which we were never, and in a crucial sense, of which we never can be *informed*. The things Johnson has in mind, the knowledge he has in mind, is a knowledge that we forget because it goes dead for us, it goes dead because we abandon it, or try to, live as if we had: it is a kind of knowledge required for living well but a knowledge often bitter, a knowledge we would, and often do, disown. We could call this knowledge *practical knowledge*, but the terminology is not crucial. It is the kind of knowledge that preoccupies Johnson in his essays; he returns to it again and again in them (and in his novel, *Rasselas*).

A good example of this kind of knowledge shapes an early chapter of Jane Austen's *Persuasion* (1818). Anne Elliot has arrived at Uppercross, the home of her sister, Mary, to care for Mary, who imagines herself indisposed. The rest of Anne's family, her father and sister, have relocated to Bath, an expedient made necessary by her father's spendthrift habits. Anne arrives at Uppercross, where she has visited many times before.

Anne had not wanted this visit to Uppercross, to learn that a removal from one set of people to another, though at a distance of only three miles, will often include a total change of conversation, opinion, and idea. She had never been staying there before without being struck by it ... yet with all this experience, she believed she must now submit to feel that another lesson, in the art of knowing our own nothingness beyond our own circle, was become necessary for her.[2]

---

[2] *The Oxford Illustrated Jane Austen*, ed. R.W. Chapman, vol. v (Oxford University Press, 1933), 42.

Austen achieves tremendous depth with an assured economy. Anne arrives at Uppercross already schooled: she knows that the concerns of her immediate family at Kellynch Hall will not be the concerns of the families at Uppercross: she *knows* or *knew* but yet she has, in a way, forgotten. Her remembrance of it comes by way of submission – a crucial term in Austen's vocabulary – to a fresh lesson in the art of knowing her own nothingness. Such lessons are lessons Anne can only learn for – and can only teach – herself. Others can of course say the words to us, but only we can embrace the lesson in the practical act that is their knowing, their acknowledgment. And we do not like these lessons, hence Austen's weighty choice of "submit." We submit to these lessons, we suffer them. Anne is not informed by what happens at Uppercross; Uppercross reminds her afresh of a knowledge that a long period of saturation in the cares of Kellynch had made go dead for her, had made welcomely forgettable, welcomely easy to stop acknowledging. (And it was so even for Anne – who is more mistress of this art than any other Austen leading character, except perhaps Fanny Price.)

★

Johnson's essays return obsessively to such topics as the art of knowing our own nothingness. In Johnson's heightened sense, the essays remind, they do not inform. And that is both a source of their sometimes neglect and their perennially discoverable and rediscovered freshness.

For anyone familiar with Stanley Cavell's essay, "Kierkegaard's *On Authority and Revelation*," the paragraphs above should be alive with echoes. I have discussed Johnson and Austen to reactivate various concepts central to Cavell's essay.

★

Of the essays in *Must We Mean What We Say?*, this essay is perhaps the most peculiar. It seems less unified: if it contains a doctrine, so to speak, it is one only of scattered occasions. The essay begins with an attempt to illuminate Kierkegaard's *qualitative dialectic* but then ends in hints and gestures about Kierkegaard and modern art, enticing hints and beckoning gestures, but, they are hints and gestures. I will address some of those as I finish. For now, I want to consider the beginning discussion of Kierkegaard's qualitative dialectic. My hope is to walk one path through Cavell's essay. Consider my essay a selective, investigative commentary on Cavell's.

★

Cavell approaches that discussion by first dwelling on the oddities of Kierkegaard's book, oddities to which Kierkegaard himself draws attention. The book centers on a man, a minister, Magister Adler, but it does not center on him as a biography centers on a person, although it crucially remains in contact with certain biographical episodes, and it does not center on him as an exemplar, as someone who is presented for imitation – far from it.

No, it seems that Adler matters for Kierkegaard in a *Nestroyan* way: it is Johann Nestroy who writes, "No man is good for nothing; he can always serve as a *bad* example." But that is not quite all that needs to be noted, because Adler is not a simple bad example, one that might or might not speak to me (as a reader of Kierkegaard's book), depending on my particular circumstances, the shape of my life. I cannot ignore him because I am not a minister or involved in the ministerial. I cannot ignore him because he is older or younger than I. No, Adler is at once more intimate and more estranged from me than that. Adler is a *Phenomenon* – a transparency in which an (our) age is caught. By means of him I see myself, myself as implicated in an age, as implicated in the case of Adler, however removed from him my professional or personal circumstances might seem to be.

And so what does Adler, so presented, teach or help Kierkegaard to teach? – He helps to teach about the confusion of, because about the forgetting of, certain concepts. Adler forms a crucial part of Kierkegaard's attempt to remind us of certain concepts, and thus a crucial part of our unconfusing them. Of course, this explanation of the use of Adler, of the specific sense in which the book is about Adler, is itself confusing.

What is it to confuse concepts? What is it to forget them? How can I confuse a concept I have forgotten? That sounds strangely like being charged with having misused what is itself missing. – And if Adler somehow helps us to answer such questions, it seems we must lack a clear sense of Adler, and that Adler must have lacked a clear sense of Adler, since Adler himself is a confuser and forgetter of the concepts of which we are confusers and forgetters, the concepts that form the true subject of Kierkegaard's book.

What are the concepts that we confuse, that we forget? The concepts of "authority" and "revelation." Those two are not a pair happenstantially: no, the confusion or forgetting of one will result in the confusion and forgetting of the other: the concepts as Kierkegaard is interested in them are fellow travelers. – But, still, this is not much help. How are we to be unconfused, made to recollect? Kierkegaard explains, as Cavell notes, that his procedure will be "to defend dogmatic concepts," "to get clarity about certain dogmatic concepts and an ability to use them."

Cavell sheds light on this procedure by negative contrast. Kierkegaard's procedure in "defend[ing]" dogmatic concepts will not be to "provide a dogmatic backing for them" – perhaps that can be done or cannot, perhaps it needs to be done or does not, but all that remains to be settled, if it can be, only after we have unconfused ourselves about the concepts, recollected them. So, the procedure will be to "defend them as themselves dogmatic," that is, to reclassify the concepts, to relocate them from one "place" to another.

Cavell offers this: "So his task is one of providing, or re-providing, their meaning; in a certain sense, giving each its definition" (*MWM* 166) But note the insistent qualification that follows hard on the semi-colon. In a certain sense. The "definition"-giving serves neither better to classify information nor better to outfit a new theory. Rather, the "definition" clarifies "what the word does mean, as we use it in our lives – what it means, that is, to anyone with the ability to use it" (166).

So it looks as if Kierkegaard's aim, as Cavell understands it, is to re-equip us with an ability, if possible, one that we have lost, but do not recognize we have lost, that has fallen into disuse. We are, unaware, the victims of a loss. But why are we unaware? Because we still have other abilities that we confuse with the one we have lost. How do we manage that? By still using the words that express the concept we are confused about, that we have forgotten – but using it to express other concepts, or, perhaps, none (it is empty in, and empty of our lives). It is the presence of those words in our lives, and the fact that we take those words as saliences of linguistic abilities (we might even call them *signs* of abilities), that confuses us.

Kierkegaard knows we still have the words "authority" and "revelation": we still use those words in our lives. But their use in our lives is wholly undogmatic, except we do not notice that; it fails to register with us. – So, the point then is not just that the "definition"-giving clarifies what the word means to anyone with the ability to use it. It clarifies what the word means to anyone *with the ability to use it a specific way*, i.e., *dogmatically*. We use the word "authority," and we use it in a, or perhaps in several, specific ways. We may even believe we are using it dogmatically, that at least one among our uses of it is dogmatic – but we are not, none is. If we ever had that specific ability we have lost it, forgotten how to use the word dogmatically, but we do not own our forgetfulness. We take ourselves to remember, still to be equipped with the requisite ability, because the word itself continues to populate our lives. Signs surround us. Kierkegaard aims to show that we do not remember, that we are not using the word dogmatically. We misunderstand the signs.

This activity of leading a person from confusion to clarity through the definition of concepts is one that Cavell thinks has, since Socrates, been regarded as a philosophical activity. It may not be the *only* philosophical activity – Cavell does not insist that it is – Kierkegaard's own activities may include others that are not philosophical – Cavell does not insist that they do not – but this activity is at the heart of Kierkegaard's efforts in *On Authority and Revelation.*[3]

★

Cavell undertakes to clarify the activity. To do so, he (1) compares the activity to Wittgensteinian *grammatical (conceptual) investigation*, and its contrast with empirical investigation, and then (2) highlights the sense in which the activity is *dialectical*. I want to explore both the comparison and the highlighting.

(1) Kierkegaard often shows that a question taken to need answering by empirical means or by formal argumentation is a *conceptual question*, and so one that needs an "answering" that is *grammatical* (169).

Cavell's example is taken from John Stuart Mill on revelation. Mill asserts that if a person were to claim that something we have from him came ultimately from God and not from him, we are within our rights to say that there is nothing about such a supposition so incredible that we might not hope it is true.

Cavell responds to this by doing something other than simply denying it. Instead, he notes that "A revelation cannot be proven by evidence," is not an empirical discovery, nor an appropriate topic for debate *pro* and *con*. Cavell compares it to a grammatical remark, a note that "places" the concept of revelation in the believer's life: for Kierkegaard, a revelation's authority in a believer's life is never a matter of accrued or accruing evidence for it. Anything with that sort of "authority" is simply not a revelation. This is not to deny that believers have *hopes*, they do; but those hopes are not for items to be borne out to be revelations; instead, the believers' hopes flow from acknowledged revelations. (In the words of a Christian hymn: "My hope is built on nothing less / than Jesus' blood and righteousness ... On Christ the solid rock I stand / all other ground is sinking sand ...")

(2) Kierkegaard often uses what he calls "qualitative dialectic," a form of the dialectical examination of a concept (169).

---

[3] Kierkegaard, despite his invocations of Socrates, and despite his irony, is not "defining" concepts in quite the way that Socrates was, and he does not have in mind by forgetting quite what Plato had in mind when he thematized ignorance as forgetfulness. Kierkegaard's reminders are closer to Johnson's than to (most of) Plato's.

Cavell takes this to be done by showing how a concept changes, and how the subject of which it is the concept changes, as the context of its use changes. Such a dialectical examination results in a history or a confrontation of these changes, these differences.

More specifically, the examination typically contrasts the concept in context with other concepts in the same context, and highlights how the pattern of contrasts changes as we consider the concept in another context – such pattern-of-contrast change (pattern-of-contrast contrasts) can be termed the "negation" of the concept's use in one context by its use in the other.[4] Cavell's useful example is *silence*.

> For example, an examination of the concept of *silence* will show that the word means different things – that silence is different things – depending on whether the context is the silence of nature, the silence of shyness, the silence of the liar or hypocrite, the short silence of the man who cannot hold his tongue, the long silence of the hero or apostle, or the eternal silence of the Knight of Faith. (170)

Cavell does not explore his example, but I want to do so.

Start with the silence of nature: this is, first of all, even when unbroken, not a noiseless silence, though it is not noisy: the wind may blow, leaves rustle, birds cry, a nearby stream may gurgle, or, to change the natural scene, gulls may scream, waves break on the shore, thunder rumble in the distance, and yet the silence of nature remains unbroken, not noisy. That silence is not noiseless, but it is also not willed. It simply occurs: it is nature's natural state, and it contrasts with the noise of human habitations, the hum of human voices, the whir of machinery, the ringing of a bell, the wail of a siren: these sounds are will, or are the consequences of will, of human business. Nature is never, in that sense, at work; nature has no business. The silence of nature is something we can hear, and we are often drawn to seek it out, listen for it, as a relief from the noise of human habitation, a refuge from will and business.

The silence of shyness is another silence, not of nature but natural, at least to the shy person. It may be unnoticed by him or her, or it may be noticed, accepted or borne or perhaps regretted, struggled against. But it is dispositional, natural to him or her. It is his or her auditory retirement, a manifestation of being withdrawn, say. It is a silence from which he or she may, by another, be drawn. It is often bound up with diffidence, or

---

[4] 'Negation' here is a term of *linguistic phenomenology*, we might say, referring not to Jane Austen, but (with apologies) to J.L. Austin. The term belongs itself to dialectics, and refers to a relationship between "heterological" items, not "homological" ones, and, since the items are "heterological," the relationship is not simple negation, but something more like a relationship of eclipsement or displacement, a shift of perspective, something with an ineliminable phenomenological dimension.

fear, or humility. Austen's Anne Elliot, already mentioned, is silent, both out of shyness and humility. No one listens to her, but all around her want her to listen to them. Her long, silent grief for the loss of Frederick Wentworth is so silent that almost no one around her notices it, attends, and she will not draw attention to it; she will not ask for, much less demand, its indulgence. The only person who notices it to any degree is also a person who is implicated in her grief's history, Lady Russell, and Anne is too delicate to share her grief openly with Lady Russell, and so it is not a topic of conversation between them. Anne's silence is noiseless silence, a silence generally natural to her but here specifically chosen. Even if she could break her silence, she has no one to listen to her. – Such a shyness can be broken, but only by the shy person. – Part of what makes the ending of *Persuasion* so satisfyingly lovely is that Wentworth, contrite and humbled, acknowledging at last that he remains desperately in love with Anne, finds himself forced by circumstance to choose to write – a method of silence – his confession and proposal, and not to speak it. He hears, attends, listens to Anne as she talks – to Wentworth's friend, Captain Harville, and what he hears demands his heartfelt and heartful response.

The silence of the liar or hypocrite responds to discovery as such; it is the silence of frustration or mortification. It is not chosen, but forces itself upon him or her, and it is bound up with shame or at least defeat, the silence of a loss, not so much of voice as of face. It is a silence not broken but recovered from or forgotten.

The short silence of the chatterer, the man who cannot tame or hold his tongue, is the silence of inhalation or of being spoken over: it is unwilling and suffered as such, a muzzling. It is not the silence of audition, because, although silent, the chatterer's head is full of his own forthcoming chatter. He listens only to what he is about to say. He does not enjoy even the brief respite from his own voice his interlocutors do – he knows no voiceless silence, only the difference between his voice sounding internally and it sounding externally. He hears others only over the sound of his own voice, if he does.

I will end this compact exercise in qualitative dialectics by mentioning one final, still qualitatively different silence, one Cavell omits to mention – the silence of the tomb. This is a final, funereal silence, the silence of the body doomed, in Shakespeare's frightful phrase (a phrase that made Samuel Johnson tremble): "to lie in cold obstruction and to rot." Such a silence that can be spoken into but not spoken from, save the Second Coming, the sounding of the trumpet blast of the Resurrection, an in-the-twinkling-of-an-eye Reanimation. It is a silence that will end, if it ever ends, in *Hosanna!*

It is worth lingering here to consider Kierkegaard's chosen term "qualitative dialectic." Why call this qualitative dialectics? – Cavell rightly concentrates on the notion of perspective when elucidating dialectics.

The "qualitative" adjective here is not as baffling as it may seem, but it has to be seen in relation to another crucial term of Kierkegaard's, a term for a crucial fallacy, a term he borrows from Aristotle. Here's a succinct description of the fallacy as Aristotle understood it: *For Aristotle each subject matter had its own principles or causes. It was for Aristotle a serious fallacy to transport techniques germane to one subject matter to another subject matter.* He dubbed the fallacy: Μετάβασις εις άλλο γενός.

We may think of this as an inflection of *ignoratio elenchi*, and it stands in close relationship to Kant's warning about trespassing sciences: "We do not enlarge but disfigure sciences, if we allow them to trespass upon one another's territory,"[5] and to Bradley's similar, successor caution: "Everything is justified as being real in its own sphere and degree, but not so as to entitle it to invade other spheres, and, whether positively or negatively, to usurp other powers."[6]

I am not here concerned to do more than to touch on the similarities of Kierkegaard to Aristotle, Kant, and Bradley – and similarity is the right term, not sameness, of course – but it is worth recognizing that their "family resemblance" does not result from Transcendental or Absolute Idealism, but from a similar commitment to deep-going, sensitive anti-reductionism. Wittgenstein will later make manifest his own membership in the family: "I will teach you differences."

I take a moment to rehearse all of this not to drop ancient or Victorian names or indulge in gnomic quotations, but rather to clarify why Kierkegaard's dialectic is qualitative. To understand the exercise that produced the different and differentiated silences is to understand it as baring the Μετάβασις εις άλλο γενός, *the transition to another type of thing,*[7] that is the crux of the exercise. Since such transitions, at least in the Greek, require a *shift* of *genus*, we could say that such dialectical exercises reveal differences in *kind*.

By contrast, the revelation of differences *within* a genus could be thought of as the revelation of differences in *degree*. That last term might not seem to fit snugly here, or to offer much independently, but the point

---

[5] Immanuel Kant, *The Critique of Pure Reason*, trans. Norman Kemp Smith (New York: Humanities Press, 1950), 18 (B xi).

[6] F.H. Bradley, *Essays on Truth and Reality* (Oxford University Press, 1914), 470.

[7] For more on this sort of distinction, "distinction without a genus," see my *The Concept 'Horse' Paradox and Wittgensteinian Conceptual Investigations* (London and New York: Routledge, 2007), *passim*.

188   *Kelly Jolley*

is to take the terms as a pair, to mark the contrast between dialectical exercises that reveal shifts of genus and those that do not, those that differentiate only within a genus. Note that the contrast between qualitative and quantitative dialectic is itself something that can only be revealed by qualitative dialectic. We have recourse to the practice to clarify the practice. To shift from the first kind of difference to the second is, we might say, itself an instance of Μετάβασις εις άλλο γενός: qualitative dialectic contrasts are different in kind from quantitative ones – for instance, the sense of "negation" that characterizes qualitatively dialectically contrasted senses will not characterize quantitatively dialectically contrasted ones. (Consider more humdrum cases of homonomy.)

Among the permanent contributions of Cavell's essay is his clarification of "dialectics," even if he shys away from "qualitative." In what is perhaps the axial passage of the essay, Cavell characterizes dialectic in terms borrowed from Wittgenstein:

"To imagine a language," says Wittgenstein in one of his best mottoes, "is to imagine a form of life." When a form of life can no longer be imagined, its language can no longer be understood. "Speaking metaphorically" is a matter of speaking in certain ways using a definite form of language for some purpose; "speaking religiously" is not accomplished by using a given form, or set of forms, of words, and is not done for any further purpose: it is to speak from a particular perspective, as it were to mean anything that you say in a special way. To understand a metaphor you must be able to interpret it; to understand an utterance religiously you have to be able to share its perspective ... The religious is a Kierkegaardian Stage of Life; and I suggest it should be thought of as a Wittgensteinian form of life. (172)

Cavell's brilliant elucidation seems to me helpfully to reveal something about what "qualitative" means, even if Cavell does not (explicitly) present it as doing such. That should emerge as I proceed.

At the center of the elucidation is the contrast between speaking metaphorically and speaking religiously. Each involves a *form* but a different (kind of) form: to speak metaphorically is to speak using a particular, identifiable piece of language for a particular purpose, to use "a definite form"; to speak religiously is not so to speak – the religious speaker does not use "a given form or set of forms of words" and does not speak for any particular purpose. The religious speaker speaks out of a form of life, "speak[s] from a particular perspective," means all that is said in a special way.

A metaphor is an identifiable use of language. It is not as simply identifiable as a simile, because, unlike a simile, it does not typically turn on an identifiable use of a particular sub-sentential unit, a word like "like." But that difference does not make the identification of metaphors particularly fraught. Practiced speakers of a language by and large know them when they see – or hear – them. The most difficult instances to identify are also the ones usually least worth identifying: the dead ones. The quick ones are the ones that matter and their quickness is typically palpable; their pulse registers. But the important thing is that the distinction between the metaphorical and the literal is itself a distinction within the language: this bit here, so spoken by him or her, is a metaphor and this other bit here, differently spoken by him or her, is not a metaphor, indeed is literal. If the metaphor provokes us, puzzles us, we interpret it – we work it out, aided, presumably, by our grasp of the non-metaphorical use of the terms and our schematic grasp of metaphor itself. However exactly such interpretation goes (and I am not here to advance any particular theory of it), it is something we do, and that we (practiced users of a language, on pain of not so counting) know how to do, whether we can particularize or regularize what we know in the form of some explicit, manageable *How-To*. We do not have to share a perspective with the speaker of the metaphor: the speaker is using some bit of the language in a special way, but not language as such in a special way. If, trying to understand the odd relationship between Lady Catherine de Bourgh and her daughter in *Pride and Prejudice*, I am moved to say: *Anne de Bourgh seems less Lady Catherine's flesh than an elaborate shadow that Lady Catherine casts upon the surrounding furniture* – you can interpret what I mean, work it out. You might agree, you might not, you might find it insightful, you might not, but though not perhaps easy to explain, we can all interpret it.

The religious speaker is not using a definite form of a language for a particular purpose: He is using the language in a special way, speaking it from a particular vantage point. He may use metaphors or he may not, but it is not the case that his speaking religiously is his speaking meta-phorically. To take it that way is to locate the difference in the wrong place. To understand a religious speaker is to do something that con-trasts markedly with what is done in interpreting a metaphor. If we try to understand the religious speaker as speaking metaphorically, then we would have to understand everything he says as a use of metaphor, but it is unclear what that could come to. Such an attempt would resemble the attempt to understand everything a given author wrote as irony. As C.S. Lewis remarks (in an essay on Austen), "Unless there is something about which the author is never ironical, there can be no true irony in the work. 'Total irony' – irony about everything – frustrates itself and becomes insipid," that is, *mutatis mutandis*, "total metaphor."[8] To

---

[8] C.S. Lewis, "A Note on Jane Austen," in *Jane Austen: A Collection of Critical Essays*, ed. Ian Watt (Englewood Cliffs, NJ: Prentice-Hall, 1963), 25–34 (at 33). The point matters not just for understanding Austen, but for understanding (Plato's and Kierkegaard's)

understand the religious speaker is not to understand, interpret, his words, his form of words, it is to understand *him*, his speaking itself, his form of life. It is to work myself into his perspective, to see not just *what* but *as* he sees, totally, to appreciate the new pattern-of-contrast among the visible and the invisible. Because only then can I really understand him. The shift from a form of words to a form of life is a radical shift, as is the shift from attempting to understand what had been spoken to understanding the speaker. If a person moves from one of Kierkegaard's *Stages of Life* to another, from the aesthetic to the ethical or the ethical to the religious, the person changes perspectives. This is not to say that each perspective change is specifically the same, but generically, each is a radical shift.

It is also important to see that the perspective is not a "means" to an "end." It is not adopted pursuant to a particular purpose. A shift into a religious form of life transvalues purposes as much as it does forms of language: this does not mean all purposes survive such a shift, nor does it mean that the shift is for the sake of the surviving (or perhaps, added) purposes. The shift no more has a purpose than language itself does.

So, speaking religiously is not as such to speak metaphorically, but is also not as such to speak literally. The distinction between speaking metaphorically and speaking literally is a different distinction than the distinction between speaking religiously and speaking secularly.

To speak as a Christian, as Kierkegaard understands it, then, is to speak from a particular perspective. It is to live a particular life, one lived in Christian categories, one distinguished by an existential structure, not by one or more striking experiences or by a pervasive mood or moods, or by a particular feeling or set of feelings. A Christian life is structured by the mutual implication of these categories, these words in this pattern-of-contrast ("authority," "revelation"). The perspective is not a psychological matter, even if it has psychological consequences. (The imitation of Christ, what Kierkegaard terms *faith*, is a matter of living a certain kind of life, not of cultivating particular psychological states.) Cavell's reaction to the oft-repeated claim that Kierkegaard is a profound psychologist matters here:

Socrates, and for understanding Kierkegaard himself. I will not develop the point about Kierkegaard here except to say that it matters both to our understanding of Kierkegaard's *Point of View of My Work as an Author*, to our understanding of the pseudonymous/non-pseudonymous strategy, and to Kierkegaard's own qualitative dialectical shifts on the word "irony," which is sometimes used as a term for a rhetorical figure (like "metaphor" as Cavell uses it) and sometimes as a term for a certain point of view.

while I do not wish to deny him that, it seems to me attractively misleading praise, especially about such efforts as [*On Authority and Revelation*]; because what is profound psychology in Kierkegaard's work is Christianity itself, or the way in which Kierkegaard is able to activate its concepts ... (*MWM* 168)

What Cavell sees here, and gets right, matters, and it is all-too-often missed. (It captures an important recognition about Christianity that Kierkegaard shares with both Gabriel Marcel and Alan Donagan. Each recognizes the depth of Christian psychology.) Kierkegaard's psychological depth – a very real depth – is a matter not of his creation of concepts not yet uncreated, but of his masterful activation of concepts already created by and on offer in Christianity. (Kierkegaard would have been mortified if it were otherwise, and so would have been mortified by a great deal of what has been said in his praise, superficially attractive though it may be.) To speak from other categories, from another perspective, no matter how religious the life of the speaker might be *in some sense or other*, however replete it might be with high and noble feelings, internal prostrations before sublimity, or long moments laced by intricate emotion, the life is not Christian.[9]

★

Cavell writes: "I do not insist that for us art has become religion ... but that the activity of modern art, both in production and reception, is to be understood in categories which are, or were, religious" (*MWM* 175). Cavell adds: "Kierkegaard's description of the apostle's position characterizes in detail the position I take the genuine modern artist to find himself in" (177). To say that the modern artist lives in the categories of apostleship (religious categories) and not the categories of genius

---

[9] It is instructive to read William James' *The Varieties of Religious Experience* with Kierkegaard in mind. James, always an able discriminator, often sees the kind of difference that for Kierkegaard would be *qualitative*. James rarely casts the point as Kierkegaard would, although there are exceptions or near-exceptions. In the Lectures on Healthy-Mindedness (Lectures 4 and 5), James quotes a passage from a 'Mind-Cure' writer, Henry Wood, and then comments on it: "Although the disciples of the mind-cure often use Christian terminology, one sees from such quotations how widely their notion of the fall of man diverges from that of ordinary Christians." The "how widely" here marks, in vaguely quantitative terms, what is instead a qualitative difference. That James senses this is shown in his lead-up to the Wood quotation, when he notes the crucial replacement of "forward" in ordinary Christianity by "fear" in the Mind-Cure disciples. James sees the difference between the patterns-of-contrast. Unfortunately, from a Kierkegaardian point of view, James fudges on frowardness and fear in the next paragraph, when he quotes (with apparent deference) J. Harnak, who attempts to turn the contrast into a textual disagreement between different "exegetists." Still, despite James' fudging (and Harnack's exegesis), this serves as a useful instance of a Kierkegaardian qualitative dialectical difference.

(aesthetic categories) is useful, and Cavell has done a great service in saying it – but it remains importantly misleading. It is not fully sensitive to a qualitative dialectical difference.

The categories of Kierkegaardian apostleship are not the categories in which the modern artist lives, because the artist, as such, is not living in Christian categories. However burdened the modernist artist may feel by something demanding its expression, however necessitous the modernist artist may be in available techniques of expression, that something demanding expression cannot be a Christian revelation as one would be given to an Christian apostle, that destitution of techniques is not the apostle's destitution. However shocked or bewildered the recipient of modernist art is, that reception is not to be understood in terms of Christian obedience to authority, the particular authority of a religious revelation. – The pattern-of-contrast, while "similar" to Christian apostleship, is not the same (it is a "similarity" across a shift of genus, Μετάβασις εις άλλο γενός). "Comparing" the predicament of the modern artist to the predicament of the Christian apostle helps us in important ways, in part because it helps us to see our past understanding of the modernist artist as caught in a simple continuation of the predicament of the premodern artist. It helps to make salient existential features of the modern artist's predicament, and helps to differentiate it from the predicament of the premodern artist, the genius. For example, it helps to show that what a genuine modernist novelist will mean by "novel" cannot be, as it once arguably was, established by membership in either a large, open-textured class that contains almost all prose fiction, *Moby Dick* to *Mansfield Park*, or a smaller, close-textured class that counts Austen's six novels not just as members, but centralizes them as paradigms.[10] Whether something counts as a novel will now no longer be a question answerable as it was when these options structured the meaning of the question. – No doubt, there were hard cases when those options structured the meaning of the question, but their hardness was not the hardness we now face, where fraudulence and fakery enormously complicate the issues, opening them to existential worries about both the writer and the critic or reader.

For Cavell, taking up the point in more detail, the modern artist faces a predicament that exhibits the features of apostleship. I will list those features and comment on why they differ from the features of apostleship, despite a "similarity": (1) The modern artist is pulled out of the ranks by a message he must, on the pain of a loss of self, communicate.

---

[10] For more, see Northrop Frye, *Anatomy of Criticism* (Princeton University Press, 1957), 303–04.

The apostle is not just pulled out, but called, and literally *called* – spoken to by Another, and given not just a message, but a charge, and the apostle is normally called by *name* ("Samuel, Samuel ...," "Saul, Saul ..."). (2) The modern artist goes through a long period of silence until he finds a way to say what he must say. The apostle's waiting period, if there is one, is decided by the Other who called the apostle, and it is the Other that ends it. (3) The modern artist has no proof of authority, or genuineness other than the artwork. The apostle has no proof of authority, but only has the message – and the message *does not take the form of an artwork*. (4) The modern artist makes the artwork repulsive because of an eschewal of mere attractiveness. The apostle is simply unconcerned with attractiveness or repulsiveness: the apostle knows that the message is dangerous to those who hear (and so to the apostle) – as a result, those who hear may find it, and perhaps the apostle, repulsive. (5) The modern artist must deny his personal or worldly authority in accomplishing what he has to do. The apostle's personal or worldly authority is irrelevant, the only relevant authority is the authority of the Author of the message. (6) For the modern artist, each artwork requires a new step, reinvention, not the resumption of a tradition (into which an artist could be apprenticed), not even one created by himself. The apostle requires a new directive for each step, a fresh revelation for each new message; each new step requires a new call, another charge, revistitation by the Caller. The relation between the new message and the old is not a relevant interest of the apostle – or if it is, that relevance is itself part of the new revelation. (7) The burden the modern artist accepts in becoming the communicator of the message finds a match in the risk of accepting the message (in accepting or rejecting, the recipient's heart is revealed). The apostle has been called to communicate a message that will judge those who hear it, reveal their hearts, but that judgment is not the apostle's to make, and the revelation of their hearts is, properly speaking, the purview of Another.

Does Cavell not recognize these differences in the mist of "similarity"? He does and he does not. He wavers. As he lists the features (and I have stayed close to his language), he sometimes allows himself *qualifiers* like "artistically speaking," or "religiously speaking," but it is as though he treats them as *mere* qualifiers, and not, in this case, as the markers of *qualitative differences* that they are. What Cavell has done is not to assume the modern artist into the Kierkegaardian category of apostle, but rather to show that the predicament of the modern artist has a striking structural "similarity" to the predicament of the Kierkegaardian apostle, and that the Kierkegaardian category can be used to highlight those features. The modern artist is not an apostle, but, so long as we remain mindful of the shift of genus involved, a "comparison" of the modern artist with the apostle is instructive. Cavell is right about that, even if he waffles on exactly how the instruction is to be understood – as a comparison across genuses or a subsumption into a genus. There is no one genus to which the modern artist and the apostle belong, however "similar" the structures interior to their respective genuses may be, how instructive that "similarity" may be.[11]

My concern here is not in correcting Cavell for the sake of correcting Cavell. Rather, the correction is itself more instruction in Kierkegaardian qualitative dialectics. Perhaps the correction will seem small, and in one way I intend it to be small and I intend it to be friendly. Cavell's basic insight, thus qualified, remains. – But while I intend the correction as friendly, small, I also insist that understanding it is no less important than understanding qualitative differences among silences. Out of such differences are differences of lives made.

⋆

Cavell terms the change in pattern-of-contrast that becomes visible when we situate the modernist artist alongside the Kierkegaardian apostle "the un-aestheticizing of aesthetics," and I take that to parallel the "undoing the psychologizing of psychology" that Cavell understands as a central burden of Wittgenstein's *Philosophical Investigations*. (The passage is, by neither mistake nor accident, in "Aesthetic Problems of Modern Philosophy"; see *MWM* 91.)

The two tasks are even closer than the structural similarity of Cavell's descriptions suggest, since the unaestheticizing of aesthetics is largely a matter of resolutely turning from the inspection of items in an individual's psychology as a revelator of aesthetics and turning in another direction.

---

[11] This section of Cavell's essay ends with what might be taken to be a recognition of my correction. He quotes Kierkegaard on the difference in appearance of apostles, applying what Kierkegaard says to the modern artist, but then, it seems, taking it back. Cavell cautions: "All this does not mean (it is not summarized by saying) that the artist *is* an apostle; because the concept of an apostle is, as (because) the concept of revelation is, forgotten, inapplicable. So, almost, is the concept of art" (*MWM* 178). This is a difficult, darkling moment in the essay. But I take it that Cavell is not actually taking back what he said, but modulating it in a "negative" way, a Kierkegaardian way – say he is modulating it dialectically. Cavell is saying that for us, in our forgetfulness of the concepts of revelation and (so) apostleship, we are unlikely to be able to *hear* what Cavell is saying as he wants it to be heard. Since we do not really have the concept of an apostle, Cavell's calling the modern artist an apostle is all-too-much like calling the modern artist a *whazzit*: it is a statement that has the form of a categorization but which, for us, *fails* to categorize.

In *Philosophical Investigations*, Wittgenstein nowhere expresses his depsychologizing with more compact power than he does in §314: "It indicates a fundamental misunderstanding, if I am inclined to study my current headache in order to get clear about the philosophical problem of sensation."[12] We can imagine an un-astheticized aesthetical equivalent: "It shows a fundamental misunderstanding, if I am inclined to study the pleasure I now feel in order to get clear about the philosophical problem of aesthetics." Although each of these remarks but sets keel to breakers, and although the crossing to the hoped-for shore is long and perilous, each is a decisive departure, a turning away from a demand that seems compulsory but produces no durable satisfaction. Each indicates a willingness to go in search of a new understanding of such demands, one that frees us from their compulsions, and reorients us on our real needs.

No psychological item, stared at in cheek-by-jowl, squinting introspection, reveals anything but itself. That revelation may be complete, but it is also utterly inarticulate and completely static. Such items exist, effervescently, and they may be the referents of terms like "sensation" or "pleasure" but they are not the senses of the terms, and no amount of introspective peering at the items will discover anything that speaks to philosophy.

When calling attention to Wittgenstein's depsychologizing of psychology in *Philosophical Investigations*, Cavell notes (implicitly) that an air of paradox attends the depsychologizing, since Wittgenstein's work "seems to turn all of philosophy into psychology – matters of what we call things, how we treat them, their roles in our lives" (*MWM* 91).

Cavell lets that air of paradox linger there, but the shortest way to dispelling, or at least challenging it, is to insist that *Philosophical Investigations'* seeming to turn all of philosophy into psychology results from the willfulness of psychologizing itself: as psychologizing is driven *from* (purely) psychological items in individuals' psychology to matters of what we call things, how we treat them, their roles in our lives, it carries its "squint" with it: now *psychologizing* the *we* (the *first-person* plural, note) and the *callings*, the *treatments*, and the *roles*. Undoubtedly, there is a sense in which these are rightly termed psychological,[13] but Wittgenstein's interest in them is in revealing the "necessities" that control human psychological and behavioral categories; Wittgenstein's

---

[12] Ludwig Wittgenstein, *Philosophical Investigations*, rev. 4th edn, trans. G.E.M. Anscombe, P.M.S. Hacker, and Joachim Schulte, ed. Hacker (Malden, MA: Wiley-Blackwell, 2009), §314.

[13] Note Cavell's important parenthetical on "psychology" on 93 of *MWM*.

interest, in Cavell's ringing phrase, is in "the necessities in human action and passion themselves" (91).

Such "necessities" extend into human *artistic* action and passion, and Cavell's unaestheticized aesthetics responds to them. The "comparison" of the plight of the modern artist to the religious apostle helps to make the necessities of the former's plight easier to recognize, turns us in the right direction.

★

Let me end by recirculating to my beginning.

One use to which Kierkegaard puts qualitative dialectic is the distinguishment of words used in a heightened sense and words that are not. Johnson's motto is an example of such heightened uses, involving heightened uses of "remind" and "forget."

Kierkegaard often dubs such contrasted uses of words "transcendental" and "immanent." I am not going to dub Johnson's heightened uses "transcendental." – I can imagine Johnson rounded on me in supercilious bombast, and demanding: "Sir, clear your mind of cant!" But I hope that the Johnson motto helps to show why Kierkegaard would believe some such contrasts worth marking, and, since each set of philosophical term is, like each unhappy family, unhappy in its own way, I believe we can indulge Kierkegaard in his, remembering that they gain their sense from his philosophical practice: his philosophical practice is not explained by them. (It is a recurring feature of philosophical terms that we do not understand them until we no longer need them.)

Such heightened uses can puzzle us, not because we cannot feel the contrast – we can – but because, as Cavell helpfully notes at the beginning, we can fail to know what to make of them or of our knowledge of them. We can wonder how we can know the pieces of practical wisdom Johnson has in mind in his motto, and wonder how, once we know them, however we know them, we could so much as forget them. What we did not learn by explicit instruction, what we forget because we would rather not acknowledge it, these things can puzzle us. Neither Cavell nor Kierkegaard offers us an explanation – as we often understand explanations – of these things, but both help us to understand that they exist, and that we can so live that we deepen our own forgetfulness or blindness, and so live that we lose touch with our own lives, the sense that they make or the nonsense.

Consider Austen's Emma Woodhouse, faced with Harriet Smith and Harriet's confidence that Mr. Knightley returns her affections. Emma suffers the final convulsions of her self-deception, knows it for what it is, and realizes not just that she loves Mr. Knightey but also that she loves him in a heightened sense (call it "transcendent" if you wish), with a love not open to her, or indeed, anyone's artful direction or complete comprehension (the "immanent" sense that has deformed Emma's words and deeds throughout the novel). Her new understanding not only shames her, it "negates" her old one. Her understanding has not merely been deepened; it has been reborn. Emma sits still – and comes to herself:

Emma's eyes were instantly withdrawn; and she sat silently meditating, in a fixed attitude, for a few minutes. A few minutes were sufficient for making her acquaintance with her own heart. A mind like hers, once opening to suspicion, made rapid progress. She touched – she admitted – she acknowledged the whole truth. Why was it so much worse that Harriet should be in love with Mr. Knightley, than with Frank Churchill? Why was the evil so dreadfully increased by Harriet's having some hope of a return? It darted through her, with the speed of an arrow, that Mr. Knightley must marry no one but herself!

Her own conduct, as well as her own heart, was before her in the same few minutes. She saw it all with a clearness which had never blessed her before. How improperly had she been acting by Harriet! How inconsiderate, how indelicate, how irrational, how unfeeling had been her conduct! What blindness, what madness, had led her on! It struck her with dreadful force, and she was ready to give it every bad name in the world ... The rest of the day, the following night, were hardly enough for her thoughts. – She was bewildered amidst the confusion of all that had been rushed on her within the last few hours. Every moment there had been a fresh surprise; and every surprise must be a moment of humiliation to her. – How to understand it all! How to understand the deceptions she had thus been practising on herself, and living under! The blunders, the blindness of her own head and heart![14]

---

[14] *Oxford Illustrated Jane Austen*, vol. IV, 407–08, 411–12. C.S. Lewis comments on this passage so as to make clear his sense of the radical shift in perspective: "All [her] *data* had to be reinterpreted ... Emma's conduct and 'her own heart' appear to her, unwelcome strangers both, 'in the same few minutes'" (Lewis, "Note on Jane Austen," 27). To put this in Cavell's Kierkegaardian/Wittgensteinian terms, as he comments on Kierkegaard's notion that a person can fail to be at home – i.e., fail to be at home with herself, that she can be *out* without knowing it, cursed by an unacknowledged unhousedness (I change the pronouns to key the passage to Emma):

A human being can be a complete enigma to herself; she cannot find her feet with herself. Not because a particular thing she does puzzles her – her problem may be that many of the puzzling things she does do *not* puzzle her – but because she does not know why she lives as she does, what the point of her activity is; she understands her words, but she is foreign to her life. (*MWM* 173)

Thus does Cavell disclose the depths of Emma, of *Emma*, of Austen.

12   Tragic Implication

Sarah Beckwith

The vast majority of critical work on Cavell and tragedy, especially Shakespearean tragedy, has been concerned to link the *last* two essays of *Must We Mean What We Say?* and to draw out of them the concept acknowledgment. Different dimensions of the interrelationship between ordinary language philosophy and tragedy are opened out by concentrating on the first and the last essay, written some ten years apart. Writing in the Preface to the updated edition of *Must We Mean* in 2001, Cavell says that he could still sense the initial exhilaration "in finding ways to mean everything I was saying" and he notes there that friends often told him that they found later preoccupations anticipated in the title essay (*MWM* xix, xvii). In her recent introduction to the French translation of *Must We Mean*, Sandra Laugier has superbly tracked some of the sources of interconnection both between the essays and into Cavell's continuation (to use the terminology of this volume) of himself.[1] Cavell has always engaged in radical revisions and extensions of Austin's work, whether *The Claim of Reason*, where what differentiates Austin and Wittgenstein is their understanding of criteria, or later still in his exchanges with Derrida in the very important and rich essay, "Counter-Philosophy and the Pawn of Voice," along with the meditations on performative and passionate utterance in *Philosophy the Day after Tomorrow*. These continuations of Austin have relevance to the question of tragic implication in ordinary language philosophy which I take, along with comic implication, to be one of the great bequests of Cavell's writing to humanistic inquiry, taking us into the sources and resources of shared grief and shared laughter.

"The tragic" (small t) is first invoked on page 14 of the title essay at the point where Cavell is elucidating the element of necessity in statements

---

[1] Sandra Laugier, "Introduction to the French Edition of *Must We Mean What We Say?*," *Critical Inquiry* 37/4 (2011), 627–51. See in particular Laugier's comments at 647, linking the early essays on OLP with the last essay as a question of the recovery of ourselves and our voices.

whose implications we understand. A usage of a particular term entitles us to draw certain inferences; this is a question of the normativity of language, an implication obscured when rules are understood as imperatives or commands. This is what the learning of language comes to: we are responsible for the implications of our speech. We are responsible for those implications even when we may not know what we are saying and doing. We may not, often we cannot, sometimes we do not, foresee how our words will go out into the world. Like other forms of action, the effects of our speech are "irreversible" – we can recant, abjure, revoke, retract, but not unsay what we've said; unpredictable, for if we must understand what we are doing in certain explicit performatives for them to do the work they do, even in those cases what follows is unforeseen – we know that the judge's verdict will result in a prison sentence but not how that verdict will resound in the defendant's life or those of his loved ones; they are boundless in their effects. (What Hannah Arendt said of human action, that it is boundless, unpredictable, and irreversible, what is done not being capable of being undone, is true of speech acts.)[2] We can begin to see some implications of implication here: inference, imputation, indication, or suggestion; implication as involvement, connection, and entanglement in bonds, as Kent puts it in *Lear*, "too intrince t'unloose"; and lastly implication in the quasi-legal sense as bearing guilt, hence responsibility.

Perhaps the tragic contours of responsibility for what Cavell will later call the necessity of sense are already emerging. Cavell is here explaining that when we ask the Austinian question: what we should say when, it is importantly a question about the first person plural. Sometimes I might be just plain wrong, and here it might be indeed a question of evidence at stake. But if I am mistaken about what we do, that is (and here is his invocation of tragedy) "liable, where it is not comic, to be tragic" (*MWM* 14). We, as native speakers, are the authority for what we say: and these systematic agreements in judgments display accord in our practices and apprenticeship in learning word and world together inseparably. To be wrong about what we say and do is to mistake the very conditions and consequences of speech, to exile ourselves from the shared and necessary conditions of our existence. To be wrong here is not to be put right "with a more favorable position of observation or a fuller mastery of the recognition of objects: it requires a new look at oneself and a fuller realization of what one is doing or feeling" (*CR* 179).

---

[2] See also *LDIK*: "I can no more take back the word I have given you and you have acted on than I can take back my touch. Each has entered our history" (322).

I note first of all that Cavell's talk is of "the tragic," not of tragedy. Much later on in an interview transcribed in *Philosophical Passages* based on a series of lectures and workshops at Bucknell when he was working on "Counter-Philosophy and the Pawn of Voice," he said that he never sought a theory of tragedy, perhaps because he both disbelieves and believes all the theories.[3] (And tragedy is the philosopher's favorite literary genre: as if the focus on failure, catastrophe, remorseless inevitability, vulnerability, and fragility in the Greek and Shakespearean variants troubles a sovereign picture of reason's agency.) The point of invoking the tragic as opposed to tragedy is to show that the moment when one occludes consciousness of the other, and so chooses the other's death so as to avoid recognition (always self-recognition) can show itself in the smallest of denials. Cavell's examples include a momentary irritation, a recurrent grudge, an unexpected rush of resentment, a false silence, a fear of engulfment, a fantasy of solitude, any occasion where "the problem is to *recognize* myself as denying another."[4] The tragic is a potentiality of just such lapses and errors: *hamartia* is just such waywardness. Tragic implication lines our dealings with each other; it can happen at any time. The fact of our attunement when we are attuned, the fact of our disharmony, our conflict, cannot be explained by any theory for nothing is deeper than the fact of agreement. Our natural history with words opens us to tragic implication: it is a natural history as much as the history of one particular genre.

The excoriating group of plays including and following *King Lear*, that Shakespeare composed during the period 1604–09, inaugurate, I believe, a new tragic idiom, one concerned with the possibilities and consequences of speech as action. *Hamlet* (most complexly but definitively) finishes off the heroic idiom of tragedy and a new beginning is made in *Lear*. Cavell's brilliant elucidations of *King Lear* are internal to his articulation of the radical project of ordinary language philosophy.[5] Shakespearean tragedy and ordinary language philosophy are thus implicated in each other, as is the title essay with the culminating essay of *Must We Mean What We Say?*

King Lear thinks that his language is identical with his will. He does not see that language bears its own necessity outside of his control, because he occludes the responses of others, and he imagines that he is

---

[3] I feel this is a point easily forgotten.

[4] Cavell, "What Is the Scandal of Skepticism?," *PDAT* 151.

[5] Laugier in her "Introduction to the French Edition of *Must We Mean What We Say?*," *Critical Inquiry* 37/4 (2011), 627–51 (at 628). has said: *Must We Mean* "is the only work of what is called contemporary thought to carry the project of ordinary language philosophy through to its end."

the very source of all that can be given ("I gave you all"). Until the advent of grace in this play he will harp on ingratitude. Lear's ceremony of flattery in the first scene of the play is a denial that there are others in his world, and when he so banishes love, so he banishes truth and his own grip on reality, for love, as Iris Murdoch has said, is disclosive of reality. Here love is not so much an experience as a concept, honed in the use of words, and Lear learns what it is as a matter of painful biography. Although *King Lear* explores the language of the social outcast more systematically than any other play, the exile from sense is where the play devastates most utterly, stripping us of all our lendings.

It is Timon's misanthropy which, allowing him no distinctions in his universal, all-pervasive hatred, makes him a skeptic in relation to language. For him now all words must fail, must lead to mistrust and scorn. His fully generalized distrust will defend him preemptively from all others, and from the risk of any and all relation. To refuse a relationship with all humankind is to refuse a relationship with any human being; it is to discount even the possibility of a claim on you. The sheerly hyperbolic quality of Timon's hatred gets him off the hook of the need to make any responses, and so from the responsibilities entailed in such responses.

Macbeth stupefies himself to what he knows is the logic of action. His wish is to eradicate thought altogether, to remove the very possibility that there could be a conceivable answer to the question, "Why are you doing that?"

In the most overtly political play about whose voice counts, Coriolanus tries to shape a world solely out of his own assertion, in structuring his relations with others on a refusal of the natural exposures of human form, human language, and human feeling.

In language we make commitments, avowals, and promises to each other, and we enter agreements with each other,

> agreements we do not know and do not want to know we have entered, agreements we were always in, that were in effect before our participation in them. Our relation to our language – to the fact that we are subject to expression and comprehension, victims of meaning – is accordingly the key to our sense of our distance from our lives, of our sense of the alien, of ourselves as alien to ourselves, thus alienated. (*In Quest of the Ordinary*, 40)

But we do not merely bind ourselves in our words in ways we do not know or understand; our words bind us not simply to each other but to the world. Language words the world, binds us to it and not by reference alone: we are bound by the challenge and difficulty of reality even when truth and reference are out of play (*PP* 188). Thus OLP gives us a vision of language in which our adequacy to reality is central but such adequation is now extended to the full play of language, and is no longer restricted to reference.

King Lear teaches Cavell his differences with Austin in ways which emerge in his later engagements with Austin. Recall that in *Little Did I Know*, Cavell tells us that his work in theatre in Berkeley, writing the musical score for a production of *King Lear* and involving himself in the production of live theatre, was an "early, specific preparation for my eventual conviction in the interest and importance of Austin's practice of philosophizing out of a perpetual imagination of, as Austin put the matter, 'what is said when,' why a thing is said, hence how, and in what context" (*LDIK* 217). It is philosophy's excision of occasion that exorcised Austin; it was the same amnesia that led literary critics to make controversies over criticism focused on either words or character, Cavell's target in the opening pages of the *Lear* essay. What he could not quite say at the time of *Must We Mean*, but what he thinks is implied in Austin, is that the connection between knowing and promising comes in the idea of giving others your word. What the advance, as he puts it, from knowledge to acknowledgment required "was coming upon a way to make sense of the mysterious and grave events of Lear" (*LDIK* 322). In the next section I would like to return again to Cavell's unsurpassable reading of the opening scene of Lear, and finally to return to some of the differences with Austin that are so fruitful in Cavell's later philosophy.

Love and Charity in *King Lear*

Cavell says King Lear is avoiding love and requesting flattery in the first act of *King Lear* when he asks the question of his daughters: "Which of you shall we say does love us most?" Under these circumstances he *cannot* be requesting love. Under these conditions, as Cordelia so rightly sees, love cannot be spoken without becoming something else – flattery, emotional extortion, competition, rivalry, deceit, or bribery. For Cordelia to say how much she loves him under these conditions, would be to rival her sisters, to flatter her father, to take part in a cynical show of obedience in exchange for land and status, converting her words into play acts, rendering them hollow. What she tells us in her first aside – "Love, and be silent," a form of words both overheard and underheard, as Cavell points out – is that she does love her father, but that her love cannot be voiced – she cannot speak it. *Can't*, not won't. It is a grammatical and not a psychological point.

So her resounding "nothing" reveals the problem with his command/ request and shows its incoherences. But her words also expose Lear's request, in Cavell's argument, as an avoidance of love's knowledge, love's exposure, for love is mutual where flattery is not. There is no necessity to reveal yourself in flattery. King Lear is not revealed but concealed in the unctuous exaggerations and hyperbole of Goneril and Regan who never have to reveal themselves in the proclaimed "love." There is mutual revelation in love of lover and loved. The play will explore the devastating consequences of the silencing of love, and the evasion of mutuality. Lear may not have known what he was doing but he will come to know what he has done. Cavell argues that Lear precisely understands that he is asking for flattery and not love; but he does not know the utterly devastating implications of the casting out of love that follow from his words.

If "love" is the word evoked and evaded in the first scene, the Gloucester subplot consistently uses the word "charity." Shakespeare extends exile of love into a picture of a vicious outcasting of charity. The distinction between love and charity had some weight in sixteenth- and seventeenth-century translation debates. In Thomas More's compendious debate with William Tyndale, the translation of "love" for the Vulgate's "caritas" had infuriated More. To More's ear the idea of charity was bound up with the pax of the mass, reflecting the idea that charity is something you are in. The difference in a vocabulary of love and charity in More's ideas bears on the charitable and loving relation not alone between a human soul and God, but between neighbor and neighbor, self and soul, self and God as an indissoluble aspect of each other. If you leave out the neighbor, then love is between soul and God alone. It is a private and not a social love. The soul that seeks its direction from God absent the neighbor has ceased to encompass our mutual imbrication, mutual dependence, ceased to find it obvious that there can be no such thing as a private relation with God.

I have argued, following Stanley Cavell, that love is banished in the first scene with devastating consequences, and I've insisted that this is a grammatical and not a psychological point. For love is disclosive of reality; a world in which the honest expression of love is impossible is a world of predation and the universal wolf, appetite. If love discloses the reality of someone, if it is bound up in and with acknowledgment, then the play extends the grammar of acknowledgment into every imagined social relation and traces the avoidance of charity as an aspect of the avoidance of love. The exploration of the avoidance of charity is naturally most evident in the figure of Poor Tom, but it emerges forcefully and pervasively throughout the Gloucester subplot.

The dispossession of Lear and the exile of charity are from the beginning bound up with the terrifying extension of the Cornwalls' jurisdiction. For the coming of the Cornwalls to Gloucester's household, where fully fourteen of the play's twenty-six scenes take place, their assumption of complete authority over Gloucester's home is a gradual, remorseless evacuation of all and any form of charitable love.

Before Lear is barred from Gloucester's household – for his own good, so he can taste his folly – before charity is prohibited by the Duke of Cornwall and his wife – their jurisdiction and its terrifying implications are established. Kent is stocked – a punishment reserved for rogues and vagabonds – the doors are barred to Lear following the pitiful and painful negotiation to keep at least some of his followers, and finally the home itself is turned into a torture chamber, where the Cornwalls reveal their lust for domination and where power is nakedly exercised because it can be:

> Though well we may not pass upon his life
> Without the form of justice, yet our power
> Shall do a courtesy to our wrath, which men
> May blame but not control.[6]

"When I desired their leave that I might pity him," says Gloucester, "they took from me the use of mine own house, charged me on pain of perpetual displeasure neither to speak of him, entreat for him, or any way sustain him." After Regan's cruel housekeeping ("this house is little; the old man and's people / Cannot be well bestowed"), charity must hide itself. Gloucester fatally asks his son Edmund to cover for him with the Duke when he decides to help the king, "'that my charity be not of him perceived" (*Lear*, 3.3.15), and he appears himself transformed out of listlessness and moral stupidity by the depravity of the Cornwalls' unceremonious takeover of his house. He seeks out Lear "against the injunction" of the Cornwalls.

In *The Claim of Reason* Cavell spells out the centrality of the question of acknowledgment to the figure and idea of the outcast, a condition shared by the witless men on the heath. "So far as we think that the human being is naturally a political being, we cannot think that some human beings are NATURALLY outcasts. So if there are outcasts, we must have, or harbour, *sub specie civilitatis*, some explanation of their condition" (*CR* 437).

The condition of the outcast is one that fundamentally entails the idea of recognition at its heart. The kinds of explanations called for by the outcast may encompass the following, all of which are rehearsed in *King*

---

[6] William Shakespeare, *King Lear*, ed. R.A. Foakes, Arden Shakespeare, Third Series (London: Thomas Nelson and Sons, 1997), 3.7.24–27.

Lear and in Part 4 of *The Claim of Reason*. The condition of the outcast is deserved – this is essentially the position of Goneril and Regan, who feel that he has brought his outcast status on himself – he must taste his folly. Or it may be the outcast is simply unfortunate – and his situation lies at the gates of chance. Each of these positions is a denial of the responsibility of the one who casts out. There is another fantasy rehearsed about the outcast – this is that the outcasts are mysteriously in league with each other. The brother Edmund is displacing, Edgar, as poor Tom chooses a disguise that complexly exemplifies the theatricalization of charity that is central to its evasion and avoidance.

Poor Tom is the most obvious instance of the play's complex and comprehensive extension of love to charity. Edgar's disguise as Poor Tom bets on the double invisibility of "the basest and most poorest shape" (*Lear*, 2.2.176). He won't be recognized as the Earl of Gloucester's erstwhile son, he will be unseen, avoided, unrecognized because to remain unseen and unrecognized is the very condition of the "bedlam beggar." Edgar relies on his culture's fear of beggars. "Although most people recognize that all of us are in some respects dependent upon each other, says Kelly Johnson in her book *The Fear of Beggars*, "the sight of a stranger asking for help outside the public order of rights and the private affection of the family shakes us up."[7] The figure of the Bedlam beggar adopted by Edgar is itself a theatricalization of charity. If poverty is a disguise for the purposes of extortion we will not feel obliged to respond to it. This attitude is nurtured and conjured, fed by the proliferation of literature about the vagrant. It emerges straight out of an inventive, long-lived literature of cony-catching, a literature that began with the epistemological drive to distinguish the deserving from the undeserving poor.

In England, laws dealing with poverty and laws mandating labor had for two centuries worked hand in glove. In examining Langland's complex exploration of the figure of Need in his great allegorical poem *Piers Plowman*, Kate Crassons has shown the costs and longevity of this mode of depiction which renders the question of need as a problem of knowledge rather than a problem of response. Poverty, she suggests, and Langland shows, requires acknowledgment. It privileges the category of human response.[8] Langland is responding to the complexity of poverty in his own culture, which was innovative for establishing an

[7] Kelly Johnson, *The Fear of Beggars: Stewardship and Poverty in Christian Ethics* (Grand Rapids, MI: Eerdmans, 2007), 3.
[8] Kate Crassons, *The Claims of Poverty: Literature, Culture and Ideology in Late Medieval England* (University of Notre Dame Press, 2010), 11.

ambitious system for documenting and identifying the poor in the legislation of 1376 and 1388. The Commons Petition against Vagrants and the subsequent Cambridge Statute of Labourers (1388) establish a scheme for documenting and identifying mobile workers. It combined – as later poor laws were to do for a considerable period of time – both a regulation of work and a regulation of poverty, attempting to make possible the discrimination of the deserving and the undeserving poor. Kate Crassons insightfully says that "the single feat of asking someone for some identification was meant to replace other more challenging forms of human response that required people to exercise moral judgment by acknowledging need, dismissing its real presence, or refusing to scrutinize what they thought ultimately unknowable." Langland brilliantly insists, as does *Lear*, on the opacity of need: that it can't be reasoned in the way such legislation presumes. Paul Slack, one of the leading historians of the Elizabethan and Jacobean poverty legislation, has said that the system "made paupers and delinquents by labelling them."[9] The unsettled poor lacked recognition for they inhabited a society where identity was still defined by place. The unsettled were whipped and sent back to their parishes; the mobility of the poor was only consciously separated from vagrancy as a punishable offence in 1662 when the Settlement Act made provision for the return of migrants to their parishes without punishment.

When Shakespeare wrote *King Lear* the mobile workers of the land lacked political recognition. Cavell's work helps us see that the entwined epistemologies of deserving (old or otherwise impotent) and undeserving poor (idlers and loungers), the question of political recognition, is also a question of human worth and an indistinguishable linguistic and ethical competence. The fantasies about the lines between deserving and undeserving poor replace the difficulties of acknowledgment with the certainty of knowledge avoiding charity, thus the bonds we are in.

Not the least of Cavell's major contributions to a philosophically inflected literary criticism is to provide a non-moralistic account of the relationship between linguistic and ethical competence, to recall that every encounter is moral, inviting us to see what positions we are prepared to take responsibility for, to show us that our positions need sometimes to be discovered and learnt because we learn about ourselves not through introspection of a mind's internal objects but through our time-bound encounters with each other, and through trial, through error, encounter, in short through our recognitive relations with each other.

[9] Paul Slack, *Poverty and Policy in Tudor and Stuart England* (London and New York: Longmans, 1988), 107.

Hence moral discourse is not to be located in a particular domain of language, with its own subject matter and restricted vocabulary, but is an aspect of our language, therefore implicating us at every turn.[10] Cavell's account is non-moralistic because of this implication, because our responses to each other are the form of recognition, the mode of acknowledgment. What suffering is is given through responses such as pity.

It was precisely the full dimensions of response in moral encounter that Cavell thought Austin had short-circuited in his focus on explicit performatives, the illocutionary rather than perlocutionary dimensions of speech acts where successes and failures were better defined. "Austin's theory of the performative utterance struck me as leaving out half the world of responses to the demands and the presumptions of one's utterances," he will say in *Little Did I Know* (303).

In his later work Cavell becomes more and more attuned to the differences in Austin's and Wittgenstein's understanding of criteria, and Austin's preference for the illocutionary speech act over the perlocutionary one. The consequences of this, as he brilliantly outlined it in "Counter-Philosophy and the Pawn of Voice," concern Austin's inability to see the tragic dimensions of his understanding of speaking as acting.

Whereas Austin had a special category for commissives in his analysis of explicit performatives, those speech acts which commit us to future actions, at the root of his idea of language is the sense that to speak at all is to commit yourself in words.[11] When Austin invokes the saw, "our word is our bond," he does so to caution us against taking binding words, such as that in a marriage service, as "the outward and visible sign, for convenience or other record or for information, of an inward and spiritual act," as a description (true or false) of the "occurrence of the inward performance."[12] This was the recourse of the reneger, the bigamist, and the welsher, or those who sought to vitiate their obvious and public commitments with a claim of an inner quality so deep and true as to be inaccessible in mere words (enter Wittgenstein's private linguist, enter the suspicion of expression and the fear of its fatality). At this point he cites the classic expression of this idea by citing Euripides' play *Hippolytus*, in which Hippolytus says, "my tongue swore to, but my heart did not." In his essay "Counter-Philosophy and the Pawn of Voice," Cavell comments on this interesting choice as an index of Austin's

---

[10] See Lars Hertzberg, "Moral Escapism and Applied Ethics," *Philosophical Papers*, Special Issue on Ethics in the Light of Wittgenstein, 31/3 (2002), 251–70 (at 255).

[11] On commissives, exercitives, behabitives, expositives, and verdictives, see J.L. Austin, *How to Do Things with Words*, 2nd edn, ed. J.O. Urmson and Marina Sbisà (Cambridge, MA: Harvard University Press, 1979; 1st edn 1962), 151.

[12] *Ibid.*, 9.

inability to see the potential tragedy in "our word is our bond." For Hippolytus dies by being bound to his oaths. Firstly, he enrages Aphrodite for not showing due reverence because he has sworn a vow of chastity; secondly, he swears to his stepmother Phaedra's nurse that he will not reveal what she has told him: that Phaedra is obsessed by love for him. After Phaedra's death by suicide, he will not break his vow to correct Theseus' erroneous assumption that he has raped Phaedra. Here the keeping of a bond is utterly fatal. And though there are innumerable examples of the rash oath formula, especially in medieval literature such as Chaucer's exquisite Breton lai, *The Franklin's Tale*, where what drives the story is the impossibility of not keeping the word you've given, Austin chose his example of a protagonist who dies of keeping his word, where keeping his word curses him. Perhaps Austin took the words out of context, betrayed his own sense that what should be under analysis was the total speech act in the total speech situation, where Hippolytus' words by no means excuse him but could be understood to mean something more like, "I swore though I did not want to; I swore though everything in me would prefer to go back on my word. Nevertheless I swore." Austin, conjectures Cavell, might have wanted to forget several things: he might have wanted to forget that our word may be no more than our bond, that this might be more a matter of "mundane credit," everyday credence, than religious faith, that it might sometimes be rightly broken. One way of glossing my word is my bond, is that any word of mine commits me, marks me out in relation to you in a specific way; the bonding cannot be reserved alone for explicit binding performatives, as in I promise, I swear, I vow, but is part of a routine and fundamental way in which we offer and take each other's words. We naturally have trust in each other's words, such trust is implicit in every speech act. It is distrust that makes trust only retrospectively come into view. Although the promise is singled out for philosophers as foundational, it is my word, no particular word, but all my words which are my bond, as I, unremarkably, take your words to be too. Secondly, Austin might have wished to forget that although Theseus in that play longs for a "token, or mark" to make clear who is friend and who is foe, there are no such marks because sincerity is unfathomable. In *How To Do Things with Words*, he had reminded us that insofar as performatives did things, they would be subject to infelicity, and insofar as they were utterances, they would be subject to abuse: insincerity was one such abuse.[13] Insincerity renders your words hollow but not void – you have still promised if you have no

---

[13] *Ibid.*, 40. Austin's examples here are relatively innocuous: "I congratulate you" when I do not feel at all pleased; "I condole with you" when I feel no sympathy, and this lends

intention on delivering on it – a point he makes in the fourth lecture of *How To Do Things with Words*. Austin did know that some actions such as stepping on a baby were not going to be encompassed in the field of excuses as he knew that contradiction was not the only outrage to and in speech. But Cavell's point in outlining the difference between Wittgensteinian and Austinian criteria is one indication of how extensive an infelicity insincerity might be, how hard it might be to discern whether, say, a smile is real. Whereas Austin had chosen examples where expertise might well be able to tell the difference, say between a goldfinch and a goldcrest, Wittgenstein's choice of examples showed the limits of criteria: that they could tell *what* something is (what we call it) but not whether or not it actually exists (whether it is in a dream or real, for example), whether you are delighted to see me or insincerely expressing delight so as not to disappoint me, whether you are smiling or merely pretending to. Wittgensteinian criteria are open to skepticism in a way, suggests Cavell, that Austin did not see or want to see. And this meant he did not see that the impotence as well as the power of words must both be part of a natural history of language. If Austin charted the vulnerabilities of human action, he perhaps failed to see how far tragedy dealt with what was not capable of being excused, what precisely we cannot get out of. He also failed to see that human utterances as actions are "essentially vulnerable to insincerity" (*PP* 86, 93).

I would like to end with the great continuation of himself that Cavell undertakes when, under the suggestion of his analyst, he takes up his dissertation again, the great dissertation put away in files and boxes. Start, said the analyst, by taking it out and putting it on your desk. "It's clear," he said, "that you have access to many continuations." He suggested that Cavell find a place for it on the desk in full sight without feeling obliged to continue it. When asked what the results were of this interesting experiment, Cavell replied first of all, like Cordelia, "nothing." But then he said – "Well, except I guess for a mild pervasive sense of pleasure." After the stunned silence, "we broke into the greatest of laughs we had had together." Tragic implication is, if caught in good time, comic implication too.

strength to Cavell's idea that in citing *Hippolytus* in apparent oblivion to what he might elsewhere call the "total situation" of the speech act he has also passed over the dangers and difficulties of insincerity in actual cases. In the Shakespearean oeuvre, of course, insincerity is sometimes malicious, comic when found out and exposed, but often tragic because insincerity works off the naturalness of trust.

13 Gored States and Theatrical Guises

Paul Standish

> That an actor can represent grief shows the uncertainty of evidence, but that he can represent grief also shows the reality of evidence.
>
> Ludwig Wittgenstein[1]

> There is a relation between discipline and the theatrical sense. If we cannot imagine ourselves as different from what we are and try to assume that second self, we cannot impose a discipline upon ourselves, though we may accept one from others. Active virtue as distinguished from the passive acceptance of a current code is therefore theatrical, consciously dramatic, the wearing of a mask. It is the condition of arduous full life.
>
> W.B. Yeats[2]

Lendings

In an essay published in 1958, "Change the Joke and Slip the Yoke," Ralph Ellison quotes these lines from Yeats in illustration of an irony he finds in the "old American problem of identity."[3] This is an irony that he seeks to understand in the light of "what Robert Penn Warren has termed the 'intentional' character of our national beginnings." He comments:

For the ex-colonials, the declaration of an American identity meant the assumption of a mask, and it imposed not only the discipline of national self-consciousness, it gave Americans an awareness of the joke that always lies between appearance and reality, between the discontinuity of social tradition, and that sense of the past which clings to the mind. And perhaps even an

---

I thank the editors and especially Suzy Harris for comments on earlier versions.

[1] Ludwig Wittgenstein, *Last Writings on the Philosophy of Psychology: The Inner and the Outer*, vol. II, ed. G.H. von Wright and H. Nyman, trans. C.G. Luckhardt and M.A.E. Aue (Oxford: Blackwell, 1992), 67.

[2] W.B. Yeats, undated journal no. 34, in *Autobiographies*, ed. W.H. O'Donnell and D.N. Archibald (New York: Scribner, 1999), 347.

[3] Ralph Waldo Ellison, *Shadow and Act* (New York: Random House, 1964), 53; hereafter cited parenthetically as *SA*. Ellison's quotation gives a very slightly different wording, concluding with "Active virtue, the passive acceptance of a current code, is the wearing of a mask. It is the condition of an arduous full life."

awareness of the joke that society is man's creation, not God's. Americans began their revolt from the English fatherland when they dumped tea into the Boston Harbor, masked as Indians, and the mobility of the society created in this limitless space has encouraged the use of the mask for good and evil ever since. As the advertising industry, which is dedicated to the creation of masks, makes clear, that which cannot gain authority from tradition may borrow it with a mask. Masking is a play upon possibility and ours is a society in which possibilities are many. When American life is most American it is apt to be most theatrical. (*SA* 53–54)

The irony is but one facet of the "old American problem." The active virtue of imagining ourselves as different from what we are is something that Yeats associates with writers as different as Oscar Wilde and Walt Whitman. Wordsworth, by contrast, so often "flat and heavy," is singled out "partly because his moral sense has no theatrical element, it is an obedience, a discipline which he has not created."[4] It is part of the burden of Ellison's essay that the literal assumption of the mask by the ex-colonials, their pretense at disguise, is matched by a more covert masking in the Declaration of Independence, which in turn surfaces theatrically in Jim Crow racism and blackface – a theatricality that is reiterated relentlessly in America's treatment of its black population. Counterfeiting came in to contain the problem, but it turns out that it makes it worse. Out of the counterfeiting of the black American's identity there arises a "profound doubt in the white man's mind as to the authenticity of his own image of himself" (*SA* 53) – his image also of the country that is his.

Profound doubt in the human mind as to the authenticity of what we say and mean might be taken as a signature feature of the plays of Shakespeare, and so it is apt that the pondering of these matters in Stanley Cavell's first book should culminate in "The Avoidance of Love," his extended essay on *King Lear*. But the notion of authenticity is now more philosophically weary than it was during the decade that spans Ellison's and Cavell's essays. Moreover, a temptation to be avoided, if we are to become clearer about these matters, is offered by the all-too-familiar assessment that a major theme of Shakespeare's plays is the relationship between appearance and reality. What matters is not what we see but what is going on underneath. The neatness of this neo-Platonist distinction scarcely does justice to the complexity of what "Must We Mean What We Say?" means, and it might easily become a barrier to exploration of what Cavell writes. (Ellison, emphasizing irony, has something else in mind.) It would erect a problem of the kind that

---

[4] Yeats, *Autobiographies*, 347.

Cavell is trying to resist when he writes that the teaching of the later Wittgenstein is "in service of a vision that false views of the inner and of the outer produce and sustain one another" (*CR* 329). The falsity is to be found where such contrasts part company with the rough ground of particular contexts and, in effect, turn metaphysical. Authenticity is a problematic concept, but it cannot simply be avoided. In what follows it ramifies in the finer grain of such issues as identity, authority, legitimacy, and meaning as these emerge in that essay.

Shakespeare's play raises these themes in peculiarly poignant ways, exposing them in part through testing the resources of theater itself. In the 2001 Preface to the updated edition of *Must We Mean What We Say?* Cavell ponders the "all but unappeasable craving for unreality" (*MWM* xx), which puts into question the nature of the everyday and the ordinary, and the human tendency to drift into a state of "exile from our words" (xxi). This exile can seem to coincide with what is sometimes a negative casting of theatricalization in his work. Theatricalization has often been coupled with the artificial and unreal in opposition to the natural and genuine.[5] These matters come back in newly explicit ways in this final chapter of the book.

It is important not to leave the matter there, however, with these negative connotations of theatricalization because the "play upon possibility" that Ellison sees in masking inheres in the projective nature of language,[6] without which Cavell's later Emersonian moral perfectionism[7] could scarcely come to light. Yet something holds us back. "We feel as if we had to *penetrate* phenomena," Wittgenstein writes, before countering this with the assertion: "our investigation, however, is directed not towards phenomena, but, as one might say, towards the '*possibilities*' of phenomena. We remind ourselves, that is to say, of the *kind of statement* that we make about phenomena."[8] The desire to penetrate phenomena is an accomplice to the sense of a bifurcation of appearance and reality. The possibilities of phenomena are explored in the world that appears, and these are not additions to the phenomenon – as though there was first the encounter with the actual thing and then the speculation about how it might be different. The thing is known from the start in terms of its possibilities, and these are extendable in open-ended ways. This is one

[5] See Adrian Skilbeck, *Stanley Cavell, Drama, and Education: Serious Words for Serious Subjects* (Dordrecht: Springer, 2021).
[6] See "Excursus on Wittgenstein's Vision of Language" (*CR* 168–90).
[7] The most systematic account of this unsystematic notion is to be found in *CHU* 4–8.
[8] Ludwig Wittgenstein, *Philosophical Investigations*, rev. 4th edn, trans. G.E.M. Anscombe, P.M.S. Hacker, and Joachim Schulte, ed. Hacker (Malden, MA: Wiley-Blackwell, 2009), §90.

reason why there is no one-tracked interpretation that can be applied to the various ways in which masks are put on – the variety being taken, in respect of *King Lear*, to embrace Edgar's elfing of his hair in knots as Poor Tom, Kent's rhyming to shape his old course in a country new, the sisters' hypocritical words, the Fool's antics, and countless other verbal ploys behind which or within which the characters hide. This hiding, it needs to be said, is a phenomenon that occurs within language or, say, in the behavior of beings with language (including the codes of clothing and accent and appearance); it is not something that occurs behind the phenomenon. Masks, disguises, and words that are untrue are moves within the realm of appearance; disguise is possible only within language-games; and we would do better not to posit something beyond this, for this can only distract us from the way the world is.

Clothing most obviously serves as a covering and, hence, as a covering over or covering up. Attention is drawn to it most clearly in the storm scene. Cast out by Goneril and Regan, wandering on the heath, Lear sends his Fool into the shelter of a hovel while he stands alone and in prayer, in remorse for the "too little care" he has shown for the poor, the homeless, the unclothed, and the hungry ("Poor naked wretches ..."). Taking on the lesson he has learned, he urges: "Expose thyself to feel what wretches feel."[9] When confronted soon after by the figure of Poor Tom (Edgar, naked, disguised as a madman), he laughs and says: "Ha! here's three on's are sophisticated! Thou art the thing itself: unaccommodated man is no more but such a poor bare, forked animal as thou art. Off, off, you lendings! come unbutton here."[10] And, exposed to the storm, he takes off his clothes. Against the background of the covering over of the truth in so much that has happened, the symbolism of nakedness is obvious. And yet nakedness has its familiar sense only for beings who wear clothes: rather than being a simple opposite to clothing, it is a possibility within the visual vocabulary of clothes, within the language-game of dressing and undressing, with its varying forms of adornment and revealing of the body. Poor Tom's naked body is not "the thing itself," a phrase that implies his nature is fundamentally animal: human beings are by nature accommodated, housed, clothed, and found in language, of which sometimes they are deprived. Recovery is not to be found in reversion to the condition of animals, to a natural Edenic state, but in projection toward new forms of words, new lendings: re-covering as renewal.

[9] William Shakespeare, *King Lear*, ed. R.A. Foakes, Arden Shakespeare, Third Series (London: Thomas Nelson and Sons, 1997), 3.4.
[10] *Ibid.*

The "lendings" Lear refers to are borrowed from the sheep, the cow, the silkworm, but the suggestion is perhaps that these are not our only borrowings: lendings are also words, where these are not the outer covering, the communication or coding of thought in speech, but its very possibility. This makes more pertinent to discussion of *King Lear* the continuity Cavell sees between concerns raised by Shakespearean tragedy and those that stir in ordinary language philosophy itself. Perhaps in one way this is apparent in J.L. Austin's pivotal reference, in *How to Do Things with Words*, to Euripides' *Hippolytus* – "my tongue swore to, but my heart (or mind or other backstage artiste) did not," retheatricalized in the burlesque of Austin's translation.[11] The official line is, of course, that Austin "excludes" actions performed on a stage, a topic that ignited Cavell's criticisms of Derrida's criticisms of Austin. Yet, in some degree, as Andrew Norris has helped to show, the extent to which Cavell writes against Austin has not been sufficiently appreciated. The encounter with Austin "sets the stage," Norris claims, "for all that comes after"; but Cavell will make ordinary language philosophy his own only when he shows that "Austin had not adequately appreciated the uncanny nature of the fact that our access to the ordinary is not immediate and unreflective but requires philosophical work, work that challenges our philosophical and cultural inheritance."[12] In fact, the ordinary language philosopher's testing out of what-we-say-when has its similarities to an actor's trying out of variations in verbal, facial, gestural, and bodily expression, as it does to variations in costume, set-design, music ... : this is not so much a matching of expression to predetermined meanings but an experiment that opens registers of significance where meaning is to be newly found.

It is significant, I think, that in "The Avoidance of Love" Cavell is not for the most part overtly engaging with philosophical works. Yet in a passage early in the essay that signals the way he will approach the play's most familiar, climactic scenes, attention is drawn to a distinction between Austin and Wittgenstein:

A philosopher like Austin, it is true, concentrates on examples whose meaning can be brought out by appealing to widely shared, or easily imaginable circumstances (once he has given directions for imagining them) – circumstances, roughly, that Wittgenstein refers to as "our language games." But Wittgenstein is also concerned with forms of words whose meaning cannot

[11] J.L. Austin, *How to Do Things with Words*, 2nd edn, ed. J.O. Urmson and Marina Sbisà (Cambridge, MA: Harvard University Press, 1979; 1st edn 1962), 9–10.

[12] Andrew Norris, *Becoming Who We Are: Politics and Practical Philosophy in the Work of Stanley Cavell* (Oxford University Press, 2017), 17–18.

be elicited in this way – words we sometimes have it at heart to say but whose meaning is not secured by appealing to the way they are ordinarily (commonly) used, because there is no ordinary use of them, in that sense. It is not, therefore, that I mean something *other* than those words would ordinarily mean, but rather that what they mean, and whether they mean anything, depends solely upon whether I am using them so as to make my meaning. (*MWM* 271)

Luther's remark that "Faith resides under the left nipple" is cited as an instance, and Part II of the Philosophical Investigations is said to move into this region of meaning, a region habitually occupied by poetry.

Cavell raises these points in the course of his contesting, more or less at the outset in this essay, the rise of the New Criticism and the quasi-technical critical approaches that were gaining prominence at the time of his writing, approaches that would eschew the consideration of character, associated with earlier forms of Shakespearean commentary, in favor of the identification of textual patterns and the play of signifiers. Cavell's resistance is both to traditional, staid, and sometimes moralizing read-ings, which emphasize understanding of character to the partial neglect of language, and to the purism of more technical textual analysis, sophis-ticated in such a way as to shield itself from character. "How," Cavell asks, "could any serious critic ever have forgotten that to care about a specific character is to care about the utterly specific words he says and when he says them; or that we care about the utterly specific words of a play because certain men and women are having to give voice to them?" (269). The eminently teachable techniques of the new forms of criticism in question – surely a part of what gives them credence – can themselves set up barriers to response. With the mental slack created by outlawing more morally charged engagements with the work, they tempt the reader to a kind of knowing connoisseurship: "When we are made to know that Shakespeare lived in Shakespeare's age and so dealt in his age's under-standings and conventions, we can forget that it is Shakespeare demanding of us; and so *his* Bastard slumps back into 'the' Bastard of his age, from which he had pointedly lifted it" (311). What both trad-itional and new forms of criticism miss is that the reality of character lies in language, and that language's significance lies in the lives of human beings.

The play starts in the middle of a conversation about inheritance and anticipation of the division of the kingdom, but then, almost immedi-ately, the honorable Kent asks Gloucester: "Is not this your son, my lord?" Edmund is the "Bastard" in question, the illegitimate son of Gloucester. "His breeding, sir," Gloucester replies, "hath been at my charge: I have so often blushed to acknowledge him, that now I am brazed to it." So this professed blushing is an admission of shame, but the acknowledgment is muffled and eased by the "locker-room" (276) swagger with which Gloucester tries to color this talk between men; it is a semblance of what acknowledgment might have been. Kent is surely dissembling in his own way and, perhaps as a matter of propriety and discretion, affecting not to understand. But his "I cannot conceive you" – that is, "I don't understand" – makes possible the double entendre of Gloucester's reply: "Sir, the young fellow's mother could." Gloucester goes on apparently to inform Kent that he also has "a son by order of law, some year elder than this, who yet is no dearer in my account," affirming, equally, the "whoreson must be acknowledged."

The prose of this exchange constitutes the preamble to the formal verse of the court scene – still Act 1, scene 1 – where Lear divides his kingdom. His manner of doing this, where each of his three daughters is to show that she merits her share by publicly declaring her love for him, occasions the juxtaposition of the florid hypocrisy of Goneril and Regan and the silent withholding of Cordelia. Of course, it will be said, the love expressed by Goneril and Regan is corrupted and commodified, totally debased, but let us attend rather to its presentation here. This is a theatricalization of the expression of love – most obviously in their empty avowals but also, derivatively, in the staging of the contrast between what they say and Cordelia's "Nothing, my lord." The scene is the coiled spring from which the plot is released, and some critics have seen it in more or less mechanical terms – a scene that is difficult to believe but that must be accepted at the level, say, of myth or, in myth's modern variant, psychological abnormality ("Lear is senile; Lear is puerile ..." *MWM* 285). Cavell is unimpressed by such readings and contends rather that what we see can be taken at face value: that one can imagine a father today demanding ostentatious expressions of affection from his daughter in "return" for his largesse; and surely, it might be added, one can imagine political leaders of today – or, perhaps, a royal family – requiring of family members public displays of loyalty and affection. What is happening is more familiar than conventional criticism is inclined to make out:

Lear is torturing her, claiming her devotion, which she wants to give, but forcing her to help him betray (or not to betray) it, to falsify it publicly. (Lear's ambiguity here, wanting at once to open and to close her mouth, further allows the ordinariness of the scene, its verisimilitude to common parental love, swinging between absorption and rejection of its offspring ...). (291)

Lear knows what Goneril and Regan are doing, *and* he knows what *he* is doing: he is offering a bribe for which in return he wants false love and a public expression of love (280–90). But why settle for a bribe when you can have the real thing? It is not exactly that he does *not* believe them, but the real thing is unruly: better to contract it to the order of ritual. Goneril and Regan are keeping up appearances; but Cordelia's disruption, refusing this game, is also something that appears. What is it that Lear does not want to reveal?

Cavell's reading turns on the idea of the avoidance of recognition:

> My hypothesis will be that Lear's behavior in this scene is motivated by – the tragedy begins because of – the same motivation which manipulates the tragedy throughout its course, from the scene which precedes the abdication, through the storm, blinding, evaded reconciliations, to the final moments: by the attempt to avoid recognition, the shame of exposure, the threat of self-revelation. (286)

The way for this has been laid, as we saw, by the brief exchange between Kent and Gloucester, which raised questions concerning legitimacy regarding both succession and birth. But these were given a particular shading by the mildly evasive double-gesture of Gloucester's affectation of shame and acknowledgment of Edmund, perhaps also by Kent's diplomatic reserve.

"Shame," Cavell writes, "is the most primitive, the most private, of emotions; but it is also the most primitive of *social* responses. With the discovery of the individual, whether in Paradise or the Renaissance, there is the simultaneous discovery of the isolation of the individual; his presence to himself but simultaneously to *others*" (286). But in what sense is shame primitive? Viewed from a contemporary developmental psychology perspective, this would scarcely make sense, but the reference to Paradise invites very different associations. Expulsion from Eden, the fruit of the forbidden tree having been eaten, suggests a coming into knowledge and self-consciousness, the very nature of which involves a rift with the absorption of animal nature.[13] Shame is epitomized by a bodily self-consciousness, by being seen by another, and strategies develop for subduing or stifling or screening this visibility. Gloucester and Lear flaunt their confidence in forms of expression that impose upon others verbal responses that are barriers to recognition. They suppress something in language itself, denying the human. The denial turns the other, at best, into a partner or opponent in negotiation, perhaps into an object; it neutralizes or neuters them.

Later, in *In Quest of the Ordinary*, Cavell will shift the accent in the interpretation of the story of Eden away from shame and toward fear:

---

[13] It remains something of a puzzle to me that at a later date, in *In Quest of the Ordinary*, Cavell departs from this reading of the expulsion from Eden as a scene of shame, suggesting instead that it is dominated by fear.

"The feature of the situation I emphasize is that its sense of exposure upon the birth of knowledge pertains not only to one's vulnerability to knowledge, to being known, to the trauma of separation, but as well to the vulnerability of knowledge itself."[14] This, I take it, is not to deny shame, or even to deny its primitivity, but to tie the anxiety to the fear of not knowing, to skepticism. That one can be seen by the other, that there are other minds, exposes the limits and the precariousness of knowledge itself. In *The Claim of Reason*, Cavell recalls his having spoken of "a stratum of symmetry in which what corresponds to *acknowledgment* in relation to others is *acceptance* in relation to objects ('The Avoidance of Love,' 324)" (*CR* 454). And later, in "The Scandal of Skepticism," he will suggest that doubt about the existence of other minds is the more fundamental form of skepticism. In my fantasies of "solitude or of self-destruction," the problem is "to *recognize* myself as denying another, to understand that I carry chaos in myself ... I am the scandal" of *skepticism* (*PDAT* 151). Fear turns the existence of the other into an epistemological problem (How do I know there are other minds?), hence providing one of the avenues through which avoidance of recognition is to be pursued. To speak to the (now neutered) other is then to convey information via a coding and decoding of thought, with the literary critics busily decoding text in disparagement of engagement with character.

"The world is to be *accepted*," Cavell writes, "as the presentness of other minds is not to be known, but acknowledged. But what is this 'acceptance,' which caves in at a doubt? And where do we get the idea that there is something we cannot do (e.g., prove that the world exists)?" (*MWM* 324). "The great difficulty here," Wittgenstein writes,

is not to represent the matter as if there were something one *couldn't* do. As if there really were an object from which I derive its description, but I were unable to shew it to anyone. – And the best that I can propose is that we should yield to the temptation to use this picture, but then investigate how the *application* of the picture goes.[15]

Not to think there is something one cannot do: it is precisely anxiety that there is that needs to be not so much resolved or dispelled but stilled, for this stands in the way of our seeing things as they are – that is, from attending to the reality of our life in words. Here again then the craving for knowledge blocks the path to acceptance and acknowledgment. But this is not something to be simply excised: it will recur as temptation,

---

[14] Stanley Cavell, *In Quest of the Ordinary: Lines of Skepticism and Romanticism* (University of Chicago Press, 1988), 49.
[15] Wittgenstein, *Philosophical Investigations*, §374.

insinuating itself into our thinking, in ways that exceed our anticipation and control, where to see how the application of the picture goes may depend upon receptivity to language's grace.

If ordinary language philosophy is generally a testing out of legitimacy that at the same time is a testing of the means of legitimation, this more poetic venturing of words – in Luther, in Part II of the *Philosophical Investigations* – causes the notion of the legitimate to tremble. It is relevant, I think, that Gerald Bruns' insightful reading of "The Avoidance of Love" sees the text as a further iteration of the ancient quarrel between philosophy and poetry, where the craving for knowledge confines philosophy in its skeptical dilemma: in a self-defined difference from the *Ursprung* of poetry, it shores itself up against the advent of the new. The Heideggerian inflection Bruns gives to the poetic needs to be read alongside his acknowledgment of the ordinary, the common, and the low in Cavell's writings. The implication of the reference to the ancient quarrel is, I take it, that it is as if philosophy sets the terms of argument in advance and, hence, silences or is dead to what cannot or will not speak in those terms, cutting off paths to the common and insulating itself against language's origination. "The problem with poetry," Bruns writes,

is not so much that its representations are false as that its textuality or reserve, its self-refusal, situates philosophy on the site of the skeptical dilemma and threatens to prevent it from beginning. It plays, so to speak, Cordelia to philosophy's Lear. And so it must be banished.[16]

It is out of Cordelia's reserve and self-refusal that Lear will eventually find a path toward self-knowledge of a kind, away from the self-enclosed scripting of his avoidance of recognition. Eventually, it is out of Lear's inchoate "Howl, howl, howl, howl!" that the rebuke arises ("O, you are men of stones") and hope against hope springs ("Lend me a looking-glass; / If that her breath will mist or stain the stone, / Why, then she lives").[17] Vision gives way to breath, and the stillness of the stone to the stain of life.

Legitimates

The long court scene is in effect held in place by two involving Gloucester and Edmund: in the first, we saw the urbane and somewhat

---

[16] Gerald Bruns, "Stanley Cavell's Shakespeare," *Critical Inquiry* 16/3 (Spring 1990), 612–32 (at 632).
[17] *Lear*, 5.3.

forced exchanges between Gloucester and Kent, and then the appearance of Edmund, who "studies deserving"; the second, which deserves studying, begins with the self-assured soliloquy of Edmund, extending into his deception, first of Edgar, then of Gloucester. Here is the soliloquy:

> Thou, nature, art my goddess; to thy law
> My services are bound. Wherefore should I
> Stand in the plague of custom, and permit
> The curiosity of nations to deprive me,
> For that I am some twelve or fourteen moon-shines
> Lag of a brother? Why bastard? wherefore base?
> When my dimensions are as well compact,
> My mind as generous, and my shape as true,
> As honest madam's issue? Why brand they us
> With base? with baseness? bastardy? base, base?
> ...
>
>   Well, then,
> Legitimate Edgar, I must have your land:
> Our father's love is to the bastard Edmund
> As to the legitimate: fine word, – legitimate!
> Well, my legitimate, if this letter speed,
> And my invention thrive, Edmund the base
> Shall top the legitimate. I grow; I prosper:
> Now, gods, stand up for bastards!

The service to which Edmund dedicates himself is to his instincts, and hence in a sense it is no service, and there is no law by which he is "bound." But the contempt carried by the plosive B of this word echoes through the repetitions of "bastard" and "base." It questions the hierarchies by which baseness is determined, the branding that is thereby imposed, and the very basis for such mechanisms of legitimation, a word itself alliterated through "law," "letter," "lag," and "love." Edmund lingers on the word "legitimate" ("fine word, – legitimate!"), savoring his scorn for the very idea, with repetition draining the word of meaning, questioning the legitimacy of legitimacy itself. "Edmund's stinging sensitivity to the illegitimacy of society's 'legitimacy'," Cavell writes, "prefigures Lear's knowledge of the influence of society's 'justice'" (*MWM* 308).

When Gloucester comes in, Edmund leads him quickly and adroitly to the belief that his son, Edgar, is intending to kill him in order not to have to wait for the inheritance that is his due; and subsequently, when Edmund sees Edgar, he persuades him that he should be in fear for his life as his father's mind has been poisoned against him. The scene serves to point up the dramatic contrast in character and sensibility between the half-brothers: in soliloquy again, Edmund describes Edgar as "a brother noble, / Whose nature is so far from doing harms, / That he suspects none: on whose foolish honesty / My practices ride easy!"[18] Edmund's warning leads Edgar to go into hiding, and he does this by adopting the guise of a madman, "Poor Tom." He sustains the disguise throughout the time of the storm on the heath, when the blinded Gloucester is present, and throughout the time when he escorts Gloucester to Dover cliff, the place where his father, in despair, intends to end his life.

But why does Edgar not reveal himself? At first the reason for his disguise was the judgment, so hastily made, that he could not, it was not safe to, confront his father. Now that Gloucester has been blinded and his deception by Edmund exposed, why does Edgar maintain the disguise? It is still as Poor Tom that he leads Gloucester apparently to the very edge of the cliff:

GLOUCESTER   When shall we come to the top of that same hill?
EDGAR   You do climb up it now: look, how we labour.
GLOUCESTER   Methinks the ground s even.
EDGAR   Horrible steep.
          Hark, do you hear the sea?
          …
EDGAR   Come on, sir; here's the place: stand still. How fearful
          And dizzy 'tis, to cast one's eyes so low!
          …
          I'll look no more;
          Lest my brain turn, and the deficient sight
          Topple down headlong.
GLOUCESTER   Set me where you stand.
          …
EDGAR (aside)   Why I do trifle thus with his despair
          Is done to cure it.
GLOUCESTER   O you mighty gods!
          This world I do renounce, and, in your sights,
          Shake patiently my great affliction off:
          If I could bear it longer, and not fall
          To quarrel with your great opposeless wills,
          My snuff and loathed part of nature should
          Burn itself out. If Edgar live, O, bless him!
          Now, fellow, fare thee well.
          …
EDGAR   Think that the clearest gods, who make them honours
          Of men's impossibilities, have preserved thee.[19]

[18] Lear, 1.2.   [19] Ibid. 4.6.

Why does he not reveal himself? "The answers which suggest themselves to that question," Cavell writes,

are sophisticated, not the thing itself. For example: Edgar wants to clear himself in the eyes of the world before revealing himself. (But he could still let his *father* know. Anyway, he does tell his father before he goes to challenge Edmund.) Edgar "wants to impose a penance on his father, and to guarantee the genuineness and permanence of the repentance" (Muir, 1). (This seems to me psychologically fantastic; it suggests that the first thing that occurs to Edgar on seeing his father blinded is to exact some further punishment. Or else it makes Edgar into a monster of righteousness; whereas he is merely self-righteous.) Edgar wants to cure his father of his desire to commit suicide. (But *revealing himself* would seem the surest and most immediate way to do that.) And so on. (*MWM* 282–83)

Cavell's dissatisfaction is not that these are psychological explanations, but that they are answers to the wrong question: they give reasons as to why Edgar delays, when we do not, at this stage, know even that he intends to reveal himself. What we do know is that Edgar is *avoiding recognition*, and this is what needs explaining.

Gloucester's avowed wish ("Oh! Dear son Edgar, …") – that he had eyes to see Edgar again – is denied by Edgar's refusal to reveal himself. He is deprived of his eyes for a second time. Symbolism of sight runs throughout the play, reminding the audience that it may not be seeing what is before its eyes. It reveals in Edgar a capacity for cruelty. Cavell does not contest the self-righteousness in Edgar, and certainly the acting out of a path toward redemption by the grace of the gods ("Think that the clearest gods … have preserved thee") suggests that Edgar is taking on the mantle of the Christian savior, albeit that the plurality of Edgar's "gods" veils this in some degree.[20] The itemizing of the sophisticated critical responses to the question of Edgar's delay has a cumulative effect that draws attention to their ingenuity in avoiding a blatantly obvious fact – that Edgar is in disguise, which by definition means that he is wanting not to be recognized. This is an ingenuity also in avoiding any more straightforward felt response. Cavell accepts the arrogation of the critic, which is like that of the philosopher, but the critic has taken on the mantle of providing explanations, and these are distractions from what is to be seen. Edgar is an illusionist: he is playing the part of "unknown redeemer" in his own miracle play;[21] and the theatricality of his rescuing of Gloucester is openly displayed by Shakespeare. Film versions of

---

[20] Religious references in the play are generally to pagan gods. Cavell's phrasing often brings out the recessive contestation with Christianity.
[21] See Sarah Beckwith, *Shakespeare and the Grammar of Forgiveness* (Ithaca, NY: Cornell University Press, 2011) for a detailed discussion of *King Lear's* inheritance and adaptation of the medieval genres of miracle and romance.

the play go badly wrong when they show the characters walking up a hill to a precipitous drop. Shakespeare's effrontery is to present this on the flat boards of the stage, to suspend the suspension of disbelief, reminding the audience of where it is, reminding them of their own awkward presence in seeing these things.

It is in the same vein, when all is said and done, that the play comes to a close with Albany's conferring of responsibility for the kingdom onto Kent and Edgar:

ALBANY Friends of my soul, you twain
        Rule in this realm, and the gored state sustain.
KENT   I have a journey, sir, shortly to go.
        My master calls me. I must not say no.
EDGAR   The weight of this sad time we must obey.
        Speak what we feel, not what we ought to say.
        The oldest hath borne most. We that are young
        Shall never see so much, nor live so long.[22]

Kent's coded anticipation of his own death is conventionalized, while Edgar's "Speak what we feel, not what we ought to say" is less than reassuring because, first, it betrays the inadequacy of the commitment to authenticity and sincerity that the play has demonstrated and, second, because "at the beginning Lear and Cordelia spoke what they felt, anyway certainly not what they ought to have said" (*MWM* 342). Hence, the harmony of the rhyming couplets comes across as a device: it does not ring entirely true to, does not resolve, except by theatrical convention, the tragedy that we have seen. It is alleviated only by the half-rhyme at the end ("young" / "long"), in a sentence that conceivably reminds us, at least so long as we remain "young," of what we fail to see. The last line is the last turn in the central motif and symbol of the play, epitomized by the gored sockets of Gloucester's eyes and the mutilated bodies in the final death scene. "To speak – the signature expression of the human life form – is to be victimized by what there is to say, or to fail to say."[23] Speech shows also what we fail to see. The stigmatism of human clear-sightedness depends, as Cavell puts this elsewhere, upon the stigma of a "hidden yet unconcealable wound."[24]

---

[22] *Lear*, 5.3.
[23] Cavell, "Companionable Thinking," in *Wittgenstein and the Moral Life: Essays in Honor of Cora Diamond*, ed. Alice Crary (Cambridge, MA: MIT Press, 2007), 281–98 (at 292).
[24] *Ibid.*

States

The shame that attaches to recognition – "the simultaneous discovery of the isolation of the individual; his presence to himself but simultaneously to others" (*MWM* 286) – is, Cavell suggests, newly discovered in the Renaissance.

Cavell's dismissal of Edwin Muir's explanation for Edgar's not revealing himself – because he "wants to impose a penance on his father, and to guarantee the genuineness and permanence of the repentance" – as "psychologically fantastic" is psychologically compelling. There is reason to squirm at Edgar's self-legitimation ("Why I do trifle thus with his despair / Is done to cure it"). But if we look again at what Sarah Beckwith has called the "complex charting of failures of acknowledgment" in Shakespeare's tragedies, a larger historical change comes into view:

The medieval home of the language of acknowledgment is the sacrament of penance, and the earliest usages of the word 'acknowe' are intimately bound up with the histories of the sacrament, especially in the act of confession. (The first definition given for confession in the *OED* is "to acknowledge," the second "to make oneself known.")[25]

Beckwith demonstrates the ramifications of changing conceptions of penitence at the time of the Reformation: penance was not to be a set of actions but repentance (*metanoia*), the "turning or returning of the whole mind and soul and life to God."[26] When people confess or forgive in the absence of a ritual, they are newly exposed to the responses of others. Far from a matter of isolated moments in our lives, this is an extension of whether we mean what we say through our ordinary lives in language, our common human bond – the significance of which in philosophy is most fully realized in its ordinary language forms. This rediscovery of speech, Beckwith writes, is the "essential medium of Shakespeare's theater."[27] Authority now depends upon each utterance, on how it is given and how received, in an interaction where each is singled out, their judgment laid bare. The salience of this with regard to Edgar is that, in casting himself anachronously as a character in a morality play, he provides an illustration of this historical shift in confession and forgiveness – and shows something further of what is at stake in recognition. The subplot echoes Lear's retrograde attempt to contain

---

[25] Sarah Beckwith, "William Shakespeare and Stanley Cavell: Acknowledging, Confessing, and Tragedy," in *Stanley Cavell and Literary Studies*, ed. Richard Eldridge and Bernard Rhie (London: Bloomsbury, 2011), 123–35 (at 126).
[26] *Ibid.*   [27] *Ibid.*, 133.

disorders of desire within a realm of law, to refuse the reality of recognition in our lives in language.

The significance of the Reformation in the play, however, has a further, more political aspect. In England, the sixteenth century was marked by instability: there was the threat both of invasion by Spain and of civil war, fueled by conflict between Catholicism and the Church of England. Elizabeth I's reign (1558–1603) had brought greater stability, but she had no heir and was slow to appoint a successor to the throne. Hence, there was fear of a division of the kingdom and renewed strife. When *King Lear* was first performed, in 1606, the division of the kingdom would have horrified the audience. This is pertinent to the way that perhaps a third of "The Avoidance of Love," principally the last third, is given to something other than direct criticism of the play – a factor that itself calls the terms of criticism into question. Attention is turned to the nature of theater and of tragedy, and to America and what it has become.

Of the great modern nations that have undergone loss of past or loss of future or self-defeat of promise, Cavell writes, "in none is tragedy so intertwined with its history and its identity as in America." Its power is so awe-inspiring, its self-defeat so heart-breaking:

> It had a mythical beginning, still visible, if ambiguous, to itself and to its audience: before there was Russia, there was Russia; before there was France and England, there was France and England; but before there was America, there was no America. America was *discovered*, and what was discovered was not a place, one among others, but a setting, the backdrop of a destiny. It began as theater. Its Revolution, unlike the English and French and Russian Revolutions, was not a civil war; its point was not reform but independence. And its Civil War was not a revolution; the oppressed did not rise, and the point was not the overthrow of a form of government but secession and union, the point was its identity ... [I]ts fantasies are those of impotence, because it remains at the mercy of its past, because its present is continuously ridiculed, by the fantastic promise of its origins and its possibility, and because it has never been sure that it will survive. Since it had a birth, it may die. It feels mortal. And it wishes proof not merely of its continuance but of its existence, a fact that it has never been able to take for granted. (*MWM* 344–45)

Writing in the decade of the Civil Rights movement and the reaction against it, of the Vietnam War and its self-destructiveness, "The Avoidance of Love" struggles with what America has become. James Conant, writing in the aftermath of 9/11, ponders the concept of America. His argument nears its close with the following words:

> America could not disguise from itself that the Vietnam War (and the War at Home it provoked) was a struggle over its own soul. But now that America can tell itself that it has been attacked, that it is vulnerable, and that it acts only to

protect itself, it has become easier than ever for it to disguise from itself how its continuance depends not only on what it does but on how it does it. America's threats from within – its triumphal assurances to itself that its constitution stands fully achieved and its equally vehement rejections of such assurances – have now become clothed in the guise of arguments about how to deal with threats from without. But if it is to have a soul worth saving, attacks on it from without must not silence its ongoing argument from within over what would count as its having a soul worth saving.[28]

Conant ends with the speculation that America's self-concept is held in place by its skepticism: if its doubts were ever dissolved it would cease to exist. The modern history of skepticism coincides with the history of America. They share a denial of what we ordinarily know – as if the Constitution were America's *cogito*. Earlier in *Must We Mean What We Say?*, in "Ending the Waiting Game," in a parenthesis regarding the Pilgrims' perception of Europe as fallen and investment in a New World, Cavell writes: "For an American, fighting for his country, that the last hope of earth should from its beginning have swallowed slavery, is an irony so withering, a justice so intimate in its rebuke of pride, as to measure only with God" (*MWM* 141).

Bonds

Pride is to be rebuked, but this should not preclude the possibility of praise.

But can there be praise in a world that is founded on injustice? Cavell later speaks of a "strain of perplexity" sufficient to brush one with madness over what America is or might become, a strain played out between the tasks of philosophy and the work that art does. (See "Fred Astaire Asserts the Right to Praise," *PDAT* 61–82.) And he formulates more explicitly his insight that the logic of skepticism threatens to debar praise of achievement and to block acknowledgment of the good in a society whose fundamental constitution is unjust. "Something maddening would be," he writes,

to have wanted so to love the world, to find it worthy of praise, that upon discovering that it is unpraiseworthy you find you cannot stop wanting its love. This is, in King Lear's process of exclusion, the occasion for cursing the world precisely for its not providing your cause of praise, hence being left with the doubt that its behavior is caused by your having cursed it with tainted love. (*PDAT* 109)

---

[28] James Conant, "Cavell and the Concept of America," in *Contending with Stanley Cavell*, ed. Russell B. Goodman (Oxford University Press, 2005), 55–81 (at 73).

The blocking of praise, as if exempting ourselves, is tantamount to a denial of the tragedies of our history (*PDAT* 79). Confronting this, he affirms his consent to America's partial democracy, with its failures and achievements. That this is something to which Cavell finds himself "bound" invokes consequences that extend to the horizons of his thought – through multiple iterations in the readings of Shakespeare, through "self-reliance's" echoes of "religion" (L. *ligare*, to bind), through Austin's insistence contra Hippolytus that "*our word is our bond*,"[29] and somewhere remembering Frederick Douglass' *Bondage*. In *King Lear*, the wheel of fortune turns from stoical Kent, facing a night in the stocks – "Fortune, good night: smile once more: turn thy wheel!"[30] – to Edmund's acceptance, having earlier declared himself bound to nature's law, now realizing he is going to die – "The wheel is come full circle; I am here"[31] – and to the extreme of suffering in Lear's own "I am bound / Upon a wheel of fire."[32] In Edmund's acceptance Cavell finds an Abrahamic thought: "That 'I am here' – imitating Abraham's response when God calls his name (*Genesis*, 22:1) – is the natural expression of the knowledge that my life is mine, the ultimate piece of fortune. That is what I understand Lear's huge lines of revelation to mean" (*MWM* 340).

Ellison identifies the acceptance of slavery by the founding fathers as initiating the nation's "drama of conscience" and as positioning the African American as "keeper of the nation's sense of democratic achievement, and the human scale by which would be measured its painfully slow advance toward true equality."[33] And in the Introduction to the thirtieth anniversary edition of *Invisible Man*, he writes: "By way of imposing meaning upon our disparate American experience the novelist seeks to create forms in which acts, scenes and characters speak more than their immediate selves, and in this enterprise the very nature of language is on his side."[34] This speaking more, going beyond the immediate, is inherent in language for reasons fully evident in Cavell's account of "projecting a word,"[35] as in the larger philosophy that he develops from this – which in turn is not so far from what Ellison goes on immediately to say:

For by a trick of fate (and our racial problems notwithstanding) the human imagination is integrative – and the same is true of the centrifugal force that

[29] Austin, *How to Do Things*, 10.   [30] *Lear*, 2.2.   [31] *Ibid.* 5.3.   [32] *Ibid.* 4.7.

[33] Ralph Waldo Ellison, *The Collected Essays of Ralph Ellison*, ed. John F. Callahan (New York: Modern Library, 1995), 778.

[34] Ralph Waldo Ellison, "Introduction," in *Invisible Man* (New York: Random House, 1981; 1st edn 1952), xxxviii.

[35] See especially "Excursus on Wittgenstein's Vision of Language" (*CR* 168–90).

inspirits the democratic process. And while fiction is but a form of symbolic action, a mere game of "as if," therein lies its true function and its potential for effecting change. For at its most serious, just as is true of politics at its best, it is a thrust toward a human ideal. And it approaches that ideal by a subtle process of negating the world of things as given in favor of a complex of man-made positives.[36]

Fictions and theatrical guises are the perfectionist element, the medium of Yeats' "active virtue," in which the world and the human come to be.

Acts

But there is a theatricalization in our failures of acknowledgment in everyday life: we keep silent and hide in the dark, and thus "convert the other into a character, making the world a stage for him" (*MWM* 333). It is by literalizing this that theater, great tragedy most obviously, brings home to us the nature of those failures. For the audience in a theater, action on the stage is made present. Cavell's proverbial "yokel" who rushes onto the stage to prevent Gloucester's blinding or Desdemona's smothering has not understood that the audience exists behind a fourth wall, the actors ignoring them, apparently unaware of them. The audience remains hidden, not in the *presence* of the characters yet in their *present*. We are spectators of the action and not seen, nor do we have the power to intervene. Hence, the conditions of theater enable and idealize what we habitually seek: avoidance of recognition and relief from the responsibility to act. And hence, Cavell can worry that in an age when the organs of news present everything happening as overwhelmingly present, when the newspaper tells him that everything is relevant (so that he no longer has one life, to which some things are relevant and some not), he no longer knows what he is responsible for and what not: feeling subsides into a generalized guilt, further confirming paralysis; and disasters become topics of conversation, in turn irritating the guilt (347–48). Fifty years on, the organs of social media mostly, massively, intensify this enervation.

Suspension of disbelief comes to an end, however, reminding us that outside the theater exemption no longer applies. "As in Plato's Cave," Cavell remarks, "reality is *behind* you. It will become visible when you have made yourself visible to it, presented yourself" (*WV* 155). The turning of the head, from the darkness of the theater toward the light outside, so richly realized at the end of *Stella Dallas*, is a turning from the world of the actors, toward the world in which we can and must act.

---

[36] Ellison, "Introduction," xxxviii.

A lesson of tragedy is to remind us of our lapse into docile assumptions of exemption. In some respects, our leaving the theater is a return to the ordinary. But the return needs to be read alongside Cavell's turning from Austin's appeal to widely shared or easily imaginable circumstances to Wittgenstein's concern with words we sometimes have it at heart to say but whose meaning is not secured by appealing to what we ordinarily say, because there is no ordinary use of them. Might this be a turn to the ordinary, the common, and the low, that attends to the poor naked wretches that are always with us; but where that poor is not accepted as a necessary, structural feature of the economy; and where race is not structural in a way that makes black people more usually poor?

But on the line of thought I am pressing, interpretation must turn away from philosophies of light, vision become breath. When we were told that Shakespeare's abiding theme was the relation between appearance and reality, and saw that the dominant symbolism in *King Lear* revolved around sight and blindness, we nearly stumbled. We saw someone dressed in disguise and knew they could uncover themselves, identity exposed by a defining mark. But this risked hiding subtler guises inherent in language itself, a subtlety amplified enormously with the reverberation of changing practices of confession and recognition through ordinary speech, which in turn conditions a more fine-grained vocabulary of clothes. (See "Stella's Taste: Reading Stella Dallas," in *Contesting Tears*, 197–222.) Subtle disguise in language is advertised in Gloucester's opening exchange with Kent.

Cavell's allusion to the Cave is dynamic. A Platonist reading, by contrast, manifests the problem with light and vision, a problem bearing on what it is to act. In the Platonist Cave, the shadows exist in a binary opposition to, as distortions of, the real, with subject and object securely positioned. But actions on the stage or screen are not simply to be contrasted with action in the world: there is a continuity through this range of acting in our experimentation with expression and imagination, with revealing and concealing, from our confessions to our continual game of "as if." This is there in our grander hopes and projects and fictions, but there also in the nuance of the everyday. It is in that experi-mentation – in the endless range of word and gesture, in the gradations of mimicking and pretending, of masking and masquerade, of imagery, irony, and allegory, and hyperbole and understatement – that we find new possibilities of living and of the way the world can be. This is where we find ourselves. Such is the grammar of our lives and world. The language-game spans the division between stage and world, extending across fiction and reality. As if there could be a real world without fiction! Imagine!

"Imagination" suggests "images," and images suggest sight, but imagination does not necessarily involve the constructing of images, rather the seeing of connections. In this modification in the concept of seeing, seeing becomes interpretation.[37] The gored state of Gloucester's eyes is the appalling reminder that he stumbled when he saw and that insight comes by different means. Does this not also suggest that we are likely to go wrong if we hanker after visualizations of appearance and reality, of shadows and true forms? The audience, the critic, is thrown back onto – depends on the gored state of – language itself. "My words are expressions of my life," as *The Claim of Reason* has it; "I respond to the words of others as their expressions, i.e., respond not merely to what their words mean but equally to their meaning of them ... To imagine an expression (experience the meaning of a word) is to imagine it as giving expression to a soul" (*CR* 355). The gored state of a body gives expression to a human soul. If we do not acknowledge the human soul, we cannot know what a human body is. The stigma of embodiment is expressed in every word we speak (*Elizabeth Costello*); and every word is touched with, is fated to express, chagrin (Emerson).[38] The mark of language is the unconcealable wound. These are the conditions to sustain in the political state, our city of words, our human condition.[39]

---

[37] See *CR* 353–54. Cavell is referring particularly to Part II, xi, of Wittgenstein's *Investigations*.

[38] Cavell relates Elizabeth Costello's remarks to "Self-Reliance," in "Companionable Thinking," 292.

[39] I thank the Editors and especially Suzy Harris for comments on earlier versions.

Bibliography

Titles by Cavell

Cities of Words: Pedagogical Letters on a Register of the Moral Life (Cambridge, MA: Harvard University Press, 2004).

The Claim of Reason: Wittgenstein, Skepticism, Morality, and Tragedy, new edn (Oxford University Press, 1999; 1st edn 1979).

"Companionable Thinking," in *Wittgenstein and the Moral Life: Essays in Honor of Cora Diamond*, ed. Alice Crary (Cambridge, MA: MIT Press, 2007), 281–98.

Conditions Handsome and Unhandsome: The Constitution of Emersonian Perfectionism (University of Chicago Press, 1990).

Contesting Tears: The Hollywood Melodrama of the Unknown Woman (University of Chicago Press, 1996).

Disowning Knowledge in Seven Plays of Shakespeare, updated edn (Cambridge University Press, 2003; 1st edn 1987).

Emerson's Transcendental Etudes, ed. David Justin Hodge (Stanford University Press, 2003).

In Quest of the Ordinary: Lines of Skepticism and Romanticism (University of Chicago Press, 1988).

Little Did I Know: Excerpts from Memory (Stanford University Press, 2010).

Must We Mean What We Say?, 2nd edn (Cambridge University Press, 2002; 1st edn 1969).

Philosophy the Day after Tomorrow (Cambridge, MA: Harvard University Press, 2005).

A Pitch of Philosophy: Autobiographical Exercises (Cambridge, MA: Harvard University Press, 1994).

Pursuits of Happiness: The Hollywood Comedy of Remarriage (Cambridge, MA: Harvard University Press, 1981).

The Senses of Walden, expanded edn (University of Chicago Press, 1992; 1st edn 1972).

Themes Out of School: Effects and Causes (University of Chicago Press, 1984).

This New Yet Unapproachable America: Lectures after Emerson after Wittgenstein (University of Chicago Press, 1989).

"What's the Use of Calling Emerson a Pragmatist?" in *The Revival of Pragmatism: New Essays on Social Thought, Law, and Culture*, ed. Morris Dickstein (Durham, NC: Duke University Press, 1998), 72–80.

The World Viewed: Reflections on the Ontology of Film (New York: Viking, 1971).

Titles by Other Authors

Adorno, Theodor W. "Trying to Understand *Endgame*," in *Notes to Literature*, vol. I, ed. Rolf Tiedemann, trans. Shierry Weber Nicholsen (New York: Columbia University Press, 1991), 241–76.

Affeldt, Steven G. "The Ground of Mutuality: Criteria, Judgment and Intelligibility in Stephen Mulhall and Stanley Cavell," *European Journal of Philosophy* 6/1 (1998), 1–31.

Ammons, A.R. *The Complete Poems of A.R. Ammons*, vol. I, ed. Robert M. West (New York: W.W. Norton, 2017).

Anderson, Luvell and Ernie LePore. "Slurring Words," *Noûs* 47/1 (2013), 25–48.

Anderson, Sherwood. *Winesburg, Ohio*, ed. Glen A. Love (Oxford University Press, 1997).

Anscombe, G.E.M. *Collected Philosophical Papers*, 3 vols. (Oxford: Blackwell, 1981).

Intention (Cambridge, MA: Harvard University Press, 1957).

Aquinas, Thomas. *Summa theologica*, trans. Fathers of the Dominican Province (New York: Benziger Brothers, 1947).

Armstrong, Louis. "West End Blues," 78 rpm recording, June 28, 1928, www.youtube.com/watch?v=4WPCBieSESI.

Austen, Jane. *The Oxford Illustrated Jane Austen*, ed. R.W. Chapman, 5 vols. (Oxford University Press, 1933).

Austin, J.L. *How to Do Things with Words*, 2nd edn, ed. J.O. Urmson and Marina Sbisà (Cambridge, MA: Harvard University Press, 1979; 1st edn 1962).

"How to Talk: Some Simple Ways," *Proceedings of the Aristotelian Society* 53 (1953), 227–46.

Philosophical Papers, ed. J.O. Urmson and G.J. Warnock, 2nd edn (Oxford University Press, 1979; 1st edn 1961).

Sense and Sensibilia (Oxford University Press, 1962).

Bamford, Kiff. *Jean-François Lyotard* (London: Reaktion, 2017).

Barth, John. *Lost in the Funhouse: Fiction for Print, Tape, Live Voice* (New York: Random House, 1988).

Baz, Avner. *When Words Are Called For: A Defense of Ordinary Language Philosophy* (Cambridge, MA: Harvard University Press, 2012).

Beckett, Samuel. *Endgame* (New York: Grove Press, 1958).

Beckwith, Sarah. *Shakespeare and the Grammar of Forgiveness* (Ithaca, NY: Cornell University Press, 2011).

"William Shakespeare and Stanley Cavell: Acknowledging, Confessing, and Tragedy," in *Stanley Cavell and Literary Studies*, ed. Richard Eldridge and Bernard Rhie (London: Bloomsbury, 2011), 123–35.

Berg, Alban. "Why Is Schoenberg's Music So Difficult to Understand?" in *Pro Mundo – Pro Domo: The Writings of Alban Berg*, ed. and trans. Bryan R. Simms (Oxford University Press, 2014), 183–94.

Bernstein, J.M. "Aesthetics, Modernism, Literature: Cavell's Transformations of Philosophy," in *Stanley Cavell*, ed. Richard Eldridge (Cambridge University Press, 2003), 107–42.

Bloom, Allan. *The Closing of the American Mind: How Higher Education Has Failed Democracy and Impoverished the Souls of Today's Students* (New York: Simon & Schuster, 1987).

Bradley, F.H. *Essays on Truth and Reality* (Oxford University Press, 1914).

Bruns, Gerald. "Stanley Cavell's Shakespeare," *Critical Inquiry* 16/3 (Spring 1990), 612–32.

Cadenas, Rafael. *Realidad y literatura* (Caracas: Equinoccio, 1979).

Chase, Greg. "Acknowledging Addie's Pain: Language, Wittgenstein, and *As I Lay Dying*," *Twentieth-Century Literature* 63/2 (2017), 167–90.

Chodat, Robert. *The Matter of High Words: Naturalism, Normativity, and the Postwar Sage* (Oxford University Press, 2017).

Colapietro, Vincent. "Experience Ceded and Negated," *Journal of Speculative Philosophy* 22/2 (2008), 118–26.

"Voice and the Interrogation of Philosophy: Inheritance, and Abandonment, and Jazz," in *Stanley Cavell and the Education of Grownups*, ed. Naoko Saito and Paul Standish (New York: Fordham University Press, 2012), 133–47.

Conant, James. "Cavell and the Concept of America," in *Contending with Stanley Cavell*, ed. Russell B. Goodman (Oxford University Press, 2005), 55–81.

Crary, Alice and Joel de Lara. "Who's Afraid of Ordinary Language Philosophy?" *Graduate Faculty Philosophy Journal* 39/2 (2019), 317–99.

Crary, Alice and Rupert Read (eds.). *The New Wittgenstein* (New York: Routledge, 2000),

Crassons, Kate. *The Claims of Poverty: Literature, Culture and Ideology in Late Medieval England* (University of Notre Dame Press, 2010).

cummings, e.e. *Complete Poems, 1904–1962* (New York: Liveright, 1994).

Cusset, François. *French Theory: How Foucault, Derrida, Deleuze, & Co. Transformed the Intellectual Life of the United States*, trans. Jeff Fort (Minneapolis: University of Minnesota Press, 2008).

Das, Veena. *Life and Words: Violence and the Descent into the Ordinary* (Berkeley: University of California Press, 2007).

Textures of the Ordinary: Doing Anthropology After Wittgenstein (New York: Fordham University Press, 2020).

Derrida, Jacques. *Points: Interviews, 1974–1994* (Stanford University Press, 1995).

Dewey, John. "The Need for a Recovery of Philosophy," in *John Dewey: The Middle Works, 1899–1924*, ed. Jo Ann Boydston, vol. x (Carbondale: Southern Illinois University Press, 1980).

Diamond, Cora. *The Realistic Spirit: Wittgenstein, Philosophy and the Mind* (Cambridge, MA: MIT Press, 1991).

Eliot, T.S. *Four Quartets* (New York: Harcourt, Brace, 1943).

Ellison, Ralph Waldo. *The Collected Essays of Ralph Ellison*, ed. John F. Callahan (New York: Modern Library, 1995).

Invisible Man (New York: Random House, 1981; 1st edn 1952).

Shadow and Act (New York: Random House, 1964).

Emerson, Ralph Waldo. *The Collected Works of Ralph Waldo Emerson*, vol. II: *Essays: First Series*, ed. Alfred R. Ferguson and Jean Ferguson Carr (Cambridge, MA: Belknap Press, 1979).

Essays and Lectures, ed. Joel Porte (New York: Library of America, 1983).

The Essential Writings of Ralph Waldo Emerson, ed. Brooks Atkinson (New York: Modern Library, 2000).

Felman, Shoshana. *The Scandal of the Speaking Body: Don Juan with J.L. Austin, or Seduction in Two Languages* (Stanford University Press, 2002).

Finlayson, Gordon. "Beethoven, Adorno and the Dialectics of Freedom," in *Aesthetic and Artistic Autonomy*, ed. Owen Hulatt (New York: Bloomsbury, 2013), 147–70.

Floyd, Juliet. "Aspects of Aspects," in *The Cambridge Companion to Wittgenstein*, ed. Hans Sluga and David Stern (Cambridge University Press, 2017), 361–88.

"Aspects of the Real Numbers: Putnam, Wittgenstein, and Nonextensionalism," *Monist* 103 (2020), 427–41.

"Chains of Life: Turing, *Lebensform*, and the Emergence of Wittgenstein's Later Style," *Nordic Wittgenstein Review* 5/2 (2016), 7–89.

"Heautonomy and the Critique of Sound Judgment: Kant on Reflective Judgment and Systematicity," in *Kants Ästhetik/Kant's Aesthetics/L'esthétique de Kant*, ed. Herman Parret (Berlin and Boston, MA: De Gruyter, 1998), 192–218.

"*Lebensformen*: Living Logic," in *Language, Form(s) of Life, and Logic*, ed. Christian Martin (Berlin: De Gruyter, 2018), 59–92.

"Teaching and Learning with Wittgenstein and Turing: Sailing the Seas of Social Media," *Journal of Philosophy of Education* 53/4 (2019), 715–33.

"Turing on 'Common Sense': Cambridge Resonances," in *Philosophical Explorations of the Legacy of Alan Turing: Turing 100*, ed. Juliet Floyd and Alisa Bokulich, Boston Studies in the Philosophy of Science (Dordrecht: Springer, 2017), 103–52.

"Turing, Wittgenstein and Types: Philosophical Aspects of Turing's 'The Reform of Mathematical Notation' (1944–45)," in *Alan Turing: His Work and Impact*, ed. S. Barry Cooper and Jan van Leeuwen (Amsterdam and Burlington, MA: Elsevier, 2013), 250–53.

"Wittgenstein on Ethics: Working through *Lebensformen*," *Philosophy and Social Criticism* 46/2 (2020), 115–30.

Floyd, Juliet and James E. Katz (eds.), *Philosophy of Emerging Media: Understanding, Appreciation, Application* (Oxford University Press, 2015).

Frege, Gottlob. "The Thought: A Logical Inquiry," in *Philosophical Logic*, ed. P.F. Strawson (Oxford University Press, 1967), 17–38.

Friedlander, Eli. "Common Sense, Communication and Community," in *The Palgrave Kant Handbook*, ed. Matthew Altman (London: Palgrave Macmillan, 2017), 407–24.

Expressions of Judgment: An Essay on Kant's Aesthetics (Cambridge, MA: Harvard University Press, 2015).

"Logic, Ethics and Existence in Wittgenstein's *Tractatus*," in *Wittgenstein's Moral Thought*, ed. Reshef Agam-Sega and Edmund Dain (London: Routledge, 2017), 97–132.

"Meaning Schematics in Cavell's Kantian Reading of Wittgenstein," *Revue Internationale de Philosophie* 256 (2011–12), 118–99.

"On Examples, Representatives, Measures, Standards and the Ideal," in *Reading Cavell*, ed. Alice Crary and Sanford Shieh (London: Routledge, 2006), 204–17.

Frye, Northrop. *Anatomy of Criticism* (Princeton University Press, 1957).

Gellner, Ernest. *Words and Things: An Examination of, and an Attack on, Linguistic Philosophy* (London: Victor Gollancz, 1959).

Giddens, Gary. *Visions of Jazz: The First Century* (Oxford University Press, 1998).

Giddens, Gary and Scott DeVeaux. *Jazz* (New York: W.W. Norton, 2009).

Gould, Timothy. *Hearing Voices: Voice and Method in the Writing of Stanley Cavell* (University of Chicago Press, 1998).

Grann, David. "True Crime: A Postmodern Murder Mystery," *New Yorker*, February 4, 2008, www.newyorker.com/magazine/2008/02/11/true-crime.

Hadot, Pierre. *Philosophy as a Way of Life: Spiritual Exercises from Socrates to Foucault*, ed. Arnold Davidson, trans. M. Chase (Oxford and Cambridge, MA: Blackwell, 1995).

Hamawaki, Arata. "Undoing the Psychologizing of the Psychological," *Conversations: A Cavellian Journal*, Special Issue, 7 (2019), 87–91.

Hart, Herbert. "The Ascription of Responsibilities and Rights," *Proceedings of the Aristotelian Society* n.s. 49 (1949), 171–94.

Hegel, G.W.F. *Phenomenology of Spirit*, trans. A.V. Miller (Oxford: Clarendon Press, 1977).

Phenomenology of Spirit, trans. Terry Pinkard (Cambridge University Press, 2018).

Hertzberg, Lars. "Moral Escapism and Applied Ethics," *Philosophical Papers*, Special Issue on Ethics in the Light of Wittgenstein, 31/3 (2002), 251–70.

Hesni, Samia. "Illocutionary Frustration," *Mind* 127/508 (2018), 947–76.

James, Henry. "Introduction" to William Shakespeare, *The Tempest*, ed. Sydney Lee (New York: Harper, 1906–07).

Letters of Henry James, ed. Percy Lubbock (New York: Charles Scribner's Sons, 1920).

James, William. *Varieties of Religious Experience* (New York: Penguin, 1982).

Jameson, Fredric R. "Beyond the Cave: Demystifying the Ideology of Modernism," *Bulletin of the Midwest Modern Language Association* 8/1 (1975): 1–20.

Postmodernism, or, The Cultural Logic of Late Capitalism (Durham, NC: Duke University Press, 1991).

Johnson, Kelly. *The Fear of Beggars: Stewardship and Poverty in Christian Ethics* (Grand Rapids, MI: Eerdmans, 2007).

Johnson, Samuel. *The Works of Samuel Johnson, LL.D.*, vol. I (London: Henry G. Bohn, 1850).

Jolley, Kelly. *The Concept 'Horse' Paradox and Wittgensteinian Conceptual Investigations* (London and New York: Routledge, 2007).

Jung, Carl G. *The Red Book: Liber Novus,* ed. Sonu Shamdasani (New York: W.W. Norton, 2009).

Kant, Immanuel. "An Answer to the Question: What is Enlightenment?" in *Practical Philosophy,* ed. and trans. Mary J. Gregor (Cambridge University Press, 1996), 11–22.

  Critique of the Power of Judgment, ed. Paul Guyer, trans. Guyer and Eric Matthews (Cambridge University Press, 2000).

  Critique of Pure Reason, trans. Allen W. Wood and Paul Guyer (Cambridge University Press, 1998).

  Critique of Pure Reason, trans. Norman Kemp Smith (New York: Humanities Press, 1950; Basingstoke: Macmillan, 2003).

Kendi, Ibram X. *How to Be an Antiracist* (New York: One World, 2019).

Krebs, Victor. "Around the Axis of Our Real Need," *European Journal of Philosophy* 9/3 (2001), 344–74.

Kripke, Saul A. *Wittgenstein on Rules and Private Language: An Elementary Exposition* (Cambridge, MA: Harvard University Press, 1982).

Lascelles, Mary. *Jane Austen and Her Art* (Oxford University Press, 1939).

Laugier, Sandra. "The Ethics of Care as a Politics of the Ordinary," *New Literary History* 46/2 (2015), 217–40.

  "Introduction to the French edition of *Must We Mean What We Say?*," *Critical Inquiry* 37/4 (2011), 627–51.

  "Popular Cultures, Ordinary Criticism: A Philosophy of Minor Genres," trans. Daniela Ginsburg, *MLN* 127/5 (2012), 997–1012.

  "This Is Us: Wittgenstein and the Social," *Philosophical Investigations* 4/2 (2018), 204–22.

  "Voice as Form of Life and Life Form," *Nordic Wittgenstein Review* 4 (2015), 63–81.

  "The Vulnerability of the Ordinary: Goffman, Reader of Austin," *Graduate Faculty Philosophy Journal* 39/2 (2019), 367–401.

  "The Vulnerability of Reality – Austin, Normativity, and Excuses," in *Interpreting Austin,* ed. Savas L. Tsohatzidis (Cambridge University Press, 2017), 119–42.

  Why We Need Ordinary Language Philosophy, trans. Daniela Ginsburg (University of Chicago Press, 2013).

  "Wittgenstein: Ordinary Language as Lifeform," in *Language, Form(s) of Life, and Logic: Investigations after Wittgenstein,* ed. Christian Martin (Berlin: De Gruyter, 2018), 277–304.

Lear, Jonathan. *Freud* (New York: Routledge, 2005).

Lewis, C.I. *Mind and the World Order* (Mineola, NY: Dover, 1991).

Lewis, C.S. "A Note on Jane Austen," in *Jane Austen: A Collection of Critical Essays,* ed. Ian Watt (Englewood Cliffs, NJ: Prentice-Hall, 1963), 25–34.

Love, Glen A. "*Winesburg, Ohio* and the Rhetoric of Silence," *American Literature* 40/1 (1968), 38–57.

Lyotard, Jean-François. *Political Writings,* ed. and trans. Bill Readings and Kevin Paul Geiman (Minneapolis: University of Minnesota Press, 1993).

  The Postmodern Condition: A Report on Knowledge, trans. Geoff Bennington and Brian Massumi (Minneapolis: University of Minnesota Press, 1984).

Mahon, Áine. "Fraudulence, Obscurity and Exposure: The Autobiographical Anxieties of Stanley Cavell," in *The Philosophy of Autobiography*, ed. Christopher Cowley (University of Chicago Press, 2015), 217–36.

McDowell, John. *Having the World in View: Essays on Kant, Hegel, and Sellars* (Cambridge, MA: Harvard University Press, 2009).

"Non-Cognitivism and Rule-Following," in Crary and Read (eds.), *New Wittgenstein*, 38–52.

Miller, Henry. "Creative Death," in *The Wisdom of the Heart* (New York: New Directions, 1941), 3–12.

Moi, Toril. *Revolution of the Ordinary: Literary Studies after Wittgenstein, Austin, and Cavell* (University of Chicago Press, 2017).

Mulhall, Stephen. "The Givenness of Grammar: A Reply to Steven Affeldt," *European Journal of Philosophy* 6/1 (1998), 32–44.

Stanley Cavell: Philosophy's Recounting of the Ordinary (Oxford: Clarendon Press, 1999).

Nagy, Peter. "The Woman in the Man: Male Modernism and Cross-Gender Identification in Sherwood Anderson's *Winesburg, Ohio*," *College Literature* 45/4 (2018), 773–800.

Norris, Andrew. *Becoming Who We Are: Politics and Practical Philosophy in the Work of Stanley Cavell* (Oxford University Press, 2017).

Ou, Li. *Keats and Negative Capability* (London: Continuum, 2009).

Pessoa, Fernando. *Poesia completa de Ricardo Reis* (Sao Paulo: Editora Schwarcz., 2000).

Peters, Michael A. *Poststructuralism, Marxism, and Neoliberalism: Between Theory and Politics* (Lanham, MD: Rowman & Littlefield, 2001).

Phillips, Adam. *On Flirtation: Psychoanalytic Essays on the Uncommitted Life* (Cambridge, MA: Harvard University Press, 1994).

Putnam, Hilary. *Philosophy in an Age of Science: Physics, Mathematics, and Skepticism* (Cambridge, MA: Harvard University Press, 2012).

The Threefold Cord: Mind, Body and World (New York: Columbia University Press, 1999).

Rawls, John. "Two Concepts of Rules," *Philosophical Review* 64/1 (1955), 3–32.

Ricketts, Thomas. "Objectivity and Objecthood: Frege's Metaphysics of Judgment," in *Frege Synthesized: Essays on the Philosophical and Foundational Work of Gottlob Frege*, ed. Leila Haaparanta and Jaakko Hintikka (Dordrecht: D. Reidel, 1986).

Rilke, Rainer Maria. "The Sonnets to Orpheus," in *The Selected Poetry of Rainer Maria Rilke*, trans. Stephen Mitchell (New York: Vintage, 1989), 225–55.

Rothman, William and Marian Keane. *Reading Cavell's The World Viewed* (Detroit, MI: Wayne State University Press, 2000).

Sanchez, Rebecca. "Shattering Communicative Norms: The Politics of Embodied Language in *Winesburg, Ohio*," *Modern Language Studies* 43/2 (2014), 25–39.

Schalkwyk, David. "Knowledge, Ethics, and the Limits of Language: Wittgenstein and Lyotard," *Journal of Literary Studies* 12/1–2 (1996), 86–111.

"Why the Social Bond Cannot Be a Passing Fashion: Reading Wittgenstein against Lyotard," *Theoria: A Journal of Social and Political Theory* 89 (1997), 116–31.

Schleiermacher, Friedrich. *Hermeneutics and Criticism*, ed. and trans. Andrew Bowie (Cambridge University Press, 1998).

Shakespeare, William. *King Lear*, ed. R.A. Foakes, Arden Shakespeare, Third Series (London: Thomas Nelson and Sons, 1997).

Sibley, Frank. "Aesthetic Concepts," in *Approach to Aesthetics: Collected Papers on Philosophical Aesthetics*, ed. John Benson, Betty Redfern, and Jeremy Roxbee Cox (Oxford University Press, 2001), 1–24.

Skilbeck, Adrian. *Stanley Cavell, Drama, and Education: Serious Words for Serious Subjects* (Dordrecht: Springer, 2021).

Slack, Paul. *Poverty and Policy in Tudor and Stuart England* (London and New York: Longmans, 1988).

Standish, Paul. "Momentous Occasions: Philosophy and Autobiography in Richard Rorty, Stanley Cavell, and Kenneth Wain," in *My Teaching, My Philosophy: Kenneth Wain and the Lifelong Engagement with Education*, ed. John Baldacchino, Simone Galea, and Duncan P. Mercieca (New York: Peter Lang, 2014), 285–302.

    "'Nothing but sounds, ink-marks' – Is Nothing Hidden? Must Everything Be Transparent?" in *Yearbook of the Danish Philosophy Association* 51/1 (2018), 71–91.

    "Public and Private: Aesthetics, Education, and Depsychologising Psychology," in *Biteki no mono: no kyoikuteki eikyo ni kansuru rironnteki bunkahikakuteki kenkyu* (*A Theoretical and Cultural-Comparative Study on Educational Influences of the Aesthetic*), ed. Y. Imai, Final Report (Tokyo: Society for the Promotion of Science, 2005).

Standish, Paul and Naoko Saito (eds.). *Stanley Cavell and the Education of Grownups* (New York: Fordham University Press, 2011).

Stevens, Wallace. *The Collected Poems of Wallace Stevens* (New York: Vintage, 1990).

Thompson, Michael. *Life and Action: Elementary Structures of Practice and Practical Thought* (Cambridge, MA: Harvard University Press, 2008).

Thoreau, Henry David. *The Heart of Thoreau's Journals*, ed. Odell Shepard (New York: Dover, 1961).

    Walden, ed. Jeffrey Cramer (New Haven, CT: Yale University Press, 2004).

    Walden and Other Writings of Henry David Thoreau, ed. Brooks Atkinson (New York: Modern Library, 1992).

Vallejo, César. *Obra poética completa* (Caracas: Biblioteca Ayacucho, 1985).

Williams, Bernard. "Moral Luck," in *Moral Luck: Philosophical Papers, 1973–1980* (Cambridge University Press, 1981), 20–39.

Williamson, Timothy. *The Philosophy of Philosophy* (Malden, MA: Blackwell, 2007).

Wimsatt, William K., Jr. and M.C. Beardsley, "The Intentional Fallacy," *Sewanee Review*, 54/3 (1946), 468–88.

    "The Affective Fallacy," *Sewanee Review*, 57/1 (1949), 31–55.

Wittgenstein, Ludwig. *Culture and Value*, ed. G.H. von Wright, trans. Peter Winch (Oxford: Blackwell, 1994; 1st edn 1980).

    Last Writings on the Philosophy of Psychology: The Inner and the Outer, vol. II, ed. G.H. von Wright and H. Nyman, trans. C.G. Luckhardt and M.A.E. Aue (Oxford: Blackwell, 1992).

Philosophical Investigations, trans. Elizabeth Anscombe (New York: Macmillan, 1953).

Philosophical Investigations, rev. 4th edn, trans. G.E.M. Anscombe, P.M.S. Hacker, and Joachim Schulte, ed. Hacker (New York: Wiley-Blackwell, 2009; 1st edn 1953).

Preliminary Studies for the 'Philosophical Investigations': Generally Known as the Blue and Brown Books (Oxford: Basil Blackwell, 1969).

Tractatus Logico-Philosophicus, trans. C.K. Ogden (London: Routledge & Kegan Paul, 1922). Originally published as *Logisch-Philosophische Abhandlung* in *Annalen der Naturphilosophie* vol. XIV, 3, 4, 185–262 (Leipzig: Reinhold Berger for Verlag Unesma GmbH, 1921).

Tractatus Logico-Philosophicus, trans. David Pears and Brian McGuinness (London: Routledge, 2001).

Wittgenstein: Lectures, Cambridge 1930–1933: From the Notes of G.E. Moore, ed. David G. Stern, Brian Rogers, and Gabriel Citron (Cambridge University Press, 2016).

Wittgenstein's Lectures on the Foundations of Mathematics: Cambridge, 1939, ed. Cora Diamond (University of Chicago Press, 1989; 1st edn 1976).

Woodard, Ashley. "Jean-François Lyotard (1924–1988)," *Internet Encyclopedia of Philosophy*, www.iep.utm.edu/lyotard/#SH4b.

Yeats, W.B. *Autobiographies*, ed. W.H. O'Donnell and D.N. Archibald (New York: Scribner, 1999).

Index of Names and Subjects

Index of Subjects

theatricalization, 212
thinking, 1, 10, 25–26, 31, 33, 35, 108–9,
    117, 119, 154, 163, 167, 171–73, 176,
    219
timing, 8
tonality, 153
tone, 4–5, 9, 17, 24, 26, 29, 32, 39, 152,
    155, 158, 161, 163, 167, 179
total metaphor, 189
Tougaloo College, 3
tradition, 2, 7, 9, 15, 34, 41–42, 48, 60, 90,
    125–26, 133, 138, 141, 165, 168, 193,
    210
tragedy, 10, 16, 45, 53, 57, 114, 167,
    198–200, 208, 214, 217, 223, 225,
    228–29
transcendence, 4, 33, 162
transvaluation, 190
trust, 140
truth, 3, 8, 22–29, 33, 46, 52, 54, 72, 79,
    82, 93, 98, 105, 107, 112, 115, 117,
    123, 148, 154, 157, 175–76, 184, 189,
    207, 213–14, 220, 227–28, 230
    and description, 73
    and meaning, 154
    and reference, 201
    conditions of, 4, 18, 33
    of art, 122
    of passion, 98
    of skepticism, 116
    of speech acts, 199
    of this world, 33
    passion for, 1, 45, 47

skepticism about, 1
    work of, 46

universal voice, 103
utterance, 139

value, 1, 4, 11, 18, 27, 38, 65, 133, 137,
    171–72, 216
Vienna Circle, 15, 47
Vietnam War, 3, 225
virtual world, 45
virtue, 165
voice, 2, 5, 8, 11, 18–19, 24–25, 28–32, 38,
    40, 44, 52, 77–80, 97, 103, 122–32,
    136, 139–43, 147–48, 151–65, 169,
    186, 201, 215
vulnerability, 46, 76, 153, 176, 200, 218

wars, 16
will, 4
wishes, 31
Wittgenstein's works
    Blue and Brown Books, 15, 21, 36
    Philosophical Investigations, 7, 24–26, 29,
        32, 36, 40–43, 54, 82, 89–90, 95, 117,
        135, 167, 194–95, 215, 219
    Tractatus Logico-Philosophicus, 49, 53
words, 15
    power of, 1
world
    aesthetic. See aesthetic, world
    of readers, 124
worth, 27

Index of References to Cavell's Works

9 781009 096546